Debt and the Twin Deficits Debate

JAMES M. ROCK, General Editor
University of Utah

Bristlecone Books

Mayfield Publishing Company
Mountain View, California
London • Toronto

Library of Congress Cataloging-in-Publication Data

Debt and the twin deficits debate / James M. Rock, editor.
    p.   cm.
    "Bristlecone books."
    Includes index.
    ISBN 1-55934-040-1
    1. Budget deficits—United States. 2. Debts, Public—United
States. I. Rock, James M.
HJ2051.D43   1991
339.5;23;0973—dc20

                                        90-46310
                                        CIP

Manufactured in the United States of America.

10   9   8   7   6   5   4   3   2   1

Bristlecone Books
Mayfield Publishing Company
1240 Villa Street
Mountain View, California

Sponsoring editor, Gary Burke; managing editor, Linda Toy; production editor, Carol Zafiropoulos; copy editor, Peggy Monihan; cover design, Jeanne M. Schrieber; production artist, Jean Mailander; illustrator, Linda Salmon. The text was set in 10/12 Meridien and printed on 50# Butte des Morts Smooth by Banta Company.

Contents

iii

PART THREE: OPINION OF THE VARIOUS OPINIONS

Preface

This book is the result of a lecture series I organized in early 1990 at the University of Utah during my tenure as University Professor. The purpose was to focus attention on the reasons for and the results of people and nations going into debt. Whether debt—personal, national, or international—is seen as a burden or a benefit is tied closely to the creditworthiness of persons and nations and to whether it is voluntary or not.

In the spring and summer of 1989 as I began to organize the debt lectures, Americans' ears were still resounding with President Bush's pledge of "Read my lips, no new taxes." At the same time Americans were just beginning to realize that the flood of failing savings and loans needed to be bailed out. November 1989 brought the tearing down of the Berlin Wall and the Iron Curtain. Eastern and Western Europe were reunited, as were East and West Germany. The end to the Cold War promised taxpayers a peace dividend.

The expectations of a sizeable peace dividend were quashed in January 1990 when Senator Moynihan charged that the surplus in the Social Security trust fund, generated by a substantial hike in payroll taxes, was being used to finance part of the federal budget deficit, and that the dividend should be used to reduce the budget deficit. Any last hopes for a peace dividend were swept away shortly thereafter by a fuller realization of the true savings and loan bailout costs. At the same time, the dissolution of the "Evil Empire" became a possibility as the wind of Eastern European independence blew through the Union of Soviet Socialist Republics, offering a new and better peace dividend. The chapters in this book were written in that ambiance.

Unlike November 1989, August 1990 brought no tearing down of barriers but the setting up of Operation Desert Shield: the American response to Iraq's takeover of Kuwait. American taxpayers have been, and continue to be, on an emotional roller coaster about the benefits and burdens of federal government actions—a ride that shows no signs of slowing down. The time is past when we could isolate ourselves from the rest of the world and from the rest of America. Where do we go from here? Join the debate.

I wish to thank President Chase Peterson and Provost James Clayton, Dean Jack Newell of the Liberal Education Program; the Department of Economics, the College of Business, the Hinckley Institute of Politics, Harris Simmons, and the large and enthusiastic audiences from "town and gown" for their support and encouragement.

In particular, I want Bob Eisner to know I'll always be indebted to him, and I am benefited, not burdened, by my debt. Many thanks go to Alan Blinder for being willing to act as the summarizer and commentator on the opinions of others and for his fair assessment of the joys of being the editor. An unexpected joy was getting to know Gary Burke, publisher of Bristlecone Books.

For Bonnie, my love

Introduction

Debt is always a controversial subject, along with taxes, inflation, and employment quotas. Even so, nations may use all four to solve their problems. People, however, can use only debt.

Although debt is sometimes an acceptable solution for both people and nations, they may be forced into debt against their will. Still, most people and nations would rather have the option of going into debt—even involuntarily—than to exhaust their creditworthiness and have to rely on the charity of others. America is proud to be portrayed as a nation built on self-reliance.

Because of our growing national and international debt, however, our land of democracy, laissez faire capitalism, and limitless opportunities is increasingly portrayed as a land of debt-ridden big government and restricted choices. America's economic woes, some would say, are impinging on our private economic lives, and look to economists for a solution. Economists, however, are divided over two policy prescriptions: increasing investment by reducing consumption or increasing investment by stimulating aggregate demand. The best plans for reducing consumption demand may be at odds with those for raising investment demand. Neither plan has overwhelming popular support. A minority even suggests going back to Reaganomics.

President Reagan emphasized, both as candidate and then as president, that his economic policy would reclaim America's world economic leadership by reversing the tax-and-spend Keynesian policies of the Democrats; his administration would be fiscally responsible and deliver a balanced budget. Reaganomics was presumably supply-side economics, in contrast to demand-side Keynesian economics. Price stability and economic growth were the goals, in contrast to the Keynesian goals of full employment and economic growth. The economic problem of scarce resources was to be solved by emphasizing the efficiency of the market mechanism, in contrast to the Keynesian solution of emphasizing more jobs.

In retrospect, the impact of Reagan's economic policy on national debt and on income and wealth distributions should have been obvious. His call for reductions in non-military government purchases, reductions in government transfer payments, and reductions in income tax rates, but increases in military spending and increases in social security payroll tax rates caused both a spectacular increase in national debt and an equally spectacular widening of the divide between the rich and the poor. A similar widening of the divide between rich and poor nations was going on at the same time.

1

Beliefs about the impact of debt—personal and national—can be forced, for the purposes of discussion, into three categories. Some believe that debt is a sin (a moral burden) for nations as well as for persons. Others know that any nation has the power to create its own revenues—be they generated by taxes or by printing presses. With this revenue-producing potential, a nation is more financially flexible than a person and perhaps better able—some of the time—to benefit from debt. And still others would change the division from one between nations and persons to one between credit-worthy and uncreditworthy nations and persons. The last category encompasses my own belief and the reason for comparing the impact of debt on disadvantaged children and Latin America in Part I and its impact on the advantaged United States in Part II. Part III critiques the first two parts.

What do economic experts think should be done to improve our personal, national, and international standards of living for the "haves" and "have-nots"—both now and in the future? Are personal, national, and international debt often defined as a problem because of personal and national values rather than because of economic constraints? A debate is needed to clarify the issues. This book provides a wide and wise variety of views about the national debt and the twin deficits, that is, the federal-budget deficit and the international current-account deficit.

Throughout our peacetime history, until the Great Depression of the 1930s, a balanced budget was the 11th commandment of the U.S. government. Since then, economists and politicians have continually debated whether government should intervene in the marketplace to promote full employment and equality. In general, classical economists and Republicans have emphasized market efficiency over personal equality; Keynes (1936, ch. 24) and Democrats have traded away some efficiency for more equality.

In Chapter 1, I discuss how one's view of debt—its causes, consequences, and remedies—depends on one's emphasis on maximum employment or price stability as the key economic goal. The importance of saving and investment to these goals is interpreted from three different perspectives: history, economic theory and accounting definitions, and creditworthiness. All three are reasons why debt is so often a topic of heated discussion.

The future of disadvantaged children is the topic of Chapter 2, and the future of the disadvantaged countries of Latin America is the topic of Chapter 3. In Chapter 2, Timothy M. Smeeding examines the growing inequality between families with children and other groups, especially childless couples and the elderly. His concern is the impact on disadvantaged children of changes in the distributions of income and wealth brought about by the tax and expenditure policy of the 1980s.

In Chapter 3, Kenneth P. Jameson looks at Latin America, the disadvantaged half of our continent. Latin America, like poorer families, is not creditworthy. Jameson examines the various plans that have been put forth to solve Latin America's debt burden and, like Smeeding, comes to the conclusion that our national and international debt reduction and relief plans are not for the benefit of the disadvantaged.

Part II presents the issues in the debate about the national debt and the twin deficits. Although the American public generally accepts that repaying a contracted debt is a contractual burden, American economists, especially the authors of these original essays, hold differing views. They do not agree whether the debt needs to be repaid now or in the future; whether the deficits need to be reduced, left constant, or increased; whether indebtedness weakens our world leadership or our moral fiber; whether partial repudiation of our debt burden through inflation or monetization is a good business practice. These economists probably do agree, however, that full repudiation is inconsistent with long-term optimal stabilization policy, but even here some others may disagree. Agreement before the fact that we do not wish to be irresponsible and turn our collective backs on our creditors is a slender reed upon which to hang our future domestic and foreign policy.

The controversy over our creditworthiness—the stability and strength of our present economic state—breeds controversy over the need for and the type of stabilization policy. Differences in theory, measurement, and policy leave economists deeply divided on whether the debt and the deficits are a burden.

Charles Schultze (1989), chairman of President Carter's Council of Economic Advisers, defined the positions in the debt debate in animate terms: pussy cat, termite, and wolf. Pussy cats are unmoved by the gloomy rhetoric of the debt/deficit doomsayers. Termites worry that the private capital base of our economy is being eaten away. Wolves (as in the phrase "The wolves are at the door!") believe that the national debt and the twin deficits are an immediate, current menace.

Robert Eisner, Peter Bernstein and Robert Heilbroner, and Robert Barro are all pussy cats but of rather different stripes. Benjamin Friedman is a termite regarding the domestic budget deficit but almost a wolf on the international deficit. Edward Gramlich is a self-proclaimed termite, and Gordon Tullock agrees with Gramlich that the economy can continue, in its present deplorable state, perhaps indefinitely, but that future generations will suffer.

The policy recommendations of these authors do not correspond perfectly to their animate categories, however. On the one hand, Eisner and Bernstein and Heilbroner advocate greater government spending on our human and nonhuman infrastructure, although Eisner wants easier monetary policy now while Bernstein and Heilbroner demur. On the other hand, Barro and Tullock point to the size of the federal government as an important cause of the economy's current problems, although Barro's Ricardian approach is quite dissimilar to Tullock's public choice approach. Friedman believes we have broken our trust with future generations by frivolously spending their inheritance and we should hasten to cure our full-employment economy's "chronic fiscal imbalance" through some mix of spending cuts and tax increases. Friedman thinks such a policy would also turn around our current-account balance and reestablish our world leadership. Gramlich sees the developments in Eastern Europe and the slight reduction in deficit burden here at home as positive but thinks the budget deficit needs to be reduced another 3 to 4 percent of net national product to give future generations the opportunity to enjoy the standard of living that we have taken for granted.

In Part III, Alan Blinder carefully summarizes the opinions of all the authors and concisely explains in what way his opinion differs from theirs. Blinder is an unconventional termite who advocates increased government investment in America's future, particularly in public infrastructure and on behalf of children at risk, even if it raises the budget deficit by a like amount.

Both investments, I believe, are eminently worthwhile and profitable. In fact, I would urge him to consider a third government investment in the future—paying off the international debt of potentially our best trading partner, Latin America. Latin American debt erasure could be accomplished at a cost of only one-fourth to one-third of the saving and loan bailout.

Our current national debt-gross national product ratio is the same as it was before World War II. Five years later in 1945 the ratio was almost three times as large. Our national reaction then was to embark on the Marshall Plan—unparalleled international investment—especially in our former enemies, Germany and Japan. How far-sighted are we today? In a democracy, our children and granchildren's futures are everyone's concern.

Part One

The Debt: National and Personal, Past and Present

1 History, Analytics and Accounting, and Analogies of Debt

JAMES M. ROCK

To understand why debt is controversial, it is important to first understand that economic history, economic theory, and national income accounting are often reconstructions of the past to serve the present and future purposes of the interpreter (Plumb, 1970). My interpretative focus is on the creditworthiness, or lack thereof, of nations and persons. Savers provide credit. Investors need credit. Saving is aided by high interest rates. Investment is discouraged.

The analogy I use to explain the burden or benefit of debt is based on creditworthiness and the voluntariness of the indebtedness. In our modern monetary credit economy—of leverage, trust, and uncertainty—the divide that separates the "haves" and the "have-nots" is their access to monetary credit. Creditworthy persons and nations function well in a capitalistic world where the morals and efficiency are those of a giant vending machine that only accepts good monetary credit. In such a world, individual human worth and national prestige derive from the willingness of others to trust your creditworthiness.

Much of the dispute John Maynard Keynes had with classical economists over the need for, and type of, government spending, taxing, and borrowing—and their apostles are now having—is about the relative importance of unemployment and inflation. This dispute is centered in the tradeoff between equality of opportunity and efficiency of the market in the past and present, and the uncertainty of the future compared to the equilibrium forces of nature and many social institutions, especially the competitive market. Arthur Okun wrote, "Tradeoffs are the central study of the economist. `You can't have your cake and eat it too' is a good candidate for the fundamental theorem of economic analysis" (1975, p. 1).

National income and product accounts are, of course, annual measures of certain economic variables. Measuring such variables year after year permits comparisons. In the national income accounts, saving and investment are defined identically. Economists argue over how the definitions for

7

consumption goods compared to investment (saving) goods are applied to real economic goods. That is because the absolute and relative amounts of consumption and saving in gross national product are good indicators of the need for and the type of governmental stabilization policy.

The current debate about private, national, and international deficits and debts is essentially about the long-term availability and stability of the transactors' credit. Debt is a benefit to those who need liquidity now and have a good credit rating. Debt is a crisis to those who need liquidity now but whose credit is nonexistent or insufficient. Liquidity is the relative ease and certainty with which the present value of one's assets can be unlocked at short notice, with or without terminating ownership (Keynes, 1930, II, p. 67).

In more and more countries around the world, democracy and capitalism are the preferred institutions of government and enterprise. They are also the "most improbable mixture" (Okun, 1975, p. 120). The efficiency of the marketplace is pitted against the equality and equity of "one person, one vote" and "equal justice for all." This tradeoff elucidates the debate about the debt and twin deficits. Thus the budgeting process in a democratic society that favors free markets requires tradeoffs between equality and efficiency. All questions of policy and budgeting are thrust under the bright light of political and economic considerations; the results cannot be predicted.

It is widely believed that the greater the inequality of income and wealth, the more likely the voting majority of poor is to support policies and budgets that stress equality. Tocqueville prophesied—with dread—that equality fostered by American democratic ideals would overwhelm American efficiency: "The gradual progress of equality is something fated. The main features of this progress are the following: it is universal and permanent, it is daily passing beyond human control, and every event and every man helps it along" (1969, p. 12).

But it hasn't happened. Okun believes the reason is that the disadvantaged want some big prizes left in the game of life so that there is still a slim chance to strike it rich, even though such a budgeting scheme favors the advantaged. "The silent majority [do] not want the yacht clubs closed forever to their children and grandchildren while those who [have] already become members [keep] sailing along" (1975, p. 49). Reaganomics and President Bush's effort to reduce capital gains taxes—two-thirds of the benefit would go to the top 1 percent of taxpayers—support Okun's reasoning and not Tocqueville's fear (Center on Budget and Policy Priorities, 1990).

THE HISTORY OF OUR NATIONAL DEBT AND TWIN DEFICITS

In one climactic year—1776—Adam Smith's *The Wealth of Nations* was published and the Declaration of Independence was signed. The first has become synonymous with self-interest and a limited role for government;

the second proclaimed "that all men are created equal," that they are endowed with "certain unalienable rights," and that, "to secure these rights, governments are instituted among men."

By 1790 we had won our freedom from Great Britain, and the new United States were concerned about their economic stability—now that their political freedom had been secured. The financial cost of the revolutionary war had been high, and there was concern that hostilities could resume at any time. The new nation needed to put its financial house in order, to conduct its finances as prudently as colonial households reputedly did. Folklore has projected an image of early Americans as thrifty, virtuous folk who bought only what they could pay cash for; however, historians now believe this is a false image (Coleman, 1974, p. viii). The United States' poor credit was generally considered its economic Achilles heel. The key to establishing creditworthiness was to convince international lenders that the United States government could balance its budget and fund its national debt. Ever since, the United States has had a turbulent romance with the balanced budget concept—forever breaking up and getting back together!

Hamilton's *Report on Public Credit*

According to the Preamble to the Constitution (September 17, 1787), the economic purposes of the new nation were to "provide for the common defense" and "promote the general welfare." Section 8 of Article One gave to Congress the power "to lay and collect taxes, duties, imposts, and excises, to pay the debts . . . [and] to borrow money on the credit of the United States." Article Six obligated the United States to pay all the debts contracted while the Articles of Confederation were in effect, from 1781 to 1788.

Consequently, the First Congress of the United States asked Alexander Hamilton, the newly appointed Secretary of the Treasury, for his recommendation on how to provide "adequate provision for the support of public credit, as a matter of high importance to the national honor and prosperity" (quoted in Kimmel, 1959, p. 9). His *Report Relative to a Provision for the Support of Public Credit* (January 9, 1790, presented to the House of Representatives on January 14) advocated payment of the national debt, both domestic and foreign, and the states' debts as well. In August 1790 Hamilton's recommendation was passed into law, after a compromise with Jefferson and Madison to move the nation's capital to the banks of the Potomac. Hamilton asserted that honoring past debts would ensure a good credit rating and a secure line of credit when needed in the future. He was looking beyond present inconveniences and concerns to future needs (see Cooke, 1964, and Taylor, 1959).

In the early days of our nation, there was no federal budget to integrate spending with taxing and borrowing. (In fact, not until the Budget Reform Act of 1921 was an administrative budget mandated.) The revenues of the new nation came almost totally from import duties, and half its expenses was interest on the debt.[1]

When Thomas Jefferson was elected president in 1801 on a platform of minimal federal government and an articulated belief that public debt is the nation's gravest danger, his procurement of new territories in the Louisiana Purchase in 1803 (which cost $15 million, including $11.25 million in new borrowings) was therefore unexpected. Likewise, when a federal surplus was run but much national debt remained, his proposal to have Congress explore the possibilities of expending federal monies on the "great purposes of the public education, roads, rivers, canals, and such other objects of public improvement" was equally unexpected. Hamilton understood the importance of organizing and administering public power; Jefferson understood the need for controlling it. Together they promoted a philosophy of government dedicated to public welfare (Caldwell, 1988).

Debt Policy Before the Civil War

To President Andrew Jackson (1829-1837), a national debt was an economic, fiscal, moral, and unpatriotic burden. In this pre-Civil War era, the principal economic arguments against the public debt were "(1) interest on the public debt was a burden on the working classes; (2) interest payments involved a redistribution of income in favor of the well-to-do; and (3) the capital freed from unproductive employment through debt reduction would find its way into productive uses" (Kimmel, 1959, p. 19).

The national debt of the Revolutionary War and the War of 1812 was finally erased during Jackson's second term as president. Shortly after he left office, however, the recession of 1837-39 began, and Congress responded by voting to increase spending to alleviate economic suffering (Webber and Wildavsky, 1986, p. 374). But President Van Buren vetoed the appropriation for the "traditional" reason: The less the government interferes with private pursuits, the better the people are served.

By the 1840s the stuttering economy caused seven states to default on their bonded indebtedness, held in part by foreigners. Although all were able to pay the accrued interest in a few years, the specter of repudiation loomed large in the minds of British investors and "poets":

> Yankee Doodle borrows cash,
> Yankee Doodle spends it,
> And then he snaps his fingers at
> The jolly flat who lends it.
> Ask him when he means to pay,
> He shows no hesitation,
> But says he'll take the shortest way
> And that's Repudiation!
> (Meyers, 1970, p. 109)

From the Civil War to 1900

In encouraging public acceptance of debt funding of the Civil War, President Abraham Lincoln (1860-1865) expressed a view some may consider modern: "The great advantage of citizens being creditors as well as debtors with relation to the public debt is obvious. Men readily perceive that they cannot be much oppressed by a debt which they owe to themselves" (Webber and Wildavsky, 1986, p. 375).

A more economically rigorous but less politically astute analysis of the Civil War "debt or taxes" issue was given by the American Renaissance man, Simon Newcomb. He noted that two hypothetical arguments could be made for financing the war through debt: (1) the national debt is a great consolidating power that binds the country together (which was Lincoln's argument), and (2) part of the burden of the war should be bequeathed to posterity, for whose benefit it is fought. Newcomb disputed both arguments. To the first argument, he countered that the many taxpayers having to pay the relatively few bond holders increases class and regional consciousness—and the associated hatred—and could even stimulate a call by the many to repudiate the debt to the few. To the second argument, he answered that the real cost of the war is the blood shed and the armies provisioned, and it cannot be passed on to another generation (Newcomb, 1865, p. 67).

Newcomb thought the war should be paid for immediately and that doing so would not have any deleterious effect on taxpayers' patriotism, productivity, and incentive. He was dead set against government bonds being tax exempt: "This 'farming out' of taxes to be collected, for this is what the contract amounts to, is the worst possible way of borrowing money" (p. 87).

Newcomb's opinions were shared by few, however, and the perception of national debt as immoral and unpatriotic was beginning to dissipate. As the war progressed, the immorality of the debt incurred to enforce the Emancipation Proclamation (1863) paled compared to the alternative.

Attitudes about personal debt and poverty were also shifting. The prevailing view had been that people controlled their own economic fate; debt and poverty were sinful because they could be avoided.[2] "Resolve not to be poor; whatever you have, spend less," exhorted Victorian-era homilist Samuel Smiles. "The first step in debt is like the first step in falsehoods; almost always involving the necessity of proceeding in the same course, debt following debt, as lie follows lie." (1889, p. 382). Not surprisingly, the traditional punishment had been to send debtors in default to prison.

In *Little Dorrit* (1857), Charles Dickens pilloried this harsh tradition, and in *David Copperfield* (1850), he examined the "criminal immorality" of being a shilling short. The popularity of these books in England and the United States reflected the changing opinion about economic misfortune. During the Civil War, Congress made the type of appropriation that had been vetoed by President Van Buren a decade or so before, and the government began to play a role in improving the standard of living of disadvantaged citizens. Federal assistance to the poor grew (albeit from "tiny to small"), even though it meant incurring additional national debt (Webber and Wildavsky, 1986, p. 383).

The rights of debtors were also improved through the passage of bankruptcy laws, but the debtors who benefited were not farmers. Before the Civil War three national bankruptcy laws had been passed but quickly repealed. After the Civil War, the new debtor class was the corporation. By 1900, two statutes were passed whose provisions still exist (Glick, 1989, p. 2). Bankruptcy law is still evolving as an efficient and equitable means of assessing costs, providing "failure insurance," redistributing resources, and facilitating reorganization. The current savings and loan scandal has furnished a huge laboratory for evolutionary experiments.

During the latter part of the nineteenth century, the United States was evolving rapidly from an agrarian economy into an industrial economy. U.S. society had great difficulty in dealing with this change, because none of its social, financial, economic, or government institutions had been designed for the new mode of production. Not surprisingly, there was great disagreement about how these institutions should be structured.

The two main political parties were joined by the Greenback, Populist, and Granger parties among others. The promise of agrarian leadership never emerged for the debtor farmer and farm laborers, however. The Greenback and Granger parties were controlled by upper-class land-owning families. A will-of-the-wisp search for a mystic commodity price formula by the Populist party left the farm laborer with land-ownership dreams and the tenant farmers struggling to retain their step on the ownership ladder with no political support.

From the Civil War to the Great Depression of the 1930s, economists' attitudes about the proper scope of government economic activity were evenly distributed along a bell-shaped curve. On one end were the laissez-faire economists with their dictum that the government that governs least governs best. On the other were the American Institutionalists, who believed that government intervention in economic affairs was absolutely necessary "if society were to progress in an orderly manner" (Kimmel, 1959, p. 135).

There was no difference of opinion, however, with regard to debt policy: Wars were the reason nations fell into debt, and peacetime was reduction-of-debt time. The only disagreement was about the rate at which the debt should be reduced. War debt was justified for two main reasons: Expenditures had to be made immediately, before revenues could be raised, and increased taxes on income and wealth would reduce private incentive and productivity—contrary to Simon Newcomb's opinion.

From the Panic of 1907 to 1930

Over seventy-five years ago, the Federal Reserve System was enacted into law to counter the problem of monetary instability. After the panic of 1907 had jolted expectations on Main Street and Wall Street, causing an increase in bank failures, Congress set up the National Monetary Commission in 1908. Its purpose was to seek some answers to why the financial sector was prone to crisis when the rest of the economy, especially the agricultural sector, was prosperous—this was the beginning of the "Golden Age" of agriculture, which ended with the outbreak of war in Europe. On December 23, 1913, after a number of political compromises, President Wilson signed into law the Federal Reserve Act (see especially Johnson, 1977). Monetary policy was born with the creation of the Federal Reserve System, but it was not expressly used as a stabilizing and growth-inducing tool of economic policy until after the onset of the Great Depression, because its function was not fully specified nor its power fully understood until the Banking Acts of 1933 and 1935.

Just before World War I, the United States, along with many other Western nations, supported minimal federal government expenditures on such items as welfare and defense with a "few low but productive indirect taxes"—mostly customs and excise taxes; tax revenues were less than 10 percent of gross national product in most industrial nations (Webber and Wildavsky, 1986, pp. 310, 354). World War I, with its large demand for federal expenditures, increased that percentage. The federal government established the income tax in 1914 (with a maximum rate of 10 percent, which was raised to 77 percent by 1918) and the federal inheritance tax in 1916, both to help pay for the war.

Although not initially of great policy importance, the Federal Reserve System was essential to the financing of World War I. The role of the Federal Reserve was to float and transfer loan funds and to issue government securities. The Treasury wanted interest rates to be as low as possible to minimize the cost of the debt. From April 1917 to June 1920, the United States spent over $35 billion on the war effort (war expenditures have the bad habit of continuing even after the hostilities are over). One-third of the expenditures came from taxes and the rest was borrowed; debt-servicing costs rose to 40 percent of outlays before falling. The U.S. gross domestic debt was $25 billion—27 percent of gross national product. It was of unprecedented size, but the prosperous Roaring Twenties enabled the United States to discharge a third of it by 1930; the GNP-debt ratio fell to 18 percent.

The post-war recession hit hard in 1920. It was over in a year or so, a year of distress for most sectors of the economy. For the agriculture sector, however, it heralded an entire decade of distress—which would be followed by another.[3]

The Great Depression and Other Economic Downturns

Every aspect of the 1930s was influenced by the Great Depression. The most important difference between it and earlier crashes was the make-up of the work force. It is estimated that in 1821 three-quarters of the nation's 2.9 million workers were in agriculture, but by 1929 only one-quarter of the labor force worked on farms. Thus, a single business failure in 1929 was likely to force the unemployment of many more workers than in 1821, and it was likely to cause greater negative effects on the interlocking grid of industrial production. Failed farms made other farms more profitable and their capital—human, land, animals, machinery—had resale value; failed firms, however, often had a domino effect on other firms and left little or no usable capital. Failed financial intermediaries, as we are currently re-learning, are the most destructive.

Most economists, trained in Adam Smith's thought through David Ricardo's extensions of his equilibrium method, knew that industrial growth meant periodic dips in activity, corrections to a too-rapidly-expanding economy. They compared business cycles to ocean waves, rolling evenly up and down. John Kenneth Galbraith's perspective of the period is different:

> The reality in the nineteenth and twentieth centuries was, in fact, much closer to the teeth of a ripsaw which go up on a gradual plane on one side and drop precipitately on the other. Or, if a wave, it was the long mounting roll and then the sharply breaking surf (1975, p. 129).

Be they depressions, recessions, or panics, these periodic downturns occurred in 1819, 1837, 1857, 1873, 1884 (to a lesser extent), 1893 (to a greater extent), 1907, and briefly but disastrously in 1921. Tension was mounting between those who maintained that a balanced budget was economically and socially the best policy and those who believed that to "promote the general welfare" was a legitimate activity of the federal government. The former asserted that a balanced budget was the solution because the market system, if left unhampered, would bring the economy back to full-employment equilibrium. The latter countered that striving for full employment was a greater good, both humanely and economically, than balancing the federal budget. They were influenced by Adam Smith's ideas about the tendency for continuing economic instability, which were expanded in the writings of Thomas Malthus. They believed that gloomy expectations had an enormous impact on long-term investment, which in turn affects future income and standards of living. To change negative expectations takes actual investment. Government purchases of goods and services and government transfer payments could dull the teeth of Galbraith's metaphorical ripsaw. The debt to GNP ratio had risen to 43 percent by 1940 aided by a slight increase in government expenditures *and* a sluggish economy.

Keynes and the Classics

John Maynard Keynes, a convert from David Ricardo's economics to Thomas Malthus's, named all the followers of Ricardo classical economists. He clearly wished to distinguish his less-than-full employment, monetary economy, uncertainty, disequilibrium approach from Ricardo's full employment, barter economy, insurable, equilibrium approach. For Keynes, macroeconomics was not just an aggregation of the microeconomies of households and firms (1936, p. 293). When classical theory was inflated to be a theory of the economy it displayed the fallacy of composition and ignored the paradox of thrift: If everyone tries to save more and consume less, saving may fall as a consequence of falling national income.

Keynes believed his approach to be the general theory—applicable to economies with all rates of employment—because it subsumed classical theory (1936, pp. 3, 378-80). When, if ever, full employment is achieved, "the classical theory comes into its own again from this point on" (p. 378). When all resources are fully employed, money is available as income earned to be exchanged in all markets. However, only Keynes' theory holds when some resources are unemployed. If resources are unsold, no income is earned and only barter exchange is possible, but not probable, because successful barter depends on the (double) coincidence of wants (Clower, 1970, p. 14).

In 1930 Keynes wrote "Economic Possibilities for Our Grandchildren" as a curative for the "bad attack of economic pessimism" the world was suffering. As he saw it, "We are suffering, not from the rheumatics of old age, but from the growing-pains of over-rapid changes" (1932, p. 358); sour expectations for the future are condemning the present. For Keynes, the solution to the economic problem is not the market system and balanced budgets but rather an expansion and upgrading of our human capital stock so that it can take full advantage of technological advances (p. 364).

Six years later, at the beginning of his last chapter in *The General Theory of Employment, Interest and Money* (1936), Keynes reiterated some of the same concerns, but now he had a theory of too little effective demand (that is, demand backed up with purchasing power) to support his earlier contentions. He stated, "The outstanding faults of the economic society in which we live are its failure to provide for full employment and its arbitrary and inequitable distribution of wealth and incomes" (p. 372).

The relevancy of Keynes' theory of unemployment to economic growth is much debated. But there are also two important ways in which Keynes felt that the distribution of wealth and income affects economic growth— consumption rates and interest rates. Reductions in the "very great disparities of wealth and income" achieved by income, excise, and death taxes are generally acceptable to the public, but the public is hesitant to carry the process further. This reluctance is partially due to a fear of making "skilful evasions too much worthwhile" and unduly reducing the "motive towards risk-taking" but mostly due to the belief—a belief also of classical economists—that investment depends on the supply of saving generated by the "rich out of their superfluity" (p. 372). Keynes accepted the "skilful evasions" and "risk-taking" arguments but rejected the "superfluity" argument. For him, high consumption and low interest rates, supplemented when necessary by government expenditures, are what induce private investment, employment, and economic growth, whereas thrift reduces consumption and consequently investment.

It was Keynes' belief that greater equality of opportunity is stimulated by greater equality of income and wealth and lower interest rates (1936, ch. 24). Superfluity is diminished as a necessary element of national economic growth on both counts.

Keynes was not for complete equality, however; he believed that there is "social and psychological justification for significant inequalities of incomes and wealth, but not for such large disparities as exist today" (p. 374). In both "Economic Possibilities for Our Grandchildren" and *General Theory*, he expressed the hope that the "necessary" human urge to accumulate wealth would also provide an outlet for a person to "tyrannize over his bank balance" rather than over other individuals, "Whilst the former is sometimes denounced as being but a means to the latter, sometimes at least it is an alternative" (1936, p. 374).

Economic Measures Since World War II

During the thirties the federal government made only halfhearted attempts at encouraging effective demand. It wasn't until World War II that Keynes' lesson was emphasized: Demand can be managed for the benefit of the nation. It was better to run a deficit than to adversely influence productivity and production; it was better to keep war goods flowing to the troops than to worry about the size of the deficit. As during World War I, the U.S. Treasury was able to control the Federal Reserve's policy agenda—interest rates were to be kept low to minimize the cost of financing the deficit and debt.

The implicit link between the U.S. Treasury and the Federal Reserve was severed with the signing of the Accord of 1951, which released the Federal Reserve from its obligation to keep interest rates low; the explicit link of the Secretary of the Treasury being a member of the Federal Reserve Board had already disappeared with the 1935 Banking Act (Federal Reserve Bank of Philadelphia, 1964). The Federal Reserve was now free to allow interest rates to rise which might aid in combatting inflation (preserving purchasing power), but might impede providing maximum employment.

In the Employment Act of 1946, Congress and President Harry Truman (1945-1953) accepted ultimate responsibility for the nation's economic performance: "The Congress hereby declares that it is the continuing policy and responsibility of the federal government to use all practicable means consistent with its needs and obligations . . . to promote maximum employment, production, and purchasing power." Balancing our international current account was not added as an additional goal for a decade or so, because we ran a huge surplus during World War II. Americans are less apprehensive about and more willing to support multiple economic goals rather than just a single one. For example, an earlier attempt, the Murray Full Employment Bill, was even more committed to employing all who wanted to work (Nourse, 1953). Attempts to make stable prices (that is, zero inflation) the statutory objective had been as unsuccessful in the 1930s (Federal Reserve of Philadelphia, 1964) as they would be in 1989 (House Joint Resolution 409, 101st Congress, 1st Session).

Although World War II ended, military expenditures continued: the Berlin blockade, beginning in 1948; the Korean War, from 1948 to 1953; and the Vietnam War, which finally ended in 1975. Even so, the U.S. economy was so large and growing so rapidly that the national debt to gross national product ratio fell during this period. The ratio between national debt (held by the U.S. public) and GNP went from a high of 114 percent in 1946 to a low of 24 percent in 1974.

The Full Employment and Balanced Growth Act of 1978 (Humphrey-Hawkins Act) established quantitative goals for the nation—a 4 percent unemployment rate and an interim target of 3 percent inflation. The Federal Reserve chairperson was directed to report to Congress annually to show that the Fed's practices are in keeping with current national goals for employment, growth, price stability, and a favorable balance of international payments—even though at times the goals are in conflict.

Legislative action was also directed to freeing business from the chafing manacles of government. Government regulation was out and the laissez faire goad was in. The Depository Institutions Deregulation and Monetary Control Act of 1980 and the Depository Institutions Act of 1982 (Garn-St. Germain) were passed to allow banks, savings and loans, and credit unions a "level field of competition"; they were now substitutes for one another rather than complements. This combined with deposit insurance of $100,000 per account and the poor or fraudulent management of a number of savings and loans has led to the current need for a bailout.[4] The estimated cost of $500 billion over 40 years is considerably more than the national debts of all the Latin America countries (Jameson, Chapter 3 of this book).

The supply-side economics that President Reagan (1980-1988) advanced in 1980—cutting taxes would so stimulate the economy that tax revenues would rise (according to the Laffer curve)—was derisively labeled "voodoo economics" by then rival candidate George Bush during the Republican primaries. (Both classical and Keynesian economists seconded Bush's appraisal of what appeared to be a "free lunch.") Nevertheless, supply-side economics was legislated by the 1981 Economic Recovery Tax Act (Kemp-Roth) which provided a 25 percent across-the-board tax cut. Capped with only a presidential pledge of a balanced budget, the deficit grew by leaps and bounds as tax revenues fell further and further below government outlays.

Public reaction caused Congress to pass the aptly named Tax Equity and Fiscal Responsibility Act of 1982; the still-rising deficit precipitated passage of the Deficit Reduction Act of 1984. Nevertheless, deficits continued to grow at what seemed to many an alarming rate. The budget hemorrhage needed a tourniquet. Two approaches were attempted: a constitutional amendment and deficit targets. After Congress rejected the Balanced Budget Amendment, it went to the states. By mid-1990, over 25 of the 34 states needed had made application for a national convention to consider a constitutional amendment mandating a balanced federal budget. America's romance with the balanced budget concept may be renewed.

The Balanced Budget and Emergency Deficit Control Act of 1985 (Gramm-Rudman-Hollings) was the beginning of the real war on the debt and the twin deficits; deficit-reducing targets were set for 1986 and 1987. The Balanced Budget and Emergency Deficit Control Reaffirmation Act of 1987 established deficit targets for 1988 through 1993, when, hypothetically, deficits will disappear. If the Office of Management and Budget's annual August estimate shows a gap of more than $10 billion between projected revenues and costs, the Balance Budget Act provides for automatic cutbacks (sequestering) on October 15. However, much spending is exempt, including Social Security, net interest on the debt, and funds already allocated, and cutbacks are limited in several other programs, notably Medicare, Stafford student loans, and veterans' medical care. The burden of sequestering falls almost wholly on defense and nondefense discretionary programs (U.S. Congressional Budget Office, July 1990 and U.S. Office of Management and Budget, August 1990).

The national debt held by the public was 26 percent of GNP when President Reagan took office in 1980. It climbed to almost 43 percent and more than doubled in real terms by the end of his second term. However, with the crumbling of the Berlin Wall and the democratic and capitalistic reforms sweeping Eastern Europe came hope of a peace dividend. But in the spring of 1990, the total amount of the savings and loan bailout was estimated at $500 billion, and the $50 billion Congress had provided to the Resolution Trust Corporation would cover only 10 percent of the costs. With that in mind, the Congressional Budget Office estimated in July of 1990 that the debt would rise to 46 percent of GNP by 1993 before beginning to fall. But that was before Operation Desert Shield; the expedition sent to the Persian Gulf region will cost at least $15 billion in the fiscal year 1991, according to the Department of Defense. The savings and loan bailout and the military buildup in the Middle East dashed all hope of a peace dividend and have greatly complicated federal debt and deficit projections.

ECONOMIC ANALYSIS AND NATIONAL INCOME ACCOUNTING

In two letters to Sir Roy Harrod (July 4 and 16, 1938), Lord Keynes stated why he felt economic analysis is relevant to real-world problems and why an economist's assumptions are critical:

> Economics is a science of thinking in terms of models joined to the art of choosing models which are relevant to the contemporary world. . . . I mentioned before that it deals with introspection and values. I might have added that it deals with motives, expectations, and psychological uncertainties. One has to be constantly on guard against treating the material as constant and homogeneous (1973, pp. 296, 300).

Sir John Hicks likened economic analysis to a language, a way to communicate: "A theory which is up-to-date—which does not forget the most pressing problems of the present day—should make communication easier" (1974, p. 8).

Keynes and Hicks, two of our greatest economists, reflect the general attitude that economic theory needs to be relevant to the pressing problems of the contemporary world. Yet among economists there is no agreement on theory or on measurement about the pressing problems of personal, national, and international debts.[5] Today, economic theory of national deficit financing may be broadly classified as classical or Keynesian. Crudely put, their basic assumptions and concerns are these: Classical theory assumes full employment and worries about inflation and saving, and Keynesian theory assumes constant prices and worries about unemployment and investment. The classical theory is usually referenced to David Ricardo (1951) and A. C. Pigou (1928), and the Keynesian theory to John Maynard Keynes and his *General Theory* (1936).

Classical theory separates the public budget into capital expenditures which are financed by debt, and current expenditures, which are financed by taxes. Borrowing for capital improvements is deemed equitable because the costs of the debt and the benefits of the capital are shared with future generations, while the costs and benefits of current expenditures are borne only by the current generation (Musgrave, 1988). Ricardo did note that hypothetically it is possible to conceive of debt and tax financing as identical—Ricardian equivalence—but rejected that conception as unrealistic (O'Driscoll, 1977; Barro, 1974).

Today's New Classical economists believe that the economy is in equilibrium at a natural rate of unemployment. (The Bureau of Labor Statistics only carries as unemployed those who have made some effort in the past four weeks to find work, such as filling out an application.) The natural rate is defined as the long-term rate of unemployment determined by structural forces in labor and product markets and associated with potential national income at which a steady, nonaccelerating inflation can be sustained indefinitely. The natural rate hypothesis further holds that government policies to achieve an actual rate different from the natural rate are ineffective in the long run and only surprise or unanticipated policies can have an effect, even in the short run, on such real economic variables as output and employment.

Keynesian economists believe that a modern monetary economy may be stuck at a less-than-full-employment equilibrium. Consequently, they advocate fiscal and monetary policies to increase the effective demand needed to move the economy toward full employment. Effective demand in a monetary economy means that creditworthiness or money is needed before a consumption or investment expenditure takes place. Although we all have a stable propensity to consume, Keynesians believe investors have a more volatile, expectational demand—influenced by nerves, hysteria, digestion, and reactions to the weather (Keynes, 1936, p. 162). Sometimes investor demand has to be induced. To do so, public debt and tax financing is expanded beyond the classically sanctioned public expenditures for wars and natural disasters to ones encouraging employment during peacetime.

When society demands public services, how to finance them is always an issue. The simple classical answer of using taxes to finance consumption expenditures and debt to finance investment is not easily put into practice. In fact, there are not any uniformly accepted definitions of consumption goods versus investment goods, not even the U.S. Commerce Department's. Theoretically, for example, investment expenditures may be defined as additions to physical, financial, and human capital; consumption expenditures are reduced to a limited few goods that provide no future stream of benefits. If economic growth is a policy goal at less than full employment, as it is for Keynesians, deficit financing may be the most beneficial; both consumption and investment expenditures expand employment and output. At full employment, however, inflation may become the policy problem.

The danger of debt financing is that it may be too intoxicating to the body politic. Reelection is most easily achieved by providing the electorate pleasure without pain—a free lunch. Thus, determining the optimal amount of government intervention in the private marketplace—through taxing, borrowing, and spending—is always a political issue.

National Income and Product Accounts

The national income and product accounts provide the most important indicators of a country's domestic and international economic health—though their adequacy is often questioned (see Eisner, 1989c, and Kendrick, 1972). Consequently, some economists adjust the official definitions to present a clearer and fuller picture of our economic status, from their standpoint and to support their convictions. National income and product accounts measure the amount of economic activity, in revenue and expenditure terms by calendar years. In contrast, the federal budget (fiscal) year begins October 1.

Although there are an infinite number of ways to subdivide an economy, most commonly economists delineate four sectors: persons or households, businesses, government, and foreign or "rest-of-the-world." Within a country's national accounts are two important balances of expenditures and receipts: government budget and foreign or rest-of-the-world. Over the decade of the 1980s, both the federal component of the government budget and the current-account component of the rest-of-the-world sector have typically been in deficit with expenditures exceeding revenues: These are the twin deficits that add to national debt and reduce net domestic ownership of foreign assets, respectively.

The federal budget is a statement of anticipated expenditures and revenues for a fiscal year. The *national debt* (or federal debt) is the total amount of net deficits piled up over the years by the federal government;

think of the national debt as a reservoir filled with about $2.3 trillion of debt held by the public. Deficits fill the reservoir and surpluses empty it. The *budget deficit* is the amount of dollars that our federal government borrows in a given fiscal year because its expenditures exceed its revenues; think of the federal budget deficit as a river currently flowing into the national debt reservoir at the rate of $150-plus billion per year. (Surpluses would be the out-flow.)

The balance of international payments is a double-entry system of accounting. Each transaction creates a flow of exports or imports and a flow of capital (capital account) to pay for it. The flow of exports and imports is stated in three basic ways: balance of trade or merchandise trade (exports and imports of goods), balance of goods and services (includes net investment income as well as goods and services), and current-account balance (includes the other two balances plus unilateral transfers). Historically, the current-account balance falls between the other two.

The *current-account deficit*, the less notorious of the "evil" twin deficits, is the *net* dollars per year that foreigners earn by trading with the United States. This deficit river of dollars enlarges the reservoir of net foreign ownership of our assets—the so-called selling of America. The size of this reservoir is the value (at time of purchase less depreciation) of United States assets owned by foreigners minus foreign assets owned by Americans. There is considerable dispute about the extent of our international debtor status, because official U.S. current-account data are not universally accepted as the last word. The *Survey of Current Business* (June 1990, p. 54) recently acknowledged the deficiencies in measurement and suspended publication of our international debtor/creditor status pending reformulation.

Part of the reason is that U.S. foreign assets were, on average, purchased earlier than foreign-owned assets here. Therefore, on the whole, U.S.-owned assets have had longer to appreciate, because the value included in the current account (purchase price less depreciation) does not reflect the almost constant inflationary pressures since World War II. U.S. gold holdings should also be evaluated at current market prices. On the other side of the ledger are unrecorded capital inflows and the evaluation at current market prices of loans to less developed countries by U.S. banks (see B. Friedman, 1988 and 1990, and Eisner and Pieper, 1990). Although this deficit and debt are not obligations of our federal government, more significantly they do constitute growing foreign claims on national income and wealth.

The United States makes little official effort to measure its net worth, even though an accurate appraisal of economic health must be done in a stock-flow (reservoir-river) context. Net worth of households and firms, the difference between assets and liabilities, is tallied on a balance sheet. The net additional flows to the stock of net worth are measured by income and product accounts. The main reason for not tallying national net worth appears to be measurement difficulties. For example, in the government sector it is difficult to impute the value of many military and nonmilitary assets, because there is no market to set their prices. It would be even more difficult to set a value on our intangible societal assets, our social institutions of democracy and jurisprudence—what businesses call "good will" and households call "reputation." It is estimated that 25 percent of the capital stock in the United States is owned by various levels of government. Local and state governments own the bulk of this capital, which consists largely of schools, roads, and water and sewer systems (U.S. President, 1990, p. 122). (The authors in Part II handle the government sector in different ways. Sometimes the national government is isolated, and the local and state governments are aggregated with households. In recent years, local and state governments, in counterdistinction to the national government, have typically run a surplus.)

Because of these measurement difficulties, GNP does not take into account the imputed income from a large share of our national tangible and intangible assets, both human and nonhuman, from all sectors of the economy (see Eisner, 1989c). Consequently, the ratio between national debt and GNP is larger and may seem more ominous under the U.S. national income accounting scheme than it would be under generally approved accounting principles used by corporations and the United Nations (1964).[6]

For these and many other reasons, there is no consensus about the extent of the "burden" or "benefit" status of our federal-budget deficit and debt and our current-account deficit. The articles in Part II of this book reflect the disagreements over whether we are too deeply in debt domestically or abroad, or both. To understand the full significance of the arguments made there, it is important to understand how the twin deficits link to each other and to the national income and product accounts. The saving-investment identity is the place to start. The federal-budget deficit (net government *dis*saving) is identically equal to the current-account deficit (*negative* net foreign investment), plus the surplus of private saving over private domestic investment, and plus the statistical discrepancy. (In the next section, the statistical discrepancy is added to saving so that gross saving plus statistical discrepancy equals gross investment; it is not listed separately.)

Saving-Investment Identity: $S \equiv I$

The saving-investment identity is basic to and is defined by the rules of national income and product accounting.[7] It holds for all consolidations of the economy, including the one-sector economy of only households, which is not discussed here. In a two-sector (households and businesses) economy, net personal saving (NPS) plus gross business saving (GBS), which is private saving, is defined as equal to gross domestic investment (GDI).

$$NPS + GBS \equiv GDI \tag{1}$$

Adding personal consumption (C) to the left side of identity (1) gives the earnings, or income, definition of GNP. Adding C to the right side gives the product definition of GNP.

In three-sector (households, businesses, and government) and four-sector (households, businesses, government, and rest-of-the-world) economies, the "simple" relationship between the saving-investment identity and GNP breaks down. In a three-sector economy, the breakdown occurs because now saving is national saving (S), which is composed of net government saving or surplus (NGS) in addition to private saving. Net government saving is defined as gross taxes (Tx) minus transfer payments (Tr) minus government purchases of goods and services (G).

$$S \equiv GDI$$
$$\text{or} \qquad NPS + GBS + NGS \equiv GDI$$
$$\text{or} \qquad NPS + GBS + Tx - Tr - G \equiv GDI \qquad (2)$$

So that the addition of consumption (C) to both sides of the identity will total GNP, it is necessary to add G to both sides as well (+ G cancels −G on the left side); this is also true for the four-sector economy.

In a four-sector economy, national saving is unchanged, but the investment side is augmented by net foreign investment (NFI), which is identically net exports minus payments to foreigners in the form of government interest and of net transfers by government and persons. Gross domestic investment plus net foreign investment is identically national investment (I).

$$S \equiv I$$
$$\text{or} \qquad S \equiv GDI + NFI$$
$$\text{or} \qquad NPS + GBS + NGS \equiv GDI + NFI \qquad (3)$$

The Twin Deficits

The twin deficits can be defined in terms of the saving-investment identity for a four-sector economy. The *budget deficit* is the negative of net government saving ($\equiv - NGS$), and the *current-account deficit* is the negative of net foreign investment ($\equiv - NFI$).

When the federal budget account and the current account are not in balance, financial flows must offset the deficits or surpluses. For the federal budget, the financial flows (besides new taxes) that can offset the deficit are newly printed money and newly issued government debt obligations—in other words, funding through money creation and borrowing. Usually only a small share of federal revenue is obtained via the printing press—$17 billion in 1987 (Barro, 1990, p. 189).

The current-account deficit (surplus) is balanced by the capital account surplus (deficit). A capital account surplus (capital inflow) is a rise, caused by a current-account deficit, in the reservoir of international debt. The net foreign capital inflow may be used to purchase private domestic assets (for example, Rockefeller Center) or to acquire accounts in U.S. banks, private or government debt obligations, or obligations of (deposits in) the Federal Reserve, or to buy U.S. assets abroad. Dollars owned by foreigners because of the current-account deficit may constitute claims on government or private assets.

The federal-budget balance is defined explicitly as the equality of government expenditures (G + Tr) and tax revenues (Tx) or

$$(G + Tr) - Tx = 0 \tag{4}$$

Allowing for money creation and federal deficits alters the federal-budget balance in two respects. First, federal revenue can come from the printing press ($\$ - \$_{-1}$) or borrowing ($B^g - B_{-1}{}^g$), as well as taxes, where $\$$ and $\$_{-1}$ are the new and old stocks of money and B^g and $B_{-1}{}^g$ are the new and old stocks of government debt—bonds, notes, and bills; it is assumed that the budget deficit ($B^g - B_{-1}{}^g$) is financed entirely by borrowing from the public and not partially by the Federal Reserve buying government debt with new money ($\$ - \$_{-1}$), that is, monetizing it. (Only a net increase in debt obligations or money produces new federal revenue; reissuing government bonds, notes, or bills as they come due or replacing money as it wears out are not net sources of federal revenue.) Second, the government's interest payments on the debt are an expenditure ($R_{-1}B_{-1}{}^g$, where R_{-1} is the interest rate and $B_{-1}{}^g$ the old debt).

The expanded federal-budget identities now may be defined:

$$G + Tr + R_{-1}B_{-1}{}^g - Tx + [(\$ - \$_{-1}) + (B^g - B_{-1}{}^g)] \equiv 0$$

where $- NGS \equiv \$ - \$_{-1} + B^g - B_{-1}{}^g \tag{5}$

As noted above, it is always true that the current and capital accounts must offset each other:

$$NFI \equiv \text{net capital outflow}$$
or $- NFI \equiv \text{net capital inflow} \tag{6}$

The saving-investment identity for four sectors (identity 3) provides a link between the twin deficits and the surplus of private saving (NPS + GBS) over private domestic investment (GDI), that is, (NPS + GBS) – GDI.

$$NGS + NPS + GBS \equiv NFI + GDI$$
or $NGS \equiv NFI - [(NPS + GBS) - GDI]$
or $- NGS \equiv - NFI + [(NPS + GBS) - GDI]$

or   federal budget deficit $\equiv$ current account deficit
                    $+$ surplus private saving   (7)

Turning to the financial flows, the newly issued government money and debt obligations (identity 5) are identical to net capital inflow (identity 6) plus surplus private saving:

$$\$ - \$_{-1} + (B^g - B_{-1}{}^g)$$
$$\equiv \text{net capital inflow} + \text{surplus private saving} \tag{8}$$

Examining identities (7) and (8) can help us think about public policy concerns caused by the twin deficits; however, caution is advised. For example, proposing a reduction on one side of identities (7) or (8) in order to reduce the other side is simplistic, because an accounting identity is not a behavioral relationship, not an equation. Even if accounting identities were behavioral relationships, critical assumptions with regard to changes in GNP, exchange rates, and interest rates would need to be addressed completely before proceeding further.

ANALOGIES BETWEEN RICH AND POOR, NATIONS AND PERSONS

The gap between rich and poor—nations and persons—is wide and growing wider. Wassily Leontief's United Nations study (1977) indicated that the rich nations will get richer and the poor nations will get poorer on into the 21st century.

In July 1990 the Center on Budget and Policy Priorities released a report showing that the distribution of income in the United States is now the most unequal ever recorded. The bottom 40 percent of Americans receive only slightly more after-tax income than the top 1 percent—14.2 percent to 12.6 percent. Between 1980 and 1990 the purchasing power of the poorest 40 percent of Americans fell by 2.5 percent, while that of the richest 1 percent increased by 87 percent.

The distribution of wealth has always been more skewed than the distribution of income. The present extent of the difference cannot be measured because the latest available wealth data are for 1983. In that year, however, one-third of the nation's privately held wealth was owned by the top 1 percent of American families, one-third was owned by the next 9 percent, and one-third was held by the remaining 90 percent of the population. Since that time, supply-side economics has probably exacerbated the inequity of wealth distribution.

In his definition of "Burden of the Debt," Robert Eisner (1987) draws a sharp distinction between the burden of debt contracted in a nation's own currency or in a foreign currency. (The debt, domestic and foreign, of poor nations is usually contracted in terms of a foreign currency.) Thomas Macaulay, writing in the mid-1800s, was eloquent in his skepticism that national debt was a burden for a rich nation, like England at the time:

> The beggared, the bankrupt, [English] society not only proved able to meet all its obligations, but while meeting those obligations, grew richer and richer so fast that the growth could almost be discerned by the eye (1978, pp. 5-6).

In the Introduction, I noted that persons and countries can be compared in terms of their relative liquidity, the relative ease of unlocking their assets' present value with or without terminating ownership. The usual difference cited between individuals and nations is that any sovereign country has the self-proclaimed right to print its own currency (create supply) and to make it legal tender to pay taxes and other obligations (create demand). However, banks have long had the right to create money, and since the Monetary Control Act of 1980, so do all depository institutions. The use of credit card money continues to increase. Gambling casinos "mint" their own money, and so do companies that issue coupons and rebates. The top 1 percent of American households can command the same economic respect—the same creditworthiness—as First World nations; the top 10 percent have better credit than most Second World nations. Neither Third World nations nor poor Americans are creditworthy.

Another advantage that a nation has over an individual, it is said, is that it is immortal and consequently never has to pay the principal on its debts—it need only service them and roll them over. However, individuals may never have to pay the principal on their debts either if they can pass their debts on to their descendants, as Keynes illustrated with Lewis Carroll's story of the professor and the tailor in *Sylvie and Bruno*. The tailor tries to achieve a "spurious and delusive immortality" by always being willing to wait another year to be paid for his suit, because the professor promises to double his money if he waits (1932, pp. 370–71).

In our modern world of credit, current income and wealth need not cover current expenditures if trust is sufficient—if others maintain confidence in our intentions or future abilities to pay our bills (Gambetta, 1988). Debts stem from the ability to buy on credit; good credit provides the means to go into debt. The better your credit, the more potential debt you can contract. But at some point which is never easily defined, when your (net) debt load increases too much, your credit rating falls. An analogy can be drawn between health and the exercise of muscles, and credit (economic health) and the exercise of debt. The question is, at what point do the aches and pains of more strenuous exercise no longer signal the building of strength but rather an impending collapse?

An indelible lesson of history is that debt and deficits affect the rich and poor—whether persons or nations—differently. Assets are a congealed flow of income that may not be able to be reliquified when they are needed. Assets can be turned into money only at the buyers' behest, not the owners'. In comparison, the reconversion of money into consumption or investment goods is constrained only by the amount you have relative to the value of the goods you wish to purchase.

Debts that rich households and rich countries amass are generally the least-cost way of achieving liquidity; when they come due, they can be paid off, rolled over, or shirked, depending on what the rich believe to be their optimal future behavior.[8] Rich nations and persons have the potential to have a reason, a plan, when they go into debt. If incurring debt is more efficient than selling present or future assets now, why not do so?

In poor households and poor countries, action is motivated by crises, not by plans. The debts and deficits of the poor—because their needs cannot be met by current income—are contracted in terms of the asset the lender wants. The assets of poor countries—undereducated populations and unwanted currency—and of poor people—unskilled labor and no credit—are normally illiquid.

In a fictional world where inflation (deflation) is anticipated perfectly, contracts can be written to take all the uncertainty out of any nominal transaction. In the world we live in, however, unanticipated inflation or deflation is part of the unfairness of an uncertain future. In our world, after a contract is signed and the terms are set, neither lenders nor borrowers want the purchasing power of the "standard of value" to change in an adverse way. When the value of this standard decreases because of credit expansion ("credit money"), monetization of the debt, or inflation, debtors rejoice, because they know a dollar is a dollar as far as repayment is concerned. Conversely, when the process is reversed and the value of the standard rises, creditors jump for joy. Stability of the standard of value is crucial in reducing risk on both sides of the market, because contract terms don't change over time—except through repudiation.

The U.S. dollar is still the currency in which most contracts are written in the United States and many other countries. In much of Latin America, contracts for nations and persons are written in terms of dollars, not in terms of domestic currency. This is so for two reasons: The lender controls the terms of the contract and secures protection against the instability of the domestic currency. Consequently, inflation in Latin American countries and most other less-developed countries is not a credit to the debtor or a tax to the creditor; the standard of value is the creditor's choice.

CONCLUSIONS

The debate over the debt and the twin deficits is about creditworthiness, saving and investment, the tradeoff between equality of opportunity and efficiency of the market, and policy prescriptions.

Nations and persons have more in common than is usually recognized with regard to the benefit or burden of debt. Advantaged nations and persons are creditworthy and go into debt voluntarily. To be disadvantaged means the opposite. The United States is an advantaged country; we control our own destiny. Our national debt and twin deficits are choices we have made. Our national budgeting decisions are motivated by our interpretation of the past, our interpretation of economic cause and effect, and our personal value systems.

Much of the dispute between economic theories concerns their interpretation of consumption and investment: definitions, measurements, and their interrelationships. If, as Keynes wrote, his theory and classical theory are no different at full employment, then the definition of the natural rate of unemployment becomes crucial if it varies, and especially if it varies with regard to the actual rate.

The tradeoff between equality of opportunity and efficiency of the market is the essence of the dispute. This discussion emphasizes equality rather than efficiency because the majority of voting Americans believe that relatively more equality is against their personal interests and that more efficiency is in their personal interests. Social philosophers as dissimilar in viewpoint as Marx and Keynes claim that the majority of nations and people would gain with more equality, but the majority of U.S. voters are currently attracted by the slim chance of large prizes.[9]

The creditworthiness of the United States—its strength, endurance, importance, and measurement—is at the bottom of the policy prescriptions debate. For some of the authors in this volume, creditworthiness is the proverbial horseshoe nail for want of which not only the horseshoe is lost but also the horse, rider, battle, and kingdom. For others, creditworthiness is assumed and assured, and debt financing is just a way of doing the nation's business of minimizing inequality and inefficiency: "Treat national economic goals as a portfolio problem, invest wherever the expected national return is the greatest" is their economic proverb. For still other authors here, creditworthiness is not an important part of their policy analysis.

A society needs to be true to its own culture to elicit its people's best efforts (Fallows, 1989). The uniqueness of the United States has lain in upward mobility which its institutions and resource base have made possible. Did the deficits of the 1980s provide for the common defense and promote the general welfare, or did we mortgage our children's and grandchildren's inheritance? Did the large deficits reduce the losses from periods of economic recession, or did they cost us our world leadership? Do government expenditures crowd out, or crowd in private investment? What is the optimal amount of government intervention in the marketplace? In the chapters that follow, noted economists give their answers to these questions.

NOTES

I am grateful for helpful comments from Barbara Armentrout, J. R. Brown, Robert Eisner, Brian Peckham, and Bonnie Rock.

1. A large share of the customs duties were "sin taxes" on wines, distilled spirits, tea, and coffee. There were no *net* revenues from the sale of public lands for almost the first 50 years of the federal government. The Louisiana and Florida purchases and other lands cost $49.7 million, and receipts were only $38.4 million as of September 30, 1832 (James D. Richardson, ed., *Messaqes and Papers of the Presidents*, Vol. 3, 1897, p. 1282; cited in Kimmel, p. 18).

2. The King James Bible was one of the original sources for the notion that sin and debt are interchangeable (see the Lord's Prayer, Luke 11:4). And the American theater has long used the "shame of debt" as one of its most powerful themes. Suicide as the means to secure life insurance to restore lost familial pride is in Eugene O'Neill's *The Iceman Cometh*, Clifford Odets' *Awake and Sing*, and Arthur Miller's *Death of a Salesman*. Linda Loman in the "requiem" section of *Death of a Salesman* speaks to Willy's grave: "I made the last payment on the house today. Today, dear. And there'll be nobody home. [A sob rises in her throat] We're free and clear. [Sobbing more fully released] We're free." (Miller, 1949, p. 133; many thanks to David Kranes for the portrayal of debt as sin and suffering in the American theatre.)

3. My 92-year-old Aunt Grace, who has ranched in Colorado for the past 70 years, always calls them the Terrible Twenties and the Dirty Thirties.

4. The original bill to set up the Federal Reserve in 1913 included a form of depository insurance to protect the solvency of banks and thereby give confidence to depositors, but that clause was taken out as part of a House-Senate compromise. The 1933 establishment of the Federal Deposit Insurance Corporation (FDIC) virtually ended runs on federally-chartered banks. Depository insurance was quickly extended to lend stability to savings and loans and credit unions as well. Over the years the amount of insurance per deposit increased tenfold. In the 1980s the insured deposits were used as collateral by Charles H. Keating, Jr. and other less notorious savings and loan executives to finance speculative ventures and for personal gain. Their actions led to the failure of many savings and loan institutions—certainly a paradoxical outcome.

5. Robert Eisner (1989a) referred to "Measurement Without Theory" in his 1988 presidential address to the American Economic Association, focusing on the problems of theory without relevant measurement. It is the title of Tjalling Koopmans' (1947) brilliant review of Burns and Mitchell's work on business cycles. A review of Jan Tinbergen's work (1939) for the League of Nations by John Maynard Keynes highlights the same problem of measuring first and doing the theorizing later (Keynes, 1973, pp. 285-320, see p. 320 especially).

6. A high-level federal government working group on improving economic statistics recently recommended that the United States move to the United Nations System of National Accounts (see *Survey of Current Business*, June 1990, pp. 20-30).

7. This model of the federal-account and current-account deficits is adapted from Baumol and Blinder (1988) and Barro (1990). The formulation used does not take into account international transfer payments or net foreign labor income (Barro, 1990, p. 373n). In addition, prices are held constant to simplify the exposition.

8. Debt repudiation has become a topic of academic interest especially since the debt moratoriums by Mexico (1982) and Brazil (1987). Recent papers by Bulow and Rogoff (1989), Calvo (1988), and Musumeci and Sinkey (1990) discuss enforcement, expectations, and pricing of less-developed-country (LDC) loans. Calvo (1988) and Kotlikoff, Persson, and Svensson (1988) both study the time consistency of optimal policy: Calvo in terms of the "credibility" dilemma faced by politicians, and Kotlikoff et al. in terms of a possible solution to it through a social contract paid for by transfers from younger to successively older generations. Regarding repudiation Keynes wrote, "Assuredly it does not pay to be good" (1932, p. 116).

9. Social philosophers frequently predict revolutions over equality. Barbara Ward says the most important revolution is that of equality—equality of men [and women] and nations (1962), and Will and Ariel Durant—summarizing what they had learned that might "illuminate present affairs, future probabilities, the nature of man, and the conduct of states"—say, "We conclude that the concentration of wealth is natural and inevitable, and is periodically alleviated by violent or peaceable partial redistribution" (1968, p. 57).

2

The Debt, the Deficit, and Disadvantaged Children: Generational Impacts and Age, Period, and Cohort Effects

TIMOTHY M. SMEEDING

INTRODUCTION

This chapter is not about how "big" or "small" the federal budget deficit or debt is. It is not primarily about the macroeconomic effects of substantial sustained deficits and the mounting debts which they bring about. Others are much more qualified than I to discuss these issues (Heilbroner and Bernstein, 1989; Eisner, 1986; Friedman, 1988; Schultze, 1989). This chapter is about the distributional burden placed on disadvantaged children by both the deficit and the debt.

It is clear to several observers (Palmer, Smeeding, and Torrey, 1988; Preston, 1984) that there is both a growing inequality in well-being among children and a growing inequality between most families with children and other groups, notably childless couples and the elderly. These inequalities are characterized by greater income inequality among families with children, by the growing number of children in single-parent families, and by the high poverty rates among children compared with other groups.

This chapter places the dilemma of disadvantaged children in the context of changes in federal taxation and expenditure policy that have both accompanied and in part caused the growth in the federal deficit over the past decade. It begins by assessing and interpreting these and other related facts using cross-sectional and time-series data. Accompanying the increase in the federal debt was a growing inequality in the underlying distribution of household income, a changing distribution of the tax burden, and differing trends in income poverty which have rewarded some and penalized others. Although these distributional patterns have largely been decided by our open political process, they are troubling to many analysts, this author in particular. Distributional choices are often viewed as being relatively costless. In other words, they are viewed as imposing no overall long-term economic burden on society. But these policies do, I argue, have a serious cost, both for the affected individuals and for society as a whole.

To assess these costs, we need to understand the differential impacts which these distributional changes are having and will continue to have on the various generations of individuals who are today's children, adults, and elderly. I begin to disentangle these impacts by differentiating three types of generational impacts: age, period, and cohort (or demographic) effects. These interact with one another to produce differential levels of well-being for each group. Next, I explain the way that patterns and changes in the deficit have impacts via each of these types of effects, and the way that these effects in turn are influencing the deficit. I end with an assessment of what I believe to be the real burden of the deficit (and federal debt) on U.S. children today, and what modest steps we as a society might make to offset this burden.

FACTS

The changing patterns of outlays, deficit, and debt are familiar to most analysts and social observers. However, a brief review of these patterns is necessary to lead us into the topic at hand. The U.S. federal government deficit as a percentage of gross national product (GNP) rose from 0.3 percent in 1970 to 5.4 percent in 1985 before falling to 2.9 percent in 1989. The Congressional Budget Office (CBO) forecasts the federal deficit to fall below 2 percent of GNP by 1994 (USCBO, 1990). In one sense then, the deficit "crisis" seems to have passed. Although we must still cut back further to reach Gramm–Rudman balanced budget targets by 1992, we are experiencing falling federal deficits as a percentage of GNP. And the federal deficit is at about the same level today as it was a decade ago. In short, taxes are failing to keep up with expenditures at about the same rate today as they were 10 years ago.

Public debt as a percentage of GNP appears to have hit a plateau as well, standing at 42.5 percent of GNP in 1989. The CBO forecasts it to decline only to about 41 percent of GNP by 1994. The opportunity cost of a substantially larger debt to be serviced by our federal tax dollars, while not growing in relative terms, will remain with us for the foreseeable future.

Gramlich (1989) points to several causes of decreases in the federal deficit during the latter half of the 1980s. These include higher taxes due to increases in the social security payroll tax, and significantly lower expenditures for nondefense discretionary spending. Outlays for nondefense discretionary spending—everything other than defense, entitlements (retirement, disability, and health care), and net interest on the debt is collapsed into this category—fell from 5.9 percent of GNP in 1980 to 3.7 percent in 1989. Many observers would see much of this decline as beneficial. Reduced enforcement of Internal Revenue Service (IRS) rules and regulations and a slightly less effective Bureau of Land Management means less bureaucratic interference with private production. On the other hand, these declines have also lessened the effectiveness of environmental programs and other regulators, particularly those who were supposed to be watching over savings and loan associations, thrifts, federal housing programs, and private pension plans. The long-term costs of these expenditure reductions have yet to be tallied, but they promise to be several times in excess of the short-term budgetary saving which they brought during the 1980s. For instance, recent congressional reports (Broder, 1990) show that individuals and corporations owe the federal government $60 billion in taxes that remain uncollected because the IRS has insufficient resources to collect them. Our collective short-sightedness in the name of deregulation has large long-term costs.

More directly linked to this chapter, declining federal discretionary outlays have also included cuts in income support and education programs for disadvantaged children. And, according to the CBO forecasts, nondefense discretionary outlays will fall to 3.4 percent of GNP in 1994 under current law. In contrast, entitlement spending, particularly for social security and Medicare, has continued to grow. Defense spending has peaked and is in decline, though perhaps not yet rapidly enough for some.

Of particular interest is the rising level of federal expenditure for net interest. More than one dollar of every seven (14.9 percent) of federal outlays now go to servicing the debt. These outlays rose by $17 billion from 1988 to 1989 alone, now standing at $169 billion. By 1994, they are expected to top $205 billion. The opportunity cost of these outlays is *not* trivial, as we shall see.

On the revenue side, a different sort of shift has taken place. Federal revenues remained at between 19.5 and 19.2 percent of GNP in 1970, 1980, and 1989, but the composition of these revenues changed dramatically. While income taxes have held constant at about 45–47 percent of total revenues, social security payroll taxes have risen from 23.1 to 36.5 percent of federal revenues. Corporate income taxes and excise taxes declined. The effect of these shifts in the composition of revenue was to make the federal tax system considerably less progressive than it had been in 1980; see Table 2-1. Though the 1986 Tax Reform Act actually increased overall federal tax rates in the upper income brackets, the net effect of the tax reduction of 1981, the federal tax reform of 1986, and the Social Security Act of 1983 was to leave us with a significantly less progressive federal tax structure in 1990 compared with 1980. Social security and Medicare payroll taxes have

TABLE 2-1
Effective Federal Tax Rates, Selected Years, 1977–90*

Year	Lowest 20%	Second	Middle	Fourth	Highest 20%
			Family Income Quintiles		
1977	9.5	15.6	19.6	21.9	27.1
1980	8.4	15.7	20.0	23.0	27.3
1985	10.6	16.1	19.3	21.7	24.0
1990	9.7	16.7	20.3	22.5	25.8
Change					
1977–90	0.2	1.1	0.7	0.6	-1.3
1980–90	1.3	1.0	0.3	-0.5	-1.5

SOURCE: U.S. Congressional Budget Office (1990).

*The method for calculating effective federal tax rates—the percentage of family income paid in taxes—for people ranked in quintiles by their adjusted pretax family income is detailed below. (Adjusted pretax income includes all cash income plus realized capital gains and is measured before all federal taxes, including those collected from business but assumed to be borne by families.) People are assigned to quintiles based on family income divided by the poverty threshold for the appropriate family size. Tax rates for the lowest quintile were calculated excluding families with negative or zero incomes. The burden of the individual income tax and the employees' portion of the payroll tax is attributed to the families who directly pay these taxes. The portion of the payroll tax collected from employers is assumed to be shifted back onto employees in the form of lower wages. Excise taxes are assumed to be passed forward to individual consumers in higher prices on goods subject to the tax. Finally, although the corporate income tax is collected from corporations, families are assumed ultimately to bear its economic burden. These estimates assume that one-half the corporate income tax is allocated to capital income and one-half to labor income. The method of allocation does not affect the main conclusions about how the distribution of the tax burden among income classes has changed over time.

increased substantially over this period. In 1990, 77 percent of families will pay higher employer and employee payroll taxes than federal income taxes (USCBO, 1990). While there is good reason for the payroll tax increase (as mentioned below), it is the main reason the federal tax system is less progressive today than it was ten years ago. If we were to add in changes in state and local taxes, the reduction in federal tax burdens among the upper income groups would be even more pronounced (Pechman, 1989) than that shown in Table 2-2.

At the same time that relative tax burdens were becoming less progressive, the pretax distribution of income was becoming much more unequal; see Table 2-2, Panel A. According to the U.S. Census Bureau, in 1988 the income share of the top 5 percent of families reached 17.2 percent, higher than any time since 1952; the top 20 percent of families had the highest share of income ever recorded, 44 percent of total income. The bottom 20 percent had an income share of only 4.6 percent that year, just one-tenth

TABLE 2-2
Before-Tax Income Shares: Selected Years, 1948–88

Panel A. Before-Tax Income Shares, Census Data,
Selected Years, 1948–88

Year	Top 5% of Families	Top 20% of Families	Bottom 20% of Families
1948	17.1	42.4	4.9
1952	17.4	41.5	4.9
1957	15.6	40.4	5.1
1962	15.7	41.3	5.0
1967	15.2	40.4	5.5
1972	15.9	41.4	5.4
1977	15.7	41.5	5.2
1981	15.4	41.9	5.0
1987	16.9	43.7	4.6
1988	17.2	44.0	4.6

SOURCE: Pechman (1990, p. 2: Table 1). Census income includes transfer payments (e.g., social security benefits, unemployment compensation, and welfare payments) but excludes capital gains. Distribution includes only families and excludes single persons living alone.

Panel B. Before-Tax Income Shares, Internal Revenue
Service Data, Selected Years, 1948–86

Year	Top 1% of Tax Units	Top 2% of Tax Units	Top 5% of Tax Units	Top 10% of Tax Units	Top 15% of Tax Units
1948	9.8	13.4	20.2	27.9	34.3
1952	8.7	12.1	18.7	26.7	33.4
1963	8.8	12.3	19.4	28.2	35.5
1967	8.8	12.3	19.6	28.3	35.5
1972	8.0	11.4	18.7	27.8	35.4
1977	7.8	11.3	18.9	28.3	36.1
1981	8.1	11.5	19.0	28.6	36.5
1986	14.7	18.2	26.6	36.8	45.1

SOURCE: Pechman (1990, p. 3: Table 2). The IRS *Statistics of Income* series uses an income concept which excludes transfer payments, but includes realized capital gains in full.

as much as the top quintile. In other postwar periods of sustained growth, such as the 1960s, the income distribution became more equal, with the shares at the top falling and those at the bottom increasing; see 1967 figures in Panel A of Table 2-2. But during the 1980s, despite eight years of con- tinuous economic growth, the income distribution continues to become more unequal. Most of this widening was due to the rapid and continuous growth in both the shares and income levels of the top 1–20 percent of families; see Table 2-2, Panel B. IRS data, which includes capital gains, show that the top 15 percent of taxpayers had 45.1 percent of pretax income in 1986, the highest share ever reported.

Pulling these distributional facts together, we find that inequality in pretax incomes grew over the 1980–90 period and that changes in federal tax policy further reinforced this change. The net impact, as shown in Table 2-3, was a more unequal pretax *and* posttax income distribution in 1988 compared with 1980 or 1977. By 1988, after-tax income inequality was higher than 1980 pretax income inequality. The modest equalizing effect of federal taxes on inequality continued to diminish over this period. Thus the supposed "progressivity" of the federal tax structure can be questioned.

The link between the growing inequality in incomes and the lessening progressivity of federal taxes may be linked to the deficit situation. As Heilbroner and Bernstein (1989) argue, the well-to-do now collect interest on their loans to the government rather than pay a like amount in income taxes. Those who are now arguing for an increase in the top federal income tax bracket from 28 to 33 percent to help reduce the deficit make similar distributional arguments and linkages. But nondistributional arguments to justify these tax developments could also be made. For instance, most economists would argue that the drop in the highest marginal income tax brackets since 1980, coupled with the broadening of the tax base in 1986, have led to a more efficient economy, one that is more driven by real economic incentives to work, save, and invest, and less driven by tax rates and tax policy. The fact that the highest income groups have benefited most from these changes, as evidenced by their rising income shares and levels, is the price that we pay for a more efficient economy. After all, changes in tax policy are openly debated on a regular basis. The Tax Reform Act of 1986 was widely hailed because one of its hallmarks was its supposed distributional neutrality. While the distribution of federal tax burdens *within* income classes was significantly narrowed by this act, analysts claimed that the progressivity of the income tax system across income classes was largely held constant (see Table 2-1). Recent tax proposals which would significantly increase or decrease federal tax progressivity (e.g., a reduction in payroll taxes or a capital gains tax cut, respectively) have not yet met with such widespread enthusiasm.

Thus, the matter of the distributional burden of the deficit is more complex than comparisons of changes in tax rates or income shares over time. The patterns of tax and expenditure which we have reviewed are a matter of social choice, not of debt burden. However, the social choice to

TABLE 2-3
Gini Coefficients of Inequality Before and After
Federal Taxes, Selected Years, 1977–88

Year	Before Federal Taxes	After Federal Taxes	Percentage Change Due to Taxes*
1948	0.4502	0.4185	-7.0
1980	0.4627	0.4320	-6.6
1984	0.4884	0.4700	-3.8
1988	0.4940	0.4722	-4.4

SOURCE: U.S. Congressional Budget Office (July 1988, p. 98).

*Percentage change is Before-Tax Gini minus After-Tax Gini divided by Before-Tax Gini.

deficit finance rather than to tax finance, to bear instead the opportunity cost of servicing the debt, and not to expand expenditures in key areas (such as Head Start and health care for mothers and infants) for budgetary reasons *does* have substantial long-run distributional effects. By changing perspectives slightly and considering the generations who are faced with repaying the federal debt, we can learn a great deal more about who is advantaged and disadvantaged (blessed and burdened) by the federal debt and its revenue and expenditure components.

GENERATIONAL IMPACTS

One way to think about the burden of the deficit and debt is to consider the way in which the deficit and debt affect various generations of individuals and families: children, adults, and the elderly. We can classify these groups in 1990 as follows: children are those aged 0–17 in 1990, adult ages are 18–64, and the elderly are aged 65 and over. Our purpose is to investigate the economic well-being of each group now and over their remaining life span. Clearly we will know with greater certainty the economic well-being of the elderly compared with adults. We will know least of all about today's children. The aged have a 65-year or longer economic history; the adults— baby boomers mainly—have some economic history, but not nearly as much as the old. Today's children, on the other hand, have a highly uncertain economic future.

At least three separate economic factors affect the economic well-being of each generation, at a point in time or over time: economic conditions, demographic changes, and public policy, especially public income support systems. These causal agents are important to both the level and trend in well-being for the elderly, adults, and children in several ways (Jencks, Palmer, and Smeeding, 1988). The following brief summary of some of these influences will provide the reader with an idea of their importance:

1. *Economic Conditions.* The overall state of the economy affects both levels and types of income received by various groups. Children's family incomes are heavily dependent on the employment status and earnings of their parents. Recent analyses (e.g., Danziger and Gottschalk, 1989) have shown how recessions affect the level and dispersion of earnings and hence the poverty status of children. While the retired elderly are less influenced by current economic conditions, they are not immune to them. High inflation can seriously deteriorate nominally (dollar) fixed income amounts (e.g., private pensions) over time or can lead to exorbitant prices for necessary items, such as health care and utilities. On the other hand, stock and bond market booms can tremendously increase the financial wealth of the elderly.

2. *Demographic Changes.* The size of birth cohorts, life expectancy at age 65, and changes in living and marriage patterns can all significantly affect the economic well-being of children and the elderly. Levy (1986) has shown how the increased labor force participation of women and the massive influx of the baby boom generation have depressed wages and earnings in the 1970s and 1980s. Life expectancy at age 65 has increased tremendously since 1960, extending the average lifespan of the 65-year-old elderly nearly 18 years. Moreover, the differential in life expectancy between women (over 19 years at age 65) and men (less than 15 years at age 65) has significantly affected the sex composition of the very old. The fastest growing age group in the United States today is aged 85 and over. Along with the growth of this group, serious chronic health problems at older ages create important patterns of special medical and social needs which must be addressed.

    Before 1950, over 60 percent of elderly widows lived with their children; in 1985, less than 20 percent did so. On the other hand, over one-half of all unmarried teenage mothers and one-third of those in their twenties share living arrangements with their parents. The causal factors which underlie the rise of single parenthood due to divorce, separation, and out-of-wedlock childbearing are not well identified. But the results in terms of higher poverty status, growing welfare dependence, and lower overall incomes are evident.

3. *Public Policy.* The aging of the population, growing numbers of single parents, and chronically high levels of unemployment have created an increased burden for public income support systems. While the antipoverty effectiveness of the income transfer system is relatively high, recent cutbacks in the growth of income support systems which largely benefit families with children (e.g., Aid to Families with Dependent Children [AFDC], food stamps, unemployment compensation, and public housing) are at least partially to blame for the rising incidence of poverty among children. In contrast, the continuing support for the social

security system and recent increases in Supplemental Security Income have significantly helped reduce poverty among the elderly.

The major task we face here is not to summarily list these changes, but rather to attempt to separate the influences of each of these components of change so that we can determine their importance as they relate to the issue of the burden of both the deficit and the debt on the coming generations. If we can separate the influence of policy, we may be able to speculate as to how past, current, and future policy regimes, and emerging changes in these regimes, are likely to affect the economic well-being of each group. Of course, it is difficult to separate the effects of economics, demography, and social policy on each of these groups not only because of their implicit interrelationships, but also because of the behavioral responses of individuals to each factor. Still, an attempt to ferret out these influences will be highly rewarding.

Our view of economic, demographic, and policy impacts considers the way that each age group or generation has moved and can be expected to move through their remaining economic lives. In order to make this intertemporal comparison, we must concern ourselves with disentangling three different types of impacts which we call age, period, and cohort effects. As each population group ages, its well-being is influenced by predictable changes in consumption, income, and assets. Economists often call these life-cycle or age effects. But to compare the life cycle of one group (e.g., the cohort of today's children born between 1972 and 1990) to others (e.g., the cohort of adult baby boomers born between 1946 and 1970, or the cohort of elderly and near elderly born between 1920 and 1935), we also have to separate cohort and period effects.

Demographic or cohort effects are those created by the relative size of various generations (e.g., today's adult baby-boom generation versus today's child and elderly baby bust groups). Differences in generation size alone often create economic and policy effects that generate distributional and budget gains or losses.

Finally, we must also disentangle period effects, the independent impact of the economic and social policy conditions through which each of these generations pass. In this way, not only are persons who are elderly, adults, or children at one particular point in time affected by economics, demographics, and policy, but entire generations are exposed to different mixes of these effects as each generation passes through its life cycle.

I will argue that the large deficits of the 1980s and the rapid increase in the debt which accompanied it will have important period and cohort effects on all three groups. In contrast, recent and expected future changes in the deficit are highly interrelated with the aging effects of the baby boom generation and the social security surplus which it is generating. Thus the "age" effects of the baby boom generation are a cause of, not caused by, some emerging patterns in the federal budget. We begin with this age effect, moving on to period and finally cohort effects, linking each to the distributional impacts of the budget deficit and debt.

While disentangling these effects is not a trivial task, there are emerging trends in measured economic well-being within and between each of these groups which are troubling and which may require significant changes in economic and social policy. These changes in policy are important to the long-run economic health of our nation. Moreover, the popular media and advocacy groups are beginning to embrace two opposite themes: Some embrace a "generational equity" theme, and others adopt an "interdependence of generations" theme. The former (e.g., Longman, 1990) claims that the elderly today are better off than other mainly middle age groups (with or without children) in the United States, and further, that we ought to redistribute income between generations to right this imbalance. The latter (e.g., Kingson, Hirshorn, and Cornman, 1986) argues that the reciprocity of giving and receiving between generations over time is overlooked by the former but is of critical importance in assessing well-being. While we disagree with the "us against them" framework of the first group out of hand, we are not yet ready to concede that richer generations will always adequately and equitably support poor ones either. Rather, we feel that it is important to thoroughly consider the relative well-being of today's elderly versus tomorrow's elderly and versus today's children in light of the current and future impacts of the deficit and debt on each group before making claims about generational equity or generational dependence, much less basing policy on either claim.

AGE EFFECTS

The aging of the baby-boom cohort and the effects of the 1983 Social Security Amendments, which were designed to provide a reserve in the social security trust fund to help pay for the retirement of the baby-boom cohort, have had a substantial positive impact on the budget deficit in recent years. This impact will grow over the next several decades. By 1994, the annual excess of revenues over outlays will be $117 billion, according to Aaron (1990). The overall federal deficit will be just about the same ($122 billion). Hence by 1994, in the absence of the social security trust fund build-up, the deficit to GNP ratio would be approximately twice as large as it is expected to be—3.6 percent instead of 1.8 percent.

The real concern over proposals to reduce social security payroll taxes is a concern about precisely this impact. If payroll taxes are reduced, the distributional burden of the federal tax system will be much less regressive. But if only this change is realized, the deficit will be much larger, the cost of servicing the debt will be much greater, *and* the social security reserve "nest egg" being built up by the baby boomers will be dissipated.[1] If another tax is levied to make up for lost payroll tax revenues, the additional deficit and debt problems would be erased. Net national saving would neither increase or decrease from its forecast level. The net distributional impact of the federal tax system would depend on the incidence of the tax which was chosen to replace the payroll tax reduction. Higher income tax rates would produce greater progressivity, a national sales or value-added tax would likely be no more progressive than the current system, and perhaps less so. But even if another tax partially replaced the payroll tax, there would be significant age effects due to the depletion of the social security trust fund. The "nest egg" of credits for future old age benefits would be lost.

As Aaron (1990) and colleagues (Aaron, Bosworth, and Burtless, 1988) and others (Myers and Schobel, 1983) have argued, today's adult baby boom generation will impose no burden on future workers if they consume no more than they produce. Because, under current tax and benefit rates, the baby boomers will receive back in social security benefits just about what they pay in taxes with a real rate of return of about 2 percent (Boskin, 1986), they will impose no burden on future generations. However, were Senator Daniel Patrick Moynihan's proposal to pass, there would indeed be a loss of social security revenues and therefore a higher social security burden on future generations.

The relationship between the social security surplus and the burden of the deficit and debt is simply one of interacting circumstances. To offset the age effects of the baby boom, payroll taxes must be raised today. Because of the cohort effect of relatively fewer elderly today compared with the next decade, these taxes are helping to build up reserves in the trust fund. Because these revenues can only be used to purchase federal government debt, the good news for the deficit is that the social security trust fund surplus, now and in the near future, helps raise national saving by offsetting some portion of the federal deficit. This in turn frees up additional saving for private investment.

The bad news is that, from a cross-sectional perspective, this trust fund is financed by a proportionate tax on earnings which, because of a ceiling ($51,300 in 1990) and because it is only levied on earnings, is regressive with respect to total income. If we wish to offset the regressivity of the payroll tax, we could continue to expand the earned income tax credit for families with children. Such a policy would provide much needed help to low-income families with children while still preserving the integrity and fiscal soundness of the social security trust fund. But the build-up of this trust fund is largely due to public policy put in place specifically to take account of the aging impact of the baby-boom generation. In my opinion, this policy should not be changed.

PERIOD EFFECTS

Much more important as a negative consequence of the federal deficit and outlays for debt service is the deleterious effect on today's and tomorrow's children. Due largely to the luck of period (and cohort) effects, and related policy inaction, the deficit is having the exact opposite impact on the elderly. But the needs of children are not now being addressed by the federal government largely because of the deficit dilemma and because of our collective unwillingness to raise taxes, lower the deficit, and undertake a new public agenda. Our vehicle for measuring unmet needs is the emergent pattern of poverty rates among children during the past decade. In contrast, the positive impacts of period (and cohort) effects on the elderly will also be apparent.

Over the past 15 years, the United States has experienced a drastic reversal of the fortunes of our two major dependent groups: children and the elderly. If the continuing dramatic decline in poverty among the elderly in the United States is the resounding success of the American system of social policy, then the deteriorating well-being of children over the past decade is its failure. National data show that from 1966 through 1978, poverty declined for all groups: children, aged, and adults. Since 1978, however, these groups have followed widely divergent paths. Despite five years of continued economic expansion, U.S. children in 1987 had an official poverty rate of 20.6 percent, almost 5 points higher than in 1978, and 3 points higher than in 1966; see Table 2-4, Panel A. Since 1982, the elderly have had poverty rates below the population average. While nonaged adults are still less poor than are the aged, the difference between these is small indeed. The largest part of the reduction in poverty among the aged is due to the growth of social security benefits over this period (Smolensky, Danziger, and Gottschalk, 1988).

But, of course, these figures do not account for the large amounts of food, housing, and other services which low-income beneficiaries receive. These benefits also come largely from federal and state governments. If we expanded the "U.S. Census" income definition to include food stamps, housing and medical benefits, implicit rent, capital gains and the like, and subtracted income and payroll taxes, would we find a different picture? A recent U.S. Census Bureau report (1988) allows us to do just that for 1986 (see Table 2-4, Panel B). These estimates indicate that the picture has indeed changed, but only to *sharpen* the differences found in Panel A of Table 2-4. Once we move to an expanded definition of income—one which places a low value on medical benefits for otherwise poor families (see first note, Table 2-4)—we find that the elderly poverty rate falls by more than one-half, to below 6 percent, while that of children drops only to 16 percent. Looking more finely within the extremes of these wide age groups does not change the picture. The youngest children are even less well off than their older siblings, while the oldest old are better off than middle-aged adults. In fact, the percentage of children poor under the expanded definition in 1986 is *higher* than the percentage poor under the official definition in 1978. The longer one goes, the more the "well-being" paths of children and elderly diverge over this period.

The final panel in Table 2-4 adds further cause for alarm. The poverty rate for U.S. children in Panel C, measured across countries using U.S. standards, is higher than that found in seven other advanced nations. While our elderly are near average, our children have a degree of poverty which

TABLE 2-4
Several Views of Poverty Among Children, the Elderly, and Adults

A. Percentage of Persons Officially Poor in United States, Selected Years, 1966–87

Group	1966	1978	1987	Percentage Change 1966–87
All Persons	14.7	11.4	13.5	-8.2
Elderly (over 65)	28.5	14.0	12.2	-57.2
Children (under 18)	17.6	15.9	20.6	17.0
Adults (18–64)	10.5	8.7	10.8	2.9

B. Percentage of Persons Poor under Two Income Definitions in United States, 1986

Group	Census Income	Expanded Income*	Percentage Reduction
All Persons	13.6	10.3	24.2
Elderly (over 65)	12.2	5.7	53.2
Elderly (over 75)	15.8	7.4	53.1
Children (under 18)	20.5	16.0	21.9
Children (under 6)	22.1	17.6	17.6
Adults (18–64)	10.9	8.7	20.1

C. Percentage of Persons Poor† 1979–82 in Various Countries

Country (Year)	All Persons	Elderly (65 and over)	Children (under 18)	Adults (18–64)	Poverty Line as Percentage Median Income‡
Australia	13.2	19.2	16.9	10.5	51.4
Canada	7.4	4.8	9.6	7.5	39.4
Germany (1981)	8.3	15.4	8.2	6.5	45.3
Norway (1979)	8.6	18.7	7.6	7.1	55.7
Sweden (1981)	5.6	2.1	5.1	6.7	50.1
Switzerland (1982)	5.8	6.0	5.1	6.2	42.3
United Kingdom (1979)	11.8	37.0	10.7	6.9	52.9
United States (1979)	12.7	16.1	17.1	10.1	42.1
Overall Average	9.1	14.9	10.0	7.7	47.4

SOURCES: Panel A—U.S. Bureau of the Census (1989, Tables 1, 2). Panel B—U.S. Bureau of the Census (1988, Table 4, Parts, A, B, C, D). Panel C—Smeeding, Torrey, Rein (1988) and Smeeding (1990).

continued

T A B L E   2 - 4   *continued*

---

*Expanded definition includes all forms of cash income (including capital gains) and noncash income from subsidized medical insurance (employer, Medicare, Medicaid), food and housing (including capital gains) and noncash income from subsidized medical insurance (employer, Medicare, Medicaid), food and housing (including implicit rent), net of federal and state income taxes and payroll taxes. Medical transfers are counted at their "fungible value" (i.e., at the market value once basic food and shelter needs have been taken into account), and at zero value if they have not. Food and housing subsidies are counted at their market value.

†Based on after direct-tax money income using the U.S. poverty line and implicit equivalence scale for the current year, converted to other currencies using U.N. Office of Economic Cooperation and Development purchasing power parities.

‡ Ratio of U.S. three-person family poverty line to (adjusted) median income in given year. Median income is median of adjusted family income using the U.S. poverty line equivalence scales and normalized to a family of three.

---

is only approached by that in Australia—a country with per capita GNP which was 82 percent of that in the U.S. in 1984. As a result, the U.S. poverty line cut the Australian income distribution at 51.4 percent of median income, compared with 42.1 percent in the United States. While these figures provide only a snapshot of the U.S. situation at the turn of the decade (i.e., back when child poverty rates were lower than today by about 5 percentage points), they are still alarming.

What has happened since 1980 across these several nations? Martin Dooley (1989) recently produced a time series of reasonably comparable data on U.S. versus Canadian poverty; see source and method statement and notes to Table 2-5. The results are shocking. The 1980 comparative picture of U.S. versus Canadian poverty in Table 2-4, Panel C, has become even more attenuated. While U.S. child poverty rose, Canadian child poverty fell during the 1980s. Why do Canadian children have poverty rates less than one-half as high as do U.S. children? The answer is *not* our racial heterogeneity—white U.S. children had poverty rates in 1986 which were nearly twice Canadian children's rates. While we have a much larger proportion of children in single-parent families than does Canada (26 versus 14 percent in 1986), the Canadians have managed to cut their poverty rate among children living with lone female parents while ours has increased. These divergent trends demand an explanation. It's not Sweden, Germany, or even the United Kingdom which we are comparing ourselves to, it's Canada! Even those Americans who "don't believe in international comparisons" must grudgingly admit to our geographic, political, and economic similarity with our northern neighbors. But how do these trends interact with the budget and the deficit? Can we lay the blame for increased poverty among U.S. children on the deficit?

If we move beyond money income alone to try to tie these explanations to budgetary outlays, some explanations begin to appear. By examining Table 2-6, we see that the United States spends about as much on health care and education as do other countries, including Canada. While the quality of the output of our education system can be questioned, and while the distribution of our health care dollars still leaves one-third of all poor

TABLE 2-5

*Poverty Rates Among Groups of Children by Family Type
in the United States and Canada: 1973, 1979, 1986*

	Canada	USA[‡]		
	All Races	All Races	White*	Black*	Hispanic*

A. Related Children in All Types of Families

1973	12.2	14.2	9.7	40.6	27.8
1979	9.7	16.0	11.4	40.8	27.7
1986	8.6	19.8	15.3	42.7	37.1
Percentage Change[t]	−29.5	39.4	57.6	5.2	33.5

B. Related Children in Lone Female Parent Families[‡]

1973	58.1	52.1	42.1	67.2	68.7
1979	45.3	48.6	38.6	63.1	62.2
1986	36.8	54.4	46.3	67.1	66.7
Percentage Change[t]	−36.7	4.4	10.0	−0.1	−2.9

C. Related Children in All Other Families[§]

1973	8.6	7.6	6.0	21.7	18.8
1979	6.2	8.5	7.3	18.7	19.2
1986	5.2	10.8	9.8	17.0	25.8
Percentage Change[t]	−39.5	42.1	63.3	−21.6	37.2

SOURCE AND METHOD: Dooley (1989, Table 18 and 19) and U.S. Bureau of the Census (1988, Table 16). All U.S. figures are taken from published U.S. Bureau of the Census reports. Canadian figures were derived by converting the U.S. poverty line into Canadian dollars using the purchasing power parities in the correct year and comparing it with Canadian household incomes using the Canadian *Survey of Current Finances* database. Income definitions, demographic groupings, and data quality are implicitly assumed to be relatively equal. Differences in definitions are discussed in Dooley (1989, pp. 20–24). *Whites and blacks include some persons who are of Hispanic ethnicity; Hispanics may be of any race. [t]Percent change is (1973–1986)/1986 times 100. [‡]Lone female parent are "mother only families" in Canada and "female householder, no husband present" in USA. Dooley (p. 23) indicates that these definitions are not fully consistent across countries. [§]All other families are mostly children living with both parents in the USA and children in married-couple families in Canada.

U.S. children without health insurance coverage (Oberg, 1988) compared with nearly zero in the other nations studied, our overall levels of expenditure are at least in the ballpark. It is in basic cash income support that we are most derelict. According to the United Nation's Office of Economic Cooperation and Development (OECD) estimates, Canada spends 1.6 percent of GNP on basic cash income support for children; we spend only 0.6

TABLE 2-6

Estimated Government Expenditures for All Children as a Percentage of Gross Domestic Product for Selected Countries: 1984

Government Expenditures	Australia	Canada	Germany	Sweden	United Kingdom	United States	Simple Average
1. Income Support, Total*	1.3	1.6	0.9	1.2	1.9	0.6	1.2
(Cash Transfer†)	(1.3)	(0.6)	(0.8)	(1.2)	(1.9)	(0.4)	(1.0)
(Tax Relief or Credit)	—	(1.0‡)	(0.1‡)	—	—	(0.2§)	(0.2)
2. Health Care‖	1.1	1.0	1.5	1.7	1.7	1.4	1.4
3. Education Expenditures#	6.0	6.1	4.6	5.9	5.3	5.3	5.6
4. Total	8.4	8.7	7.0	8.8	8.9	7.3	8.2
(Adjusted Total**)	(7.6)	(8.4)	(7.9)	(10.4)	(8.6)	(6.8)	(8.2)
Addendum:							
GDP per Capita††	10,994	14,330	11,466	12,009	10,225	15,665	12,448
(1984 U.S. Dollars)							

— = 0.0
NA = not available

*This does not include the amount of transfers that are taxed back. If net transfers were included, it would reduce Sweden's and Germany's percentages slightly.
†UNOECD-based as calculated in O'Higgins, "Allocation of Public Resources to Children and Elderly in OECD Countries" in Palmer, Smeeding, and Torrey (1988).
‡Calculation of tax benefits for children by O'Higgins, op. cit., based on UNOECD data.
§1979 tax expenditure for deduction of dependents 17 years and under.
‖Health care expenditures were calculated as part of a Luxembourg Income Study (Smeeding, Torrey, and Rein, 1988) project on estimating the value of noncash income for children and are preliminary. U.S. estimates include employment related subsidies for employee health insurance.
#Education expenditures are taken from U.N. Office of Economic Cooperation and Development (1985, 1988)
**Adjusted totals include an adjustment for the relative number of children in each country. This adjustment is made by dividing the percentage of the population which are children in each country and dividing it by 27, the overall average percentage of the populations which are children in these six countries. The results are then divided into the unadjusted figures in row 4. The divisors are Australia 1.11, Germany 0.89, Sweden 0.85, United Kingdom 1.04, United States 1.07, Canada 1.04.
††U.N. Office of Economic Cooperation and Development (1987). These figures are gross domestic product per person at current prices using current purchasing power parities in U.S. dollars.

percent. While our income tax allowance for children has grown since 1984 along with a slightly expanded earned income tax credit, we still do not provide a refundable tax credit to poor children. Of the eight nations studied, only the United States does not have some form of a refundable income tax credit or a universal child allowance.

Have relative levels of federal budgetary outlays for children and the elderly changed over the past decade as the deficit has ballooned? According to the U.S. House of Representatives Ways and Means Committee (1989) there has been a substantial shift in outlays (see Table 2-7). Expenditures for the elderly have grown 52 percent in constant dollars from 1978

TABLE 2-7
*Federal Expenditures for Children and for the Elderly
in Millions of Constant 1987 Dollars*

Category	Year		Percentage Change in Outlays
Elderly:	1978	1987	
Income (OASI)	114.0	159.4	40
Other	3.4	3.4	0
Health	34.1	67.6	98
Total	151.5	230.4	52
(As Percentage of GNP)	(4.2)	(5.1)	(+0.9)
Children:	1978	1984	
Income	20.6	18.6	−10
Nutrition	13.0	14.5	11
Education	7.6	7.0	−8
Health	3.4	3.7	10
Other	6.1	5.1	−20
Total	50.7	48.9	−4
(As Percentage of GNP)	(1.4)	(1.1)	(−0.3)

SOURCE: U.S. Congress (1989).

to 1987, while federal expenditures for children have dropped by 4 percent. Income support expenditures for families with children fell by 10 percent over this period. In terms of shares of GNP, outlays on the elderly have grown to 5.2 percent of GNP, about 5 times the level expended on children. Put differently, in 1987 we spent $138.6 billion on servicing the federal debt, almost three times the $48.9 billion we spent on income support, nutrition, education, and health for children and their families. Expenditures for education, income support, preventive health care for at-risk children, school lunches, and legal aid are less available now than they were a decade ago; see Table 2-7. Poverty has clearly increased for children and has shown a stubborn persistence to remain high in the face of sustained economic growth and high employment. The growing phenomenon of a U.S. urban and rural *underclass*, while relatively small in number, is very real (Jencks, 1989). It is becoming increasingly hard to argue that all U.S. children have equal life chances during this period of general prosperity. But we have not yet risen to the budgetary challenge to help offset these negative trends.

And so, we argue, one group which is disproportionately disadvantaged by the federal deficit and cost of servicing the debt are today's poor children. While we should be proud of our accomplishments on behalf of the elderly, social support for at-risk children has declined over the past decade: Income security against loss has diminished as divorce has risen and as unemployment insurance and means-tested benefits have shrunk in terms of both coverage and level of benefits. Our reduced capacity to meet emerging national needs because we are saddled with a too large deficit has led to a disadvantaged generation (Smeeding, 1990). It has left us in a situation where $.5 billion to expand Head Start by 180,000 children and thereby enroll up to 70 percent of eligible four-year-olds is *the* Bush administration's major initiative for poor children (Pierce, 1990) in 1991. This is only about 5 percent of the expected $20 billion increase in debt service this year (USCBO, 1990). But why all this handwringing? Isn't the distributional decision not to support poor children and their families similar to the decisions not to raise taxes on the well-to-do? Is there a real economic cost to society of this "period" effect? We now turn to this final aspect of our analysis.

COHORT EFFECTS

The final type of effect that interests us is the particular types of changes which affect a given cohort as they move through their life cycle. For instance, our comments, facts, and figures above indicate that today's elderly are a relatively advantaged group, or at least they are experiencing less poverty than previous elder cohorts. What about tomorrow's elderly? How has this cohort moved through their economic life cycle? In contrast, how will the next generation, today's children, move through theirs? And finally, how will it affect today's baby boomers?

Evidence from the 1950–1980 Censuses and from wealth surveys taken between 1962 and 1984 (Wolff, 1985; Avery et al., 1984) indicate that the next generation of elderly (i.e., those born between 1925 and 1935 who will reach age 65 between 1990 and 2000) will be even better off than today's elders. This age group (aged 25–35 in 1960) has had the good fortune to begin their prime working years during the period of maximum earnings growth of the halcyon 1960s, to find the value of their homes soaring during the inflation of the 1970s, and to be in the maximum liquid asset position to most fully capture the higher real interest rates and stock market boom of the early to mid-1980s. Indeed, individuals born in the 1930s have been dubbed the "good times" generation by demographer Carl Harter (Moon and Smeeding, 1989). A recent Federal Reserve Board study (Avery et al., 1984) indicates that the mean net worth of those 55–64 in 1983 (many of whom are good timers) was 84 percent above the national mean net worth. Similar earlier surveys for 1962 and 1969 indicated that the 55–64-year-olds in those years (whose survivors are among today's elderly) had net worth holdings which ranged only from 39 to 56 percent above the average. This generation is also more likely to have a greater fraction of long-term, two-earner families and hence a larger share of persons receiving higher average amounts of private pensions and larger entitlements to social security benefits than any preceding generation. Thus, with few exceptions, we expect continued success in meeting the social needs of tomorrow's elderly, even with continued deficits and debt service.

But our prediction of the future performance of U.S. social policy toward our children is just the opposite. Clearly, this cohort faces higher risks than faced today's adults when they were children. Single-parent families are at greater risk of economic insecurity than are married-couple families, and single-parent families are increasing rapidly. Divorce and out-of-wedlock births are here to stay for the foreseeable future; the percentage of children in such families increases annually. *Over one-half* of the children born today will spend some of their first 18 years of life in an economically vulnerable, single-parent household. Access to preventive health care is a key to normal healthy child development, but the percentage of poor children without health insurance has been constant since 1983, despite new legislation to expand and increase coverage. Deficit-driven rules and regulations are beginning to inhibit some potentially effective programs just as they are being brought to bear on low-income adolescents. For instance, state training fund allocations for the Job Training Partnership Act (JTPA) have declined with unemployment rates in the late 1980s, despite the fact that JTPA serves only 5 percent of the eligible population. At the same time that the program is being effectively targeted toward hard-to-serve populations, such as at-risk youth and school dropouts, there is less serious money to deal with their relatively large needs. The growing ineffectiveness of our child care system and education system have been widely debated. But two weeks after his "Education Summit," President Bush unveiled a 1990 budget that offered little in the way of federal budgetary efforts to help remedy either of these problems.

Will the poverty of today's children affect other generations? The answer is clearly yes. Unless we can provide the human capital necessary for today's children to afford the same rate of economic growth which today's elderly and adults have experienced, this generation will be hard pressed to pay off the social security "nest egg" claims for the baby boom's retirement next century (Smeeding, 1990a).

In fact, the current deficit and debt situation doubly penalizes children and younger workers. First of all, the net effect of the deficit is to reduce our national saving, channelling private and foreign investment to meet the public sector deficit and not the needs of private capital accumulation. While the maturing of the baby boomers into their prime saving years (40s and 50s), another cohort effect, will undoubtedly add to private saving, many analysts (e.g., Schultze, 1989, 1990) see this effect as too little and too late. The future generation of U.S. workers, today's children, will therefore be relatively disadvantaged in terms of the physical capital stock with which they will be able to work. To maintain current productivity growth, without having to rely on net inflows of foreign capital, our net public and private saving rate will have to rise from its current 3.0 percent to 8.0 percent. If private saving is the 7.0 percent which Schultze predicts during the 1990s, the public sector will have to be about 1.0 percent in *surplus* in 1995 (rather than the 2.0 percent deficit which the CBO expects us to face) to meet this 8.0 percent target.

If we are willing to accept net foreign investment as a solution to our capital shortage, we must also be willing to pay the price of not being the masters of our own fate. For instance, Reischauer (1990) argues that long-term U.S. government bond rates have risen by 0.75 percent from September 1989 to February 1990, largely due to foreign capital (Japanese and other) flowing to West Germany in anticipation of economic opportunities in Eastern Europe. If our interest rates must be kept at high levels to maintain foreign capital inflows, net private investment in real capital will be discouraged because of its high cost.

One final cohort effect deals with the job opportunities that are likely to face today's children as they begin to go off to work in the next decade. As the current baby-bust generation reaches working age, the structure of the U.S. workforce will change drastically. A recent study by the Hudson Institute finds the pattern of workforce changes shown in Table 2-8.

The U.S. workforce is in for a marked change. The key numbers in the table are those in the middle column (net new entrants). Of the 25 million *net* new U.S. workers over the 1985–2000 period, only 15 percent will be U.S. born white males. The gross flows will be much larger, but as the cohort of heavily white-male-dominated older workers (those age 47–62 in 1985) reaches retirement age, they will be increasingly replaced by other groups, particularly women (65 percent of net new workers), and minorities (43 percent of net new workers). These groups are typically less well educated than are white males, and hence are less likely to fill key occupational shortages in such areas as science and engineering (Atkinson, 1990). This demographic shift will also necessitate workplace changes, if married women are to fill career jobs. For instance, child care assistance will become a greater necessity for employers, as will flexible work hours, parental leave, sick leave to care for children, and related changes that accommodate two-earner families. The net national changes for the 1985–2000 period in Table 2-8 are much larger than the emergent composition of the labor force of 2000 (final column), but it is these net changes that employers must accommodate. By the millennium, only about two in every five workers will be white males. Superimposed on this change is that fact that between 1985 and 2000 the labor force will grow more slowly than the net number of new jobs created (Hudson Institute, 1988; Bloom and Bennett, 1989). In addition, because of low birth rates over the past 15 years, the proportion of younger workers (age 16–24) in the U.S. workforce will decline from 30 percent in 1985 to 16 percent by the year 2000. Together, these changes indicate that the demand for workers, especially younger entrants, will be higher than their supply. For those who are both younger and highly educated (for example, new college graduates), job demand will so outstrip

TABLE 2-8
Changing Composition of the U.S. Workforce

	1985 Composition of the Labor Force	Net New Entrants to the Labor Force 1985–2000	2000 Composition of the Labor Force
U.S. Born White Males	47%	15%	41%
U.S. Born White Females	36	42	37
U.S. Born Nonwhite Males	5	7	6
U.S. Born Nonwhite Females	5	13	6
Immigrant Males	4	13	6
Immigrant Females	3	10	4
Total	100%	100%	100%
Total Labor Force	115,500,000	25,000,000	140,500,000

SOURCE: Hudson Institute (1988).

supply that they are very likely to experience real wage increases similar to or greater than those experienced in the 1960s. The rate of economic return to a four-year college investment today is greater than it was in the 1960s (Smith and Welch, 1989), and it will grow to even greater levels over the coming decade.

But what about the relatively less educated and less experienced; in particular, disadvantaged minorities, high school dropouts, and single parents? In the 1960s, higher labor demand than supply pulled many of these workers into the mainstream of the economy. But the good jobs in the 1960s required much less formal education, literacy, and trainability than those that will appear in the 1990s. Several authors (for example, Bloom and Bennett, 1989; Murnane, 1988; Briggs, 1987) speculate that those who are unprepared for the labor market in terms of skill or experience are likely to fall even further behind the mainstream than today. Hence, our failure to invest in *human* capital will burden the current generation of younger Americans in the same way that our deficit continues to drain our *physical* capital needs. The economic cost of this deficit will be lower living standards for most of today's children, particularly those less well educated. Coupled with the rising debt service that we are bequeathing this generation, it may be difficult for the rich and poor together to meet the payroll tax claims necessary to finance the baby boom's retirement early next century.

TOWARD A REDRESS

The widely heralded 1988 Family Support Act (FSA) will extend Aid to Families with Dependent Children (AFDC) to unemployed two-parent families and require work from these parents and some AFDC mothers with school age children. It will also extend and strengthen enforcement of child support payments from absent fathers, and extend temporary employment and training (through the Job Training Partnership Act network in many states), child care, and Medicaid to mothers and parents working their way off welfare. While it will not increase AFDC benefits, FSA is a positive step toward reducing dependency and increasing self reliance. But, largely because of deficit-driven budgetary pressure, the total additional cost of the program is only $3.4 billion *over five years;* not enough to make a serious dent in the child poverty or child investment problem that our country faces.

Programs which will effectively reduce child poverty and provide the basis for the physical, emotional, cognitive, and educational human capital development of poor children will be more expensive than FSA. A program which costs $3.4 billion over five years is exactly one-fifth of the $17 billion in increased costs of servicing the public debt in 1989 alone. It is just about 2 percent of total *debt service outlays.*

Table 2-9 lists the modest budgetary costs of nine programs: Six programs are for direct investment in children, while three others are for safety net and earnings supplement programs to support basic living standards of children and parents. The total necessary outlays are about $20 billion in 1990, just a bit more than the increased cost of debt service this year. These nine programs are adapted from budgets compiled at the Urban Institute, U.S. Congress, and U.S. Congressional Budget Office and are in many ways similar to those advocated by the Ford Foundation (1989) in a recent report.

The first group of programs would provide the funding to help bring all needy children into our public education system in sound physical and developmental health (1, 2, 3), to help them do well once there (4, 5), and finally to help them stay in school and to find jobs when they leave it (6). These programs are separate from the second group in that they directly add to the health and developmental skills and abilities of children.

The second group would help provide basic income support to the families of poor children: a national minimum AFDC and food stamp benefit equal to 65 percent of the poverty line (7), and refundable dependent care and earned income tax credits (8, 9) sufficiently large to reduce payroll tax burdens, cover a portion of child care costs, and raise the incomes of most working poor families with children to the poverty line.

The cost of these programs is modest. All of the first six programs have been shown to be cost effective, saving far more than they cost society, almost immediately (see Children Defense Fund, 1990, and related references). Most income supplements would go to the working poor; one-half of the total increase in spending would go directly to poor children. But how will we pay for these benefits? Alternatives to a tax increase are either to set aside some fraction of the growing social security surplus for public investment in children and their families, or to direct some of the peace dividend to this purpose. Neither solution would, however, lessen the

TABLE 2-9

The Federal Budgetary Cost of a Program to Invest in Disadvantaged Children and to Provide Basic Income Support to Families with Children in 1990

Child Investment Programs

1. Special Supplemental Food Program for Women, Infants, and Children	$ 1.5 billion
2. Medicaid	2.0 billion
3. Head Start	2.0 billion
4. Compensatory Education	2.5 billion
5. School Lunch and Breakfast	.6 billion
6. Job Corps and JTPA	1.5 billion
Subtotal	$10.1 billion

Basic Income Support: Safety Net and Earnings Supplement Program

7. Aid to Families with Dependent Children and Food Stamps	$ 3.0 billion
8. Refundable Dependent Care Credit	1.8 billion
9. Earned Income Tax Credit	5.8 billion
Subtotal	$10.6 billion
TOTAL COST	$20.7 billion

SOURCE: R. Barnes et al. (1989); S. Hendricksen and I. Sawhill (1989); S. Danziger (1989).

deficit. Still, I would argue that the nation's aggregate return from $20 billion of direct investment in poor children and their families will exceed the nation's payoff from $20 billion of deficit reduction.

CONCLUSION

Serious negative economic consequences arise from our current deficit situation. The most serious opportunity cost of $200 billion in federal budgetary outlays to service the national debt each year is foregone human capital investment in U.S. needy children and youth. Ten percent of this cost, $20 billion, would begin to provide the investment in poor U.S. children which we so sorely need. This malaise is widespread. The budgetary policies of the 1980s and general social policy myopia have led to a situation which my colleague, Richard Burkhauser (1990), aptly terms "morality on the cheap." Because of our unwillingness to increase taxes and a general lack of administrative leadership, we are left in a situation where the only way to get things done at the federal level is "off the books," via mandate, legerdemain, smoke, and mirrors. The results, higher minimum wages, federal mandates to employers and states to increase social policy outlays, and deregulation in the name of short-term budgetary saving, often lead to counterproductive results and always push someone else to bear the costs of social policy expansion. Our lack of investment in U.S. children is, however, not even morality on the cheap. Rather, it is pure ignorance. The "distributional burden" of the deficit is, in fact, a real burden, shared by all Americans whose living standards will not rise as fast as those in other nations because of underinvestment in human capital.

The major institutions of U.S. social policy are still those created as a result of the Great Depression more than a half century ago, when widows, war veterans, and old people were the at-risk groups in society, and Ozzie and Harriet families were the norm. We must overcome the myopic budgetary paralysis of deficit politics and morality on the cheap. What is needed is a fresh vision of U.S. social policy which calls attention to the economic plight and vulnerable status of a large minority of our children and which convinces U.S. leaders that it is in the direct and immediate interest of all Americans to rectify this situation by investing in disadvantaged U.S. children and their families.

NOTES

The author would like to thank Jim Rock for extensive comments, and Julie Tapp and Kelly Johnson for assistance in preparing this paper. However, he retains responsibility for all errors of commission and omission.

1. Of course, payroll tax revenues are not "saved" in the traditional sense. In the short run, surpluses will build up due to contributions in excess of outlays. But over the long run, the social security system operates on a pay-as-you-go basis. Today's children will therefore have to pay future taxes that will make good the "claims" for today's workers. At some future point, taxes may have to be increased to pay off these claims, and perhaps also to pay the other government bills which today's excess payroll tax revenues are covering.

3 Latin America's Burden: The Debt

KENNETH P. JAMESON

Part Two of this volume debates whether the federal debt, which is increasing because of continued fiscal deficits, represents a burden on the economy. However, few economists would dispute the central claim of this chapter: that Latin America's large international debt, the legacy of loans to Latin American countries during the 1970s, is currently a major obstacle to any improvement in their recent pathetic economic performance (i.e., that there is a clear and heavy burden of the debt in Latin America).[1]

The debate on debt in Latin America and in other third world debtor countries centers on how the countries got into their current difficulties and what steps might be taken toward a solution, not on whether the debt is good or bad for them. There are three main benefits to a study in which the answer to the debate on debt is so clear:

1. The clarity of the Latin American debt case can focus the U.S. debt debate by specifying some of the circumstances under which the burden of the debt is different, depending on whether the country is rich or poor.

2. The Latin American case also emphasizes that the effect of debt depends in large degree on the system which defines how debt is treated; in other words, when is repayment not required, who bears the loss of defaulted debt, and what responsibility does the society at large have for absorbing losses on debt instruments.

3. Finally, the chapter may in some degree help educate us about the reality of Latin America. We know little about our hemispheric neighbors to the south, and much of what we "know" is incorrect. For example, columnist William F. Buckley (1990) recently derided democracy in Bolivia, writing that Bolivia "recently endured its 192nd coup" since its independence from Spain in 1826. In actuality, Bolivia has had two successive normal transfers of power, and its last coup was in 1981. Buckley's statement, which I never saw challenged, would be analogous to an observation that "Ronald Reagan was recently inaugurated after his victory over Jimmy Carter," a ridiculous claim, since he

became President in 1981. Such ignorance of Latin America is all the more dangerous at this point in history when it appears that the world is being reorganized into new spheres of influence, Japan dominating Asia, and Germany exercising predominant influence in Europe, including Eastern Europe (Garten, 1989). The United States will remain dominant in the Western Hemisphere, but only if we can understand Latin America better and are willing to deal creatively with the problems that the countries of the "South" face.[2]

The first section of the chapter examines the reality of the debt in Latin American countries, and the second emphasizes the burden of debt and explains its operation. The third section examines in detail how the system ensures that the burden of the debt is placed most squarely on the Latin American countries and on their citizens, in this case by functioning as a "dollar bloc" that links the Western Hemisphere economies through the central role that the dollar plays in their financial systems, either directly or indirectly. The fourth section details the recent adjustments in the system which have been designed to stabilize it but have had little effect in removing the burden of this debt from the people of Latin America. The concluding section considers the options available for moving beyond this counterproductive situation and for making some progress in advancing human welfare in the Western Hemisphere, under U.S. leadership.

DEBT AND ECONOMIC PERFORMANCE IN LATIN AMERICA

The phase of rapid increase in Latin American debt began with the OPEC oil cartel's increase in oil prices in 1974, which generated large financial surpluses for oil-exporting countries (only Venezuela and Mexico in Latin America) that were absorbed by bank loans to other countries. It ended with the Mexican debt default in 1982, partly as a result of the decline in oil prices after 1981. The Latin American debt in nominal terms was $16 billion in 1970 (IBRD, 1989, Table 24), rose to $161 billion in 1978, and then more than doubled to $360 billion by 1983 (see Table 3-1). After the Mexican default of late 1982, new foreign loans virtually dried up, unless they could be obtained through hard and long bargaining; from 1982–87, the banks "succeeded in extracting 50 cents for every dollar owed" (Bulow and Rogoff, 1990, p. 34). Nonetheless, debt continued to increase to $441 billion in 1987, and not until 1988 did it fall, to $426 billion. The economic performance of Latin American countries during the 1970s was aided by the debt increase. They were able to cushion the adjustment forced on non-oil-exporting countries by the increase in oil prices. But when the Mexican default frightened the banks and caused this source of funds to dry up, Latin American countries were left with a crushing burden, and the possibility of using new funds to grow out of the debt problem was no longer available.

TABLE 3-1
Disbursed Total External Debt Outstanding, by Country, 1978–88
(Millions of Dollars)

Country	1978	1979	1980	1981	1982	1983	1984	1985	1986	1987	1988
Argentina	13276.1	20949.7	27157.0	35656.7	43634.1	45949.2	48906.4	49148.7	49602.5	56472.1	59600.0
Bahamas	180.6	178.3	150.7	226.7	303.3	263.6	226.6	215.6	252.1	232.7	202.7
Barbados	98.3	156.1	165.9	233.5	335.6	580.2	392.3	453.2	610.4	618.7	606.0
Bolivia	2161.3	2550.2	2702.2	3220.5	3312.9	4057.8	4270.7	4736.2	5543.6	5558.6	5689.8
Brazil	53614.1	60419.0	70565.4	80373.0	91916.0	97487.5	104707.5	106472.8	112766.5	123961.8	112301.0
Chile	7360.6	9357.8	12084.0	15663.3	17313.6	18107.8	19878.8	20308.1	20181.5	21109.1	18971.0
Colombia	5101.7	5869.0	6940.5	8716.3	10306.4	11412.5	12037.3	14237.4	15366.8	17006.4	17797.0
Costa Rica	1677.7	2108.7	2736.7	3289.1	3630.6	4167.9	3977.0	4359.8	4522.0	4715.5	n.a.
Dominican Republic	1332.4	1601.6	2003.2	2294.2	2517.8	2922.7	3102.1	3418.4	3507.1	3670.2	3844.0
Ecuador	3975.8	4525.2	5996.8	7822.6	7861.8	7548.1	8262.0	8569.7	9208.3	10393.2	10549.1
El Salvador	910.0	886.4	911.2	1127.6	1419.4	1675.8	1735.2	1746.5	1711.4	1761.2	1783.4
Guatemala	813.0	1039.8	1165.8	1265.6	1537.3	1802.4	2349.9	2574.9	2758.2	2820.0	2768.0
Guyana	561.3	620.0	757.5	836.8	912.7	972.8	981.1	1101.3	1236.2	1275.9	1257.0
Haiti	200.4	253.1	302.9	423.5	536.0	570.9	659.4	697.5	705.6	811.2	836.5
Honduras	932.6	1182.1	1475.4	1708.6	1844.8	2135.3	2296.9	2731.5	2981.3	3296.9	3331.9
Jamaica	1416.4	1700.2	1909.7	2305.4	2842.8	3326.5	3473.4	3814.9	3970.9	4386.4	4250.7
Mexico	35720.6	42825.2	57450.7	78297.4	86110.7	93083.1	95015.6	96650.7	100887.7	107424.8	101807.0
Nicaragua	1429.1	1486.0	2171.8	2572.6	3330.6	4178.7	5113.1	5690.7	6204.6	7291.0	7220.2
Panama	2310.6	2603.4	2974.3	3367.5	3923.2	4392.1	4380.6	4750.3	4921.0	5292.8	n.a.
Paraguay	615.2	806.9	958.0	1149.9	1297.5	1407.1	1460.9	1791.4	2040.2	2447.2	2569.6
Peru	9647.2	9174.6	9996.9	10288.4	12285.8	12059.0	13189.3	14136.9	15925.8	17983.3	19000.0
Surinam	n.a.	n.a.	n.a.	n.a.	n.a.	n.a.	33.1	47.7	69.6	71.0	n.a.
Trinidad and Tobago	486.7	680.6	828.5	1049.8	1202.8	1438.0	1221.8	1448.1	1857.5	1801.3	2060.3
Uruguay	998.3	1323.1	1659.7	2174.4	2646.8	3297.0	3281.5	3892.8	3892.1	4199.9	4244.2
Venezuela	16568.4	23895.8	29490.1	32120.0	32045.0	37431.4	36456.6	34692.8	34708.8	36518.7	34838.1
Latin America	161388.5	196192.8	242554.5	296183.3	333076.5	360267.5	377408.9	387687.8	405431.7	441119.9	426000(est)

SOURCE: Inter-American Development Bank, *Economic and Social Progress in Latin America, 1989*, Table E.I, p. 503.

The best measure of the burden is the magnitude of the external dollar transfers the countries have made to service and retire the accumulated debt (see Table 3-2). Payments of interest and principal on public or publicly guaranteed debt (92 percent of the total) were $1.6 billion in 1970 and rose to $32.3 billion in 1982. Payments since have averaged $31 billion; that amount is transferred every year out of Latin America to the United States, Japan, and Europe. The per capita gross national product (GNP) of the United States is close to $20,000; Latin America's averages $2,336. Latin American countries are transferring to the advanced countries 3 percent of their GNP every year, increasing the already great differences in incomes.

Let us now move to the argument that the debt is a burden on Latin America, and for purposes of exposition let us cast it in the same terms that are used in the U.S. case. Economists who discount the burden of the U.S. debt, such as Robert Barro and Robert Eisner, use a variety of empirical indicators to make their argument. For example, U.S. interest rates have not risen with the debt, especially in real terms; GNP growth has not slackened measurably; national saving has fallen but has been easily supplemented by foreign saving; gross investment has not fallen, especially if purchases of durable goods are included. And finally, inflation has not increased as would be expected but has actually fallen from the early years of the decade.

Since economic performance on these indicators has not deteriorated, as the simple burden of the debt argument would predict, they conclude that concern with the debt and the deficit is unwarranted and so are described as "pussycats" on the debt. To stress the difference between the economic health of the United States and that of Latin America, I will apply their argument to Latin America and assess the effect of the debt on those economies.

Let us look at these same indicators for Latin America, especially in the period since 1982. Barro and Eisner found no deterioration in U.S. economic performance as the debt increased. But all of the measures for the Latin American countries deteriorated notably. Interest rates increased dramatically, with nominal rates often over 100 percent, and real interest rates remained at 30–40 percent in many of the countries, such as Argentina and Chile (Foxley, 1983). In most countries real interest rates continue to be well over 10 percent, compared with a rate of around 4 percent in the United States.

Growth in gross domestic product (GDP) per capita, a measure of all the goods and services produced in an economy in a given year, has been negative in Latin America since 1982; although growth has stabilized in recent years, in 1988 the hemisphere as a whole exhibited another decline in per capita GDP (see Table 3-3). This contrasts with the strong growth rate of 3.1 percent from 1961 through 1980. The debt increase of the 1970s certainly aided growth in GDP, which totaled 78 percent over the decade, raising per capita GDP in Latin America to $2,512 in 1980. Since 1980, GDP growth has totaled only 12 percent; in per capita terms, there has been a decline in living standards (per capita GDP), to $2,336 (IDB, 1988).

TABLE 3-2
Payments on the External Debt, by Country, 1970, 1978-87
(Millions of Dollars)

Country	1970	1978	1979	1980	1981	1982	1983	1984	1985	1986	1987
Argentina	343.5	1613.3	895.3	1145.8	1092.8	1010.2	963.9	482.7	835.6	1509.3	506.6
Bahamas	4.6	11.4	20.0	17.7	31.0	18.1	17.3	29.2	30.8	21.1	36.1
Barbados	0.0	4.4	6.9	8.7	7.5	7.1	11.2	13.1	23.8	25.7	38.4
Bolivia	16.8	274.7	149.7	126.3	110.1	106.4	104.6	117.3	151.0	106.4	74.3
Brazil	255.9	2635.8	3604.0	3857.5	3938.1	4200.0	2026.3	2388.1	2178.4	2590.1	2942.1
Colombia	165.8	933.7	904.0	891.2	1175.6	474.2	321.5	311.9	233.1	286.0	186.0
Chile	75.2	220.4	408.0	249.8	261.6	303.8	392.7	539.9	646.6	968.6	1263.9
Costa Rica	20.6	173.3	171.9	75.2	83.6	55.5	104.3	105.8	125.6	188.2	60.9
Dominican Republic	7.3	47.5	190.6	61.6	109.1	148.1	114.7	59.1	72.6	98.9	68.1
Ecuador	15.6	109.5	739.8	271.5	481.2	544.7	164.5	191.0	178.0	208.8	222.5
El Salvador	5.9	12.3	12.7	17.2	17.7	32.3	93.1	122.0	128.4	116.2	105.7
Guatemala	19.9	10.4	14.8	15.2	22.5	43.7	70.7	109.3	149.4	136.3	146.6
Guyana	2.2	32.2	66.1	42.8	43.6	23.4	22.8	15.2	11.3	16.1	9.1
Haiti	3.4	14.1	8.6	15.3	15.1	8.6	7.8	11.3	13.5	11.2	13.6
Honduras	3.0	28.1	59.6	38.9	37.3	51.4	38.9	47.3	69.5	79.1	142.4
Jamaica	5.9	126.5	106.9	91.7	132.2	105.0	112.7	75.5	186.5	220.3	210.9
Mexico	475.0	4404.9	7138.6	4010.1	3717.8	3241.3	4836.9	3897.3	3105.7	2571.6	3249.3
Nicaragua	16.2	47.3	15.5	44.4	70.0	53.8	45.0	29.6	18.8	11.1	22.1
Panama	23.7	442.9	190.1	214.6	213.2	280.9	188.6	232.7	107.1	148.4	157.7
Paraguay	7.0	20.0	30.9	45.0	38.9	39.6	39.2	57.5	75.6	114.7	128.2
Peru	100.2	435.9	490.5	956.0	1364.4	972.6	360.4	261.0	360.7	280.4	250.4
Surinam	n.a.	n.a.	n.a.	n.a.	n.a.	n.a.	n.a.	n.a.	n.a.	n.a.	n.a.
Trinidad and Tobago	10.0	8.8	8.9	175.6	29.5	51.1	151.4	110.4	155.2	191.1	262.8
Uruguay	47.2	366.0	54.8	93.0	60.8	70.6	93.9	126.2	124.3	87.7	134.1
Venezuela	42.0	356.2	889.7	1735.0	1399.3	1611.1	950.6	1254.7	945.6	1469.1	1209.2
Latin America	166.9	12329.6	16177.9	14200.1	14452.9	13453.5	11233.0	10588.1	9927.1	11456.4	11441.0

SOURCE: Inter-American Development Bank, *Economic and Social Progress in Latin America, 1989,* Table 8, p. 510.

TABLE 3-3
Growth Rates of Gross Domestic Product per Capita

Country	Average		Annual		
	1961–80	1981–85	1986	1987	1988
Argentina	1.7	−3.6	4.1	0.7	−2.4
Bahamas	1.2	0.3	1.2	3.0	0.7
Barbados	3.5	−1.0	4.9	2.5	3.4
Bolivia	2.2	−4.7	−5.5	−0.7	0.0
Brazil	4.6	−1.1	5.3	1.4	−2.3
Chile	1.4	−2.0	3.9	4.0	5.6
Colombia	2.8	0.1	3.6	3.1	1.6
Costa Rica	2.6	−2.6	2.7	2.6	1.1
Dominican Republic	3.0	−0.8	0.8	5.7	−1.3
Ecuador	3.7	−0.8	0.4	−7.9	5.0
El Salvador	1.5	−2.9	−1.0	0.9	−1.5
Guatemala	2.7	−3.9	−2.7	0.2	0.6
Guyana	0.9	−3.5	0.3	0.7	−2.9
Haiti	0.8	−2.8	−0.9	−2.1	−2.1
Honduras	2.2	−2.5	−0.3	0.9	0.6
Jamaica	0.8	−1.3	0.4	3.7	0.4
Mexico	3.6	−0.5	−6.0	−0.8	−1.1
Nicaragua	0.4	−2.7	−4.3	−4.0	−11.1
Panama	3.7	0.6	1.2	0.3	−18.8
Paraguay	3.7	−0.9	−3.0	1.3	3.1
Peru	1.7	−2.9	8.5	5.1	−11.1
Surinam	7.4	−0.3	0.6	−8.7	1.6
Trinidad and Tobago	3.8	−4.0	−4.3	−8.6	−5.1
Uruguay	1.6	−3.7	6.7	5.1	−0.3
Venezuela	1.5	−3.8	4.0	0.3	1.4
Latin America	3.1	−1.6	1.6	0.8	−1.5

SOURCE: Inter-American Development Bank, *Economic and Social Progress in Latin America, 1989*, Table 11-3, p. 10.

Saving in Latin American economies has declined rapidly, and net foreign saving has often been negative because the countries have had to run foreign trade surpluses to allow them to service the debt. The Inter-American Development Bank (IDB) carried out a careful study of saving during the 1980s in the seven major Latin American economies—Argentina, Brazil, Colombia, Chile, Mexico, Peru, and Venezuela (IDB, 1988, Ch. VI). The rate of national saving decreased by 6.7 percentage points (almost 33 percent) from 21.8 percent of GNP in 1980 to 15.1 percent in 1983, and then stabilized at 16 percent of GNP. External saving, the trade deficit, also declined by 6.2 percent between 1982 and 1985, and was only 1 percent of GNP in the later part of the decade. Thus the saving rate for the economies fell from 29 percent of GNP to 17 percent, a precipitous drop, and again quite the opposite of the U.S. experience, where the saving rate was relatively stable.

Gross investment in these countries also decreased from 25.8 percent of GNP in 1981 to 16.8 percent in 1983, a 25 percent decline (IDB, 1988, p. 91). This is more jarring from a long-run perspective, for it implies that the stagnation in the capital stock of these economies is likely to be a long-lived phenomenon.

Finally, how has Latin America fared on the inflation front? There were four countries with inflation rates over 15 percent in the 1960s, 10 countries in the 1970s, and 16 in 1987. Bolivia had an inflation rate of 12 million percent over the decade (see Table 3-4). Once again, the existence of the debt has not corresponded to better economic performance or even acceptable economic performance—quite the opposite.

So we must conclude that the Latin American pattern of economic performance as the debt increased is very different from that of the United States. This is not to say that the debt is the whole story. Poor economic policy in Latin America has played a role, as have external factors such as natural disasters and deteriorating prices for Latin America's export products. Capital flight from certain countries has increased the pressure on their balance of payments (Pastor, 1990). Nonetheless, debt is a central contributor to the deterioration of Latin American economic performance, and the effect of its burden is quite real and quite tragic.

Behind the bloodless figures, there are real people. My own work on Bolivia showed a dramatic increase in malnutrition among children, a drop in schooling, a drop in basic purchasing power which forced people to eat and buy only the most basic commodities (Jameson, 1989). Over time, this will show up in higher infant mortality rates and lower life expectancies. A comparison of the percentage of the population below the "destitution line," where malnutrition begins to take its toll, found that between the 1970s and 1980s the indicator rose from 12 to 22 percent in Mexico, in Peru from 25 to 34 percent, and in Venezuela from 10 to 13 percent (ECLAC, 1989).

Thus, it is quite difficult to be a pussycat on the Latin American debt. The "termite stance" that debt is eating away the foundation of the economy also seems understated, as does the "wolf at the door stance." We need a new way of describing the vantage point for viewing the effect of the Latin American debt. I would suggest the metaphor of the "anaconda" to assess the effect of the debt. The anaconda is a large South American jungle snake which wraps itself around its victims and constricts until they die. It then ingests them. I'm not sure whether the anaconda of debt has ingested most of Latin America as yet; but it has been choking the life out of those countries since 1982.

TABLE 3-4

Annual Variation in the Consumer Price Index, by Country, 1961–88
(Percentages)

Countries with relative price stability (annual rise in prices of less than 5 percent)

1961–70		1971–80	1981–85		1986		1987		1988	
El Salvador	0.7		Panama	3.3	Panama	0.0	Haiti	11.5	Haiti	0.2
Guatemala	0.8				Barbados	1.3	Panama	0.9	Panama	0.4
Venezuela	1.0				Haiti	3.3	Honduras	2.5	Honduras	4.5
Panama	1.3				Honduras	4.4	Barbados	3.3	Barbados	4.8
Nicaragua	1.7									
Dominican R.	2.1									
Honduras	2.2									
Guyana	2.3									
Costa Rica	2.5									
Mexico	2.8									
Haiti	2.9									
Barbados	3.0									
Trinidad	3.1									
Paraguay	3.4									
Jamaica	4.2									
Surinam	4.2									
Ecuador	4.4									

Countries with moderate inflation (annual rise between 5 and 15 percent)

1961–70		1971–80		1981–85		1986		1987		1988	
Bolivia	5.6	Panama	7.1	Bahamas	5.9	Bahamas	5.5	Bahamas	6.0	Bahamas	5.1
Bahamas	6.2	Bahamas	7.5	Honduras	6.9	Trinidad	7.7	Jamaica	6.7	Surinam	7.3
Peru	9.7	Honduras	8.2	Surinam	7.0	Guyana	7.9	Trinidad	10.7	Trinidad	7.8
Colombia	11.1	Venezuela	8.5	Guatemala	7.7	Dominican R.	9.8	Guatemala	12.3	Jamaica	8.2
		Guatemala	9.7	Barbados	7.8	Venezuela	11.5	Bolivia	14.6	Guatemala	12.1

continued

TABLE 3-4 *continued*

	1961–70	1971–80	1981–85	1986	1987	1988
		Surinam 9.9	Haiti 9.1	Costa Rica 11.8		Chile 14.8
		Guyana 10.3	Venezuela 11.1			
		Dominican R. 10.5	Trinidad 12.4			
		El Salvador 10.9	El Salvador 14.7			
		Haiti 10.9				
		Costa Rica 11.1				
		Ecuador 12.7				
		Trinidad 13.2				
		Paraguay 13.4				
		Barbados 14.6				
Countries with high inflation (annual rise greater than 15 percent)	Argentina 21.4	Mexico 16.8	Paraguay 15.9	Jamaica 15.1	Dominican R. 16.1	Bolivia 16.0
	Chile 27.1	Jamaica 18.5	Jamaica 16.9	Surinam 18.7	Costa Rica 16.8	El Salvador 19.8
	Brazil 46.2	Bolivia 20.2	Dominican R. 16.9	Colombia 18.9	Chile 19.9	Costa Rica 21.0
	Uruguay 47.8	Nicaragua 20.4	Guyana 19.7	Chile 19.5	Paraguay 21.8	Paraguay 23.4
		Colombia 21.3	Chile 21.5	Ecuador 23.0	Colombia 23.3	Colombia 28.1
		Peru 31.9	Colombia 22.4	Paraguay 31.8	El Salvador 24.9	Venezuela 29.5
		Brazil 36.7	Ecuador 28.1	El Salvador 32.0	Venezuela 28.1	Guyana 40.1
		Uruguay 63.1	Costa Rica 37.4	Guatemala 37.0	Guyana 28.7	Dominican R. 44.4
		Argentina 141.6	Uruguay 46.0	Uruguay 76.4	Ecuador 29.5	Ecuador 58.2
		Chile 174.1	Mexico 62.4	Peru 78.0	Surinam 53.3	Uruguay 62.2
			Nicaragua 66.9	Mexico 86.2	Uruguay 63.6	Mexico 114.4
			Peru 104.9	Argentina 90.1	Peru 85.9	Argentina 342.5
			Brazil 153.9	Brazil 145.3	Argentina 131.3	Peru 667.9
			Argentina 382.4	Bolivia 276.4	Mexico 131.8	Brazil 682.3
			Bolivia 2692.0	Nicaragua 681.5	Brazil 229.7	Nicaragua 14295.3
					Nicaragua 911.9	

SOURCE: Inter-American Development Bank, *Economic and Social Progress in Latin America, 1989*, Table II-7, p. 16.

WHY IS THE DEBT A BURDEN IN LATIN AMERICA?

If the debt is in a country's own currency, the main effect is to redistribute consumption among generations. If it is in a foreign currency, this intergenerational effect operates both domestically and internationally, and the claim of foreigners represents a real claim, for which actual goods and services must be delivered in order to generate the foreign exchange necessary to retire the debt or to pay the interest. As a result, domestic living standards may well go down.

Robert Eisner (1987, p. 296) put it very simply:

> Public debt held by other countries or their nationals is another matter. If that debt is denominated in a country's own currency, it too can always be paid off by money creation and depreciated by inflation. If there is an external debt in foreign currencies, however, there is a real burden, which can, if the debt is sufficiently large, prove overwhelming. In the case of such external debt, this burden must be carefully balanced against any benefits in terms of income or wealth or assets which the debt may have financed.

Eisner is one of the pussycats on U.S. debt, but this quote shows that he understands the very real burden of the debt in cases such as Latin America. Interestingly, a number of factors he feels should be adjusted because they contribute to overestimating the burden of the debt in the United States go exactly in the opposite direction in Latin America, again emphasizing the very real burden of the debt for those countries:

1. The real value of the Latin American countries' debt is not diminished by their inflation, since their debt is denominated in dollars.

2. In addition, the debt principal is unlikely to be paid, so interest payments are the most relevant indicator of the burden. These payments are generally based on a floating interest rate which will adjust to take account of inflationary effects.[3] So as inflation increases, the real cost to the countries will not diminish.

3. The reschedulings of debt which required up-front fees to the banks which organized the process have kept the principal well in line with inflation. As a result, increases in debt in recent years have not been the result of inflows of "new money."

4. Other adjustments which Eisner suggests when evaluating U.S. international debt, such as revaluing U.S. foreign investments to their higher current market values from the values they had at the time of purchase, would imply that the Latin American debt burden is greater than conventionally measured. Given this adjustment, the value of Latin America's capital owned by foreigners would increase as would the implied payments to its owners.

These measurement issues highlight the reality of the debt as it must be faced by Latin America: It represents a real drain of resources out of the countries, and the usual techniques of escaping debt burdens are closed for Latin America. The yearly transfer of resources denominated in foreign exchange cannot simply be inflated away. Taking on additional debt as a means of stimulating economic growth and thereby diminishing the weight of the debt over time is not an option, because the Latin American countries' access to international loans is close to nonexistent. Growing one's way out of the debt burden by increasing a country's output and production and thereby increasing the means of repaying debt is not feasible in most countries. Growth in Latin America requires imports of capital goods and of intermediate products, and there is not enough foreign exchange for such imports. In recent years growth has been slow at best, and for the most part negative. This is partly because of poor domestic economic policy, but in large measure it has resulted from unfavorable international pressures on the economies. The upshot is that these countries are not likely to be able to grow their way out of debt. The burden of the debt is real and is squeezing the life out of the Latin American economies.

At this point, the key to understanding the Latin American situation is the manner in which the international financial system has forced adjustment on those economies. How did the system keep Latin American countries from simply repudiating their debts? How did it keep them dangling by offering dribs and drabs of additional resources, at a price that was remunerative to the banks and in amounts that maintained the minimum of stability and kept the whole system functioning? How did a system operate whose result was continued stagnation and increasing debt for the debtors, while creditors were generally unaffected and at times even gained greater profits from the relationship?

At the time the debt problems became obvious, a cute saying seemed to sum up the situation: "If I owe you $10, that is my problem; if I owe you $10 billion, that is your problem." One of the remarkable things is that the problem remained almost entirely the Latin American countries' until some adjustment began in the last two years.[4]

When?,

THE DEBT SYSTEM AND THE DOLLAR BLOC

One way of understanding the rapid increase in debt during the 1970s is that the banks were "loan pushers"; they made loans that were doubtful even with the knowledge available at that point, and they abandoned the traditional prudential judgments of financial entities in the interest of greater short-run profits (Darity and Horn, 1988). There was an implicit assumption that the loans would be paid back because they had the backing of the debtor government.

The operation of the system is seen most clearly in how the banks were protected from losses on their "bad" loans. During the 1970s, after the OPEC price increases, there were excellent profits to be made from recycling those dollars through international markets, through pushing loans.

As those loans went bad during the 1980s, the large international commercial (money center) banks should have borne the burden, or at least a portion of the burden. In the Latin American case, the international financial system and the power of international politics protected the banks from these losses.

One of the earliest examples was in 1981–82, when private firms in Mexico and Chile, which had received many of the loans, were unable to repay them. The lending banks did not absorb the loss. They were able to use international pressure and the threat of closing international capital markets to force the governments of those countries to assume those private debts and to undertake refinancing and guarantee programs to protect the banks from any immediate losses. Money center bank profits in the early 1980s were heavily reliant on Third World loans, which in many cases accounted for over 50 percent of a bank's profits. And studies of bank stock prices when a rescheduling was agreed upon showed that the stock prices rose with reschedulings, especially in the late 1970s, reflecting higher profit expectations (Ozler, 1990). Political and economic power preserved the international banks' claim to contractual repayment, by the central government if necessary, much to the detriment of the Latin American countries that had to assume those obligations.

The Mexican default increased pressure on the system, but as the default option became a real threat, clever coordination among the banks, the western governments, and the international lending institutions kept the system afloat.[5] For example, friendly finance ministers were supported and co-opted. The finance minister of Mexico, who had prevented the country from a long-term default in 1982, was hailed as the "Finance Minister of the Year" by *Euromoney* magazine and has been a popular lecturer in the United States ever since. And when a country threatened to break with the rules, sanctions were carefully orchestrated to limit the damage and to dissuade other countries from following. When Alan Garcia, the president of Peru, declared in 1985 that Peru would limit its debt payments to 10 percent of its export earnings, the country suddenly could not get the short-term credits it needed to finance its trade; countervailing tariffs were placed on its textile exports, and the result was that Peru paid far more than Garcia had wished and perhaps even more than if it had simply played by the existing rules of the game.

The fundamental reason the Latin American countries have been unable to escape the burden of their debt is that they are integrated into the western economic system on which they can make few demands because of their lack of real power. It is a system whose organizing principles have been established with other purposes in mind, that is, a capitalist system in which it often seems that the "golden rule" operates: Whoever has the gold makes the rules.

In almost every case, Latin American countries opened up their economies to international competition in the 1970s, as the Eastern European economies are presently being encouraged to do. As a result, they became more closely tied to what we term a "dollar bloc," in which access to dollars became the central determinant of economic performance. The only way for their economies to prosper was through access to international capital markets, to the resources of the international lending agencies, to foreign loans, or to increased foreign investment. Once those were inadequate or had dried up, the economies were placed under severe pressure. The conclusion is that the debt represents an onerous burden because of the constraints placed on the countries by their participation in the dollar bloc. Were they more autarkic (i.e., less dependent on the international economy), the burden of the debt—the dollar drain for debt repayment—would be much less.

Not only is the dollar bloc important for its effect on the burden of the Latin American debt, but adjustments in the bloc could also have an important role in dealing with this burden and in the success of the effort to reverse the deteriorating economic performance in Latin America. Thus, a more detailed treatment of the dollar bloc is required.

There are several elements to the dollar bloc. First, almost all of the Latin American currencies are fixed or pegged to the dollar, and so the relation with the dollar is the most important price relation in those economies. All but 10 of them fixed their currency to the dollar in 1988, thus constituting a large percentage of the 36 countries in the world fixed to the dollar (IMF, May, 1989, p. 22). For the most part, the smaller countries fixed, though Ecuador, Paraguay, and Venezuela did as well. Even Guyana, which had effectively fixed to the British pound as recently as 1986, now uses the dollar as its reference. Just two countries, Bolivia and Uruguay, operated with a floating exchange rate in this post–Bretton Woods era which encourages such an approach, and Bolivia managed the exchange rate through an auction mechanism.[6] The other eight Latin American countries either had a managed float against the dollar or adjusted their currency against the dollar according to a set of economic indicators. The actual exchange rate regime in Latin America evidences the central concern of Latin American governments: stability between their national currency and the dollar.

Indeed, in the cases in which countries have been able to stabilize their domestic economy, the ability to stabilize the exchange rate has been a central element of the success—for example, in Bolivia and Chile (Sachs, 1987). The experience of Latin America in this regard is guiding many of the policy suggestions in Eastern Europe as those countries reorient their relations with the international economy (Sachs, 1990b).

The dollar bloc is also felt in many of the countries in which there is extensive use of dollars in the domestic economy, often termed "dollarization." In many Latin American countries, dollars are used for large purchases; if local currencies are used for the purchase, the price is often set in dollars. In some countries, as much as 75 percent of the savings deposits in the banking system have been denominated in dollars.

This integration into the dollar bloc was the starting point for the first U.S. effort to topple Manuel Noriega by interrupting the flow of dollars to

Panama, which is the most dollarized economy. The dollar has been its currency ever since, as former Senator S. I. Hayakawa said, "We stole it fair and square." In the recent effort to oust Noriega, the United States succeeded in interrupting the legal flow of dollars and in disrupting the economy; but our policymakers underestimated Noriega's ruthlessness and staying power and thus resorted to more direct means of action.[7]

There are previous cases in which foreign currencies were important in domestic financial systems as well as in the international financial regime. One of the most notable was the British sterling bloc, which developed in the 1930s and continued until the late 1960s (Conan, 1952; Strange, 1971). It provided a stable context for economic relations among the members of the British Commonwealth, and it was an accepted international economic arrangement—the backdrop to decolonization and the establishment of more independent states.

The second was the French franc bloc, which has continued in operation in the former French colonies of Africa. Since 1948, it has provided a stable medium of exchange and an accepted means of controlling credit creation in its member states. It has facilitated acceptable growth rates within a generally stable economic context (Devarajan and de Melo, 1987; Guillamont et al., 1988).

It is no accident that the first issue in the reunification of the two Germanies was the establishment of a common currency, or actually the replacement of the East German currency by the West German mark (i.e., the formation of a "mark bloc"). Having stable currency relations is a prerequisite for closer economic relations in other areas.[8]

The role of the dollar in Latin America and the Caribbean resembles that of sterling and the franc in their respective currency blocs, though with a much less formalized structure. A number of parallels can be noted.

In all currency blocs, participants have an obligation to support the central currency in some fashion. This generally takes the form of mandatory reserve transfers to the central country or of mechanisms which allow the central country to exert control over the movement of reserves in the whole system. The growth of the dollar-denominated debt and the current obligation of the debtor countries to transfer reserves to the United States has played this role in the dollar bloc. On average during the 1980s, $31 billion per year have been transferred from Latin America to the advanced countries in the form of debt service payments. This transfer has bound the Latin American countries to the dollar bloc more tightly.

Currency blocs have also made available to their members "reserve pools," funds which could be drawn, based upon some determination of need, and which could be used to offset negative economic developments for the short or medium term. The dollar bloc has its analogue, a dollar pool that can be used by countries according to "need." The International Monetary Fund (IMF) has traditionally been the source of such resources, and it continues to play this role. However, other pools of dollars have been found and made available to members of the dollar bloc deemed to merit access. On occasion, the U.S. government, the U.S. Treasury, and the Federal Reserve Board have pooled as much as $5 billion in short-term funds to facilitate agreements that were needed to stabilize the dollar bloc. Mexico has been the main beneficiary of such arrangements, for keeping Mexico in the bloc has been the keystone of the policy. The most recent example in early 1990 was the decision of the U.S. Treasury to transfer $350 million to Mexico as a subsidy on interest arrangements with its creditors.

Currency blocs also provide some external limits on internal domestic macroeconomic policies and performance. In the franc bloc, this is an explicit limit on credit creation in the member countries. In the sterling bloc, it was the ability of the Bank of England to drain reserves from the member countries when it needed them. Under present circumstances, the operation of the dollar bloc limits the autonomy of domestic Latin American economic policy. The three areas in which these limits operate are control of the domestic money supply, control of the exchange rate with the dollar, and loss of seigniorage revenue. Let us examine each in turn.

Latin American policymakers have little control over the size of their domestic money supplies, because the dollar is a (often preferred) substitute in virtually all transactions, and they have no control over the supply of dollars. They also may lose control over their exchange rate with the dollar, even though it is a key policy instrument and they are "obligated" to maintain a fixed rate with the dollar (Dornbusch, 1987). For example, market expectations and speculations caused the Argentine austral exchange rate to rise from 17 per dollar to 1,000 per dollar between February and December of 1989; in February 1990, it took 4,800 australes to buy one dollar.

Stanley Fischer (1982) argues that currency bloc members are also prevented from gaining revenues through seigniorage (i.e., the addition to government purchasing power from printing and using its own currency, less the cost). This might appear to be a weak argument, for only a deranged policymaker would think that the current revenues of seigniorage are worth the risk (cost) of the future inflation that an overly used printing press will surely bring. However, the high rates of inflation apparent in Table 3-4 indicate that such steps are not uncommon in Latin America. Their participation in the dollar bloc facilitates the action of citizens who opt to insulate their assets from the inflation tax by "capital flight" (i.e., converting their domestic assets to more stable foreign ones), thus frustrating the seigniorage goals of the government.

I conclude that the Latin American countries have had a heavy burden to bear as a result of their debt situation, and that this shows up clearly in the indicators of economic performance noted above. In addition, the burden has been determined not only by the size of their debt obligation, but also by the functioning of the dollar bloc into which the countries are integrated. Most importantly, this implies that solutions to the debt problem must be of a systemic nature, taking into account the system (i.e., the dollar bloc) and its effect on the countries.

ADJUSTMENTS TO MAINTAIN THE SYSTEM

Let us turn now to assess the adjustments to the system which have been made in recent years, adjustments which have been designed to maintain the system rather than to solve the burden of the debt on Latin American countries.

The poor overall economic performance and the continued centrality of access to dollars necessarily make the international bases of the dollar bloc prone to dispute and negotiation. There have been direct challenges to the strictures of the bloc. There have been efforts to form a cartel of debtors, and they will surely continue; Fidel Castro has encouraged other countries to repudiate their debt, though none have formally done so because the costs are far too high.

Brazil has offered the most direct challenge to the system by publicly declaring a moratorium on interest payments on its bank debt on more than one occasion. It has also suggested that it would deal only with governments and international agencies in finding a solution. This stance is a direct attack on the system as it has operated; its purpose is to force adjustments in the operation of the bloc so that the costs of its continuation can be more evenly shared. Brazil does not have the power to force through the changes, and it has received lukewarm support from other debtors who hope to receive added infusions of funds; so Brazil has renewed payments on its debt.

This result was a tribute to the success of the "Baker Plan," named for now Secretary of State James Baker, who proposed a debt strategy in 1985 which consciously and consistently avoided dealing with debt as a systemic issue. Every case was to be taken on an individual basis, every country's problem was to be dealt with at crisis points by negotiations between the banks, the country, and the international organizations. Once a set of policies for the domestic economy had been agreed upon, international funds would be forthcoming—a draw on the dollar pool—and debt reschedulings would be agreed to which would push the burden somewhat further into the future. Its purpose was to give the system "breathing room," not to reduce the total burden.

The hope of this plan was that renewed growth in Latin America would allow those countries to grow out of the debt problem, and that the added international resources which would be necessary to facilitate the process would be minimal. However, minimal new resources were forthcoming, few economies responded as hoped, and consequently the abysmal performance we noted above continued in most countries and in most years of the 1980s.

The pressures which this stagnation has engendered have forced some adjustments in the operation of the dollar bloc. Traditionally, agreement with the IMF was the gateway to the dollar pool, but recent years have seen much greater flexibility. "Bridge loans," short-term loans provided as an immediate bridge between a crisis and the commitment of longer term loans, have often been approved far in advance of such agreements and even when dispute with the IMF was likely. In 1988, Argentina was able to reach an agreement with the Bank for Reconstruction and Development (World Bank) and started receiving funds even though it strongly resisted the economic program the International Monetary Fund had proposed.

Countries have been allowed to adjust the basic debt contracts under certain circumstances. Agreements to allow Bolivia and Chile to buy back private debt at market value were examples of the growing willingness to reassess the arrangements that have developed. Thus, Bolivia bought back one-half of its private debt at eleven cents on the dollar, the going market rate at that time. The funds to do so were donated by several European countries. Another step has been the reduction in the face value of the debt as a result of "debt-equity swaps," the purchase of companies or land at a discount through the repurchase of loans owed by a country. Mexico and Chile have been the most active in this area, with Chile retiring over $6.5 billion of its $21 billion debt through swaps for domestic assets (Krueger, 1990, p. 23).

In addition, the role of the U.S. government as the champion of the interests of its banks has changed in recent years. Banks have been forced to write down some of their nonperforming loans (for example, the 20 percent write-down of Argentine loans in June 1989). They have been pressured to add to their loan loss reserves and have been required to increase their capital base, that is, to have on hand more real assets to protect them if the loans finally go into default. These steps have forced the banks to begin to shoulder some of the costs of keeping the bloc in operation; for example, they set aside loan loss reserves of over $17 billion during the second quarter of 1987, which generated accounting losses of over $7 billion. The banks saw this measure as a move to soften the threat of default, since it protected them from the effects of a default; however, it also made it more likely that they will "take a hit" and end up writing down, or off, portions of these loans. Further evidence is the continuation of reserve build-ups. Many banks now have reserves set aside for up to 50 percent of the Third World loans. For example, Citicorp added $1 billion to its reserves in the fourth quarter of 1989, bringing its coverage to 38 percent of its total loans. This is a more realistic representation of the actual value of those loans, for Table 3-5 shows that the market value of the debts has declined and is far from their face value. The news is not that the debts are worth less than their face value, a widely known and accepted fact, but that the banks' actions imply their agreement with this assessment.

The adjustments to the debt situation were formulated most comprehensively in the Brady Plan, offered in 1988 by Secretary of the Treasury Nicholas Brady. Much of the impetus for the plan was a new assertiveness by the Japanese (the Miyazawa Plan), who wanted to force some movement toward a solution of the debt burden. They used the Economic Summit of the major industrialized countries in Toronto in 1988 as a forum for pushing new policies. Although not changing the principle that adjustments be made on a case-by-case basis, Brady's proposal to provide debt main effect was to allow many banks to sever all relations with Mexico and thus escape further obligation. The agreement reduced the face value of Mexico's debt by about $7 billion, but the country had to borrow over $5 billion to finance the effort, so the net effect was small. Its major impact was to reduce annual debt payments by approximately $1 billion, again far less than had been hoped.

The Brady Plan was declared dead on arrival because of these meager results. That judgment may be slightly unfair as there have been four such arrangements, though all much more modest than the Mexican plan and with even more modest benefits to borrowers. In addition, after a period of domestic political instability, the Japanese may again assert their international influence, and they are the most willing to push for a meaningful solution that will relax the burden of the debt on Latin American countries.

However, the background to this situation is continued economic stagnation in a Latin America that continues to reel under the burden of the debt. The Economic Commission for Latin America and the Caribbean reports that growth last year was positive but only an anemic 1 percent overall (ECLAC, 1990). Their projection for this year is equally dismal, a growth rate of 1.5 percent, shared very unequally among the countries. A scenario of collapse and chaos in Latin America might lead to a change in U.S. willingness to take a more responsible role regarding Western Hemisphere economic performance; it could lead to more fundamental adjustments in the debt relations. However, at this point there is no reason to expect steps to be taken to change the functioning of the dollar bloc.

Nonetheless, it is important to envision now the possible solutions to the debt burden of Latin American countries. What fundamental changes in the dollar bloc might better serve the needs of Latin America?

TOWARD REMOVAL OF THE BURDEN OF THE LATIN AMERICAN DEBT

Colombia, Chile, and post-1985 Bolivia have performed better than the Latin American average in terms of financial, exchange rate, and price stability. Their experience proves the rule that only if domestic policies are combined with favorable external conditions, in this case the availability of dollars, will stability be attained. Colombia has had an ample dollar supply because of its pivotal role in the international drug trade. Drug proceeds have also found their way to Bolivia, a producer of the coca leaf, which is the base of cocaine (Naylor, 1987). In addition, Bolivia has been favored by the international system through multilateral loans and by being allowed to retire one-half of its private debt, as noted above. Chile has been supported by the World Bank and the IMF, which provided a net transfer of $1.3 billion between 1983 and 1987, giving Chile the highest debt/GNP ratio in South America. So access to the dollar pool and assurance of the ability to limit the reserve drain are central to domestic economic performance;

domestic economic policy cannot operate autonomously. And even these successes, with the exception of Chile, have not solved the problem of renewing growth. Per capita GDP fell 0.4 percent in Bolivia and rose only 0.9 percent in Colombia in 1989 (ECLAC, 1990). This indicates that a fundamental change in the handling of the debt is essential.

The Brady Plan, described above, is criticized from two directions. Krueger (1990), Bulow and Rogoff (1990), and Eaton (1990) all argue against involvement of international organizations and of developed country resources in solving the debt problem. They point to Korea, which has successfully confronted its debt; they note that the Brady Plan does improve the banks' return on these loans; they claim the debt is not a cause of the problems; and they note that the income of the large debtors is higher than that of many other countries and so they should not be given preference.

The other critique comes from Sachs (1990a) and Kenen (1990), who find that the Brady Plan underestimates the need for concerted international action. They propose a new international agency which will take over the debts, buying them at a price between the face value and the market value noted in Table 3-5. Alternatively, the institution could simply assume the debts at a far lower interest rate. Sachs estimates that about $7.5 billion of U.S. funds, spread over many years, would be required to stimulate this process, which should be self-operating once the initial debts are assumed.[9] For arguments in favor of their proposals, they point to the burden of the debt, to the inefficiencies for both debtors and creditors of the current situation, and to the inability of debtors or creditors to attain any resolution of this situation without outside intervention. This perspective has been pushed even further by Darity (1989), who proposes general forgiveness of the debt, a step which has been widely taken for the debt of poor African countries. Canada has also forgiven most of the Latin American debt owed it.

My proposal differs from both of the above. I agree with Bulow and Rogoff (1990) that involvement of international organizations such as the IMF and the World Bank have not improved the situation and have often made it difficult to reach agreements. I go further to suggest that the entire international system has operated to protect the interests of the U.S. banks which, after all, made bad loans and should have begun to bear the cost of those bad loans as far back as 1982. As noted earlier, it was sheer international political power which forced many of the Latin American governments to assume not only their own debts but the debts of their private sectors as well, political power which was wielded to protect the industrial countries' banks and banking system. So I agree with these authors and Buiter et al. (1989) that getting the international organizations and the U.S. government out of the issue in the short run is the best step. Let the governments and the banks work out the problem, which will give the banks a further incentive to settle by indicating that their effort to use the U.S. government to protect their position will no longer be possible.

This step would provide the banks an incentive to reach an agreement on their debt which would be more attuned to the market valuation of the debt. Since 1982, they have been better off to hold out because they knew the U.S. government would protect them. At present, the same strategy is encouraged by providing banks with hope that some international debt organization will assume the debt at a more remunerative rate.

The second step will be to create a functioning and positive dollar bloc in the Western Hemisphere, to exert what the Cubans call a "positive hegemony," a continuation of U.S. dominance in the Western Hemisphere, but in a policy context which is much more positive for Latin American development. The United States treats Latin American countries as competitors who must be opposed at all junctures in the interests of U.S. producers. Thus, even while we are forcing Brazil to run a $19 billion trade surplus to facilitate continued payment on its debt, we threaten countervailing duties against Brazilian exports to the United States because Brazil is attempting to develop its own computer industry. We should realize that a functioning and vibrant Latin America is very much in the interests of the United States. We export to Latin America, and could export much more if their incomes were not falling. A growing Latin America would provide less incentive for migration into the United States and free up the resources that are spent to prevent illegal immigration from Latin America. If Latin American farmers and entrepreneurs had better alternatives, drugs and the drug trade would be much less appealing to them.

But the key step in changing this situation will be the formation of a responsive, creative, and positive dollar bloc. Once the drain of dollars generated by the debt has been staunched, bilateral and multilateral negotiations can be undertaken to change the bases of economic relations in the Western Hemisphere.

The keystone of this effort must be the reestablishment of a dollar bloc of financial relations on a different basis. The Latin American countries must accept some limits on their domestic policy autonomy; in return, they should receive access to much greater international resources and support in their domestic economic efforts. There must also be better coordination of policy on trade, foreign assistance, and foreign investment. Our government must take the lead by defining the welfare of the entire Western Hemisphere dollar bloc as a central element of policy which both private and public sectors must support.

Most of all, a new vision of the Western Hemisphere must be articulated which sees those close links and which finds the possibilities for a positive relation that can serve all sides. The events in Eastern Europe and especially in East Germany show the power of such a vision, a "united Germany," in affecting economic policy and the search for viable approaches to problems. Such an effort is essential, for the world is retreating from the liberalization and internationalization of the last 20 years to spheres of influence and currency or economic blocs as noted above (Garten, 1989). The virtual absorption of East Germany by West Germany is the most tangible example, and it is likely that the rest of Eastern Europe will fade into a Western European sphere of influence. In this context the United

States must take responsibility for the area in which it continues to remain supreme, the Western Hemisphere.

The approaches taken over the last decade have failed miserably, and the proposals either to continue the current system or to set up a mechanism which will primarily protect U.S. banks are inadequate to the problems at hand. The lack of a broader vision makes one recall Keynes' 1919 observation on the debate over reparations to be extracted from Germany after World War I:

> This chapter must be one of pessimism. The treaty [of Versailles of 1919] contains no provisions for the economic rehabilitation of Europe. . . . It is an extraordinary fact that the fundamental problems of a Europe starving and disintegrating before their eyes, was the one question in which it was impossible to arouse the interest of the Four [Britain, France, Italy, and the U.S.] (1971, p. 143).

NOTES

1. We will use the term Latin America as a shorthand for the 25 countries included in Table 3-1, instead of the more complete terminology of Latin America and the Caribbean. The bulk of the debt is owed by the larger Latin American countries, which are the main focus of analysis; however, the problem exists for virtually all of the countries.

2. Bulow and Rogoff (1990) advocate that debt relief be carried out by an "International Citizenship Fund," a new grant-making arm of the World Bank, which will reward developing countries that have "responsible policies towards the environment, population growth . . ." (1990, p. 39). Contributions by industrialized countries to the fund will be based on the same criteria. The greater the industrialized country's "irresponsible policies," the greater will be its contributions to the fund.

3. By the late 1970s, the interest rate on most loans was pegged to the London Interbank Rate (LIBOR) and so increases in that rate would increase the rate of interest on the outstanding Latin American loans.

4. Eaton (1990, p. 48) notes that Keynes felt that debtor countries have no reason to repay loans, writing:

> Indeed, it is probable that loans to foreign Governments have turned out badly on balance. . . . The investor has no remedy—none whatever—against default. There is, on the part of most foreign countries, a strong tendency to default on the occasion of wars and revolutions and whenever the expectation of further loans no longer exceeds in amount the interest payable on old ones.

5. The International Monetary Fund (IMF) and the International Bank for Reconstruction and Development (IBRD or World Bank) used their substantial lending resources as carrot or stick to encourage the countries to deal with the banks and to maintain payments on the debt. Agreement with the IMF on a set of economic policies was generally required to gain access to IMF funds and World Bank loans, as well as to be able to negotiate reschedulings of private debt.

6. The weakening of the regime of fixed exchange rates, agreed to at Bretton Woods, NH, in 1944, led to the current International Monetary Fund agreement which encourages floating exchange rates.

7. Noriega was at the center of a whole web of illegal dollar transactions such as laundering drug transactions (i.e., funnelling illegal proceeds into the ordinary legal banking system) (Naylor, 1987).

8. There have been suggestions in some Latin American countries (e.g., Bolivia) that the dollar be adopted as the official currency, but they sparked a firestorm of rejection.

9. Some perspective on the issue is gained by comparing it with the savings and loan debacle in the United States. The Government Accounting Office now estimates the U.S. taxpayers will pay at least $325 billion and perhaps as much as $500 billion to "solve" the crisis, that is, to protect depositors in the S & Ls and to ensure financial stability. Recall the total Latin American debt is only $426 billion, and if its market value is 33 percent of that, the entire debt could be retired for a paltry $142 billion!

Part Two

Opinions on the Benefits and Burdens of the U.S. National Debt and Twin Deficits

4 Deficits and Us and Our Grandchildren

ROBERT EISNER

Deficits can be good for us. They can bring a better life now. And they can bring a better life in the future.

Deficits can also be bad, if they are too large—or too small. But you can't tell which unless you measure them right.

As I write, in the spring of 1990, the overall size of the deficit is probably just about right. In a fundamental sense that I will explain, the reported deficit now really represents balance, consistent with balanced growth of the economy. The composition of the deficit—the combination of government expenditures and taxes that brings it about—is another matter. I can, and will, recommend some changes in that composition which would help the economy, today and tomorrow. And I shall also recommend a change in the mix of fiscal and monetary policy, not with a view to reducing the measured deficit, although it might. The purpose rather is to improve that bottom line—or what should be the bottom line—in our national accounting, the quality of life for us, our children, and our grandchildren.

MEASURING THE DEFICIT

I am fond of asking audiences how they feel about debt. Is it good or bad? A majority of hands indicates that debt is bad. Then I ask, "How many of you borrowed to buy a house? Or how many of your parents did?" A sizable majority of hands rises in the affirmative. "How many of you think that was bad?" No hands are raised and I follow up, "Then you are not so sure that debt is generally bad!"

Of course, in terms of federal accounting the deficit is the increase in debt. If the government borrows to build housing for military personnel or to support housing for the poor, that contributes to the deficit. A road is built or a bridge repaired—that contributes to the deficit, unless taxes are raised to cover it. If the U.S. Treasury borrows to finance loans it makes to small business, that contributes to the deficit. In short, unlike any private business or the people in my audience, who recognize that borrowing to buy a house is not the same as borrowing to gamble away the proceeds in

Las Vegas or Atlantic City, the federal government budget makes no distinction among current or capital expenditures.

Private business budgets exclude capital expenditures or investment from their current accounts or income or profit and loss statements. They include as expenses in those accounts only the depreciation on existing capital assets. If we did that for the federal government, we would be subtracting out net investment, or capital expenditures minus depreciation, from the current budget.

The 1989 federal unified budget was in deficit to the amount of $152 billion. Utilizing Office of Management and Budget estimates of "investment-type expenditures"[1] and making a rough estimate of depreciation, I come up with $70 billion for net investment. Taking that out of the current-account budget would reduce the measure of the deficit to $82 billion.

But the federal government deficit is swollen by some $120 billion in expenditures for grants in aid to state and local governments. If we are interested in the total impact of government at all levels on the economy, it hardly makes sense to count the federal deficit and ignore the state and local surpluses which the federal deficit has contributed to making possible. In fiscal 1989, the state and local governments were in the aggregate in surplus by $47 billion. Count that as a counterbalance to the federal deficit and we reduce the total deficit to $35 billion.

And now we come to a critical correction if our measure of the deficit is to have much economic relevance. Recall that we pointed out that deficits add to debt. Indeed, we can readily define the deficit as the increase in debt. If anyone starts with a debt of $2,000 and spends $150 more than he or she takes in as receipts, the $150 of borrowing to finance that deficit increases the debt to $2,150. That is precisely what happens to the federal government, except that the figures are in billions.

However, suppose someone owes $2,000 and there is over the period of, say, a year a rate of inflation that lowers the real value (that is, the purchasing power) of the dollar by 5 percent. In real terms, the existing debt has fallen in value by 5 percent of that $2,000, or $100. The $150 of borrowing to finance the deficit has then left the person with a *real* debt only $50 higher than at the end of the previous year.

At the level of the federal government, this means that all those U.S. Treasury bond, note, and bill holders out there in fact pay an "inflation tax" on their holdings. Although probably, contrary to some oratory, no more cruel than any other tax, it is just as real in its impact on people's wealth and hence, ultimately, on their economic behavior. Indeed, it is closely related to the measured deficit because we count, in the expenditures that make up the nominal deficit, interest payments that must include an inflation premium to induce people to hold bonds that are depreciating in real value as the dollar keeps buying less.

Since in 1989 the federal debt held by the public averaged $2,120 billion, an inflation tax at the rate of 4.1 percent signified a loss of $87 billion in the real value of outstanding debt. We put all this together in

TABLE 4-1
Adjusted and Unadjusted Deficit, Fiscal Year 1989
(Billions of Dollars)

Federal Unified Budget, Unadjusted	$152
Minus Net Investment (Estimated)	– 70
Federal Budget Deficit, Current Account	$ 82
Minus State and Local Budget Surpluses	– 47
Total Government Budget Deficit	$ 35
Minus Inflation Tax: 4.1% of $2,120	– 87
Total Government, Adjusted *Surplus*	$ 52

Table 4-1 and what do we find? The nominal or official deficit is converted into a *real* surplus of $52 billion!

Ignoring the inflation tax is particularly mischievous and misleading in periods when inflation is substantial, and failing to take it into account as inflation varies can generate disastrous guides for public policy. A rough illustration can be provided in terms of the situation as Jimmy Carter's presidency came to a close. As shown in Table 4-2, federal debt, in very round numbers, may be put at $700 billion at the end of 1979. The dollar lost some 10 percent of its value in 1980 as a consequence of inflation that was essentially the result of huge increases in energy costs generated by the oil cartel. The inflation tax thus came to $70 billion. There was, it is true, a nominal deficit of $60 billion. Yet the real value of the debt, even with that deficit, fell by $10 billion. In the relevant sense of the change in the real value of federal debt—*the real value of wealth in federal securities held by the public*—we can well argue that the federal budget was in surplus to the amount of that $10 billion, just as surely as if the surplus had been achieved by raising explicit taxes to a point where explicit tax revenues exceeded expenditures by that amount.

Neither outside critics nor advisers within the Carter administration saw things this way. Conventional wisdom of that time insisted that the "huge" deficit was the cause of the inflation and had to be reduced. Efforts to reduce that "deficit," along with restrictive monetary policies undertaken by the Federal Reserve under its new Chairman, Paul Volcker, kept the economy sluggish, with both inflation and unemployment mounting. One may well conjecture that this, as well as those unfortunate events with the Ayatollah and the television persona of Carter's opponent, contributed to Carter's November election loss. Had the nominal deficit been seen properly as a real surplus, the existing inflation might have been recognized as a consequence of restricted supply and not general excess demand. And we might not have had the further tightening of fiscal and monetary policy through the initial years of the Reagan administration, culminating in 10.7 percent unemployment by the end of 1982, the worst recession since the Great Depression of the 1930s.

Table 4-2
Inflation Tax and Real Debt and Deficit
(Billions of Dollars)

1979 Total Debt	$700
Minus 1980 Inflation Tax (10%)	− 70
Old Debt in 1979 Dollars	$630
Plus 1980 Nominal Deficit	+ 60
1980 Total Debt in 1979 Dollars	$690
Decrease in Real Debt: 700 to 690 = 1980 Real *Surplus*	$ 10

THE IMPACT OF THE DEFICIT ON CURRENT EMPLOYMENT AND OUTPUT

Charles Schultze (1989) has characterized beholders of deficits as variously seeing wolves, termites, and pussycats. To the wolves school, a deficit is the wolf at the door threatening imminent destruction of all of the house's occupants. National bankruptcy, ruinous inflation, even somehow depression are the likely outcomes unless we promptly rid ourselves of this scourge.

After some eight years of presumably substantial deficits, disaster has still not struck. The sky has not fallen. Indeed, the economy has moved along in a record period of uninterrupted, if not always brisk, growth. Few serious, responsible observers can remain adherents of the wolves school on deficits.

But then Schultze portrays the termite school, of which he is a leading adherent or, perhaps I should say, director. It sees in deficits termites eating away at a house's foundation and slowly but inexorably bringing about its ruin. The economic rationale is that public deficits absorb private saving, thus depriving the economy of needed accumulation of capital or forcing that accumulation to be financed by other nations. In either case, the product available to us in the future is diminished. We will pay the price of our current public profligacy in the years ahead, as will those who follow us. This is indeed a serious argument, but also an argument that is fatally flawed. I shall come back to it as we proceed.

Finally, there is the pussycat school. Those accepting this label for their views tell you the deficit, at least the current deficit, is like a pussycat: "Not to worry! It won't hurt you." I am proud to have been labelled, by one *New York Times* correspondent describing pussycat economists, as "the pick of the litter," all the more so since my wife and I have a beautiful, adorable long-haired cat.

I should make clear though that I do not counsel calm because I think deficits do not matter; in this I differ, in particular, with Robert Barro.[2] I argue rather that deficits can and frequently do matter very much. But they can, as I said at the outset, matter for good as well as ill. And the size of our current deficit in current circumstances is not something to worry about.

The explanation lies in just a bit of simple economic theory, largely ignored by many, and a number of facts or empirical relations that support it. The most essential part of the theory is that what people spend as consumers depends very largely on their current and expected incomes and on the wealth that they believe they have at their disposal. This theory might be called Keynesian, as its essential formulation is indeed to be found in John Maynard Keynes's *General Theory of Employment, Interest and Money* (1936), which set the foundation for modern macroeconomics and policies that have been variously followed throughout the capitalist or free market world. But its most finished modern version is to be found in the work of Nobel Laureates Milton Friedman (1957) and Franco Modigliani.[3] And vital pieces for its application to the issue of deficits come from the work of A.C. Pigou (1943 and 1947) and Gottfried Haberler (1941), leading "neoclassical" critics of Keynes.[4]

The argument may be put as follows. For every borrower there must be a lender. The public deficit is the private sector's surplus. When the government runs a deficit, it is giving the private sector, by its spending, more than it is taking away in taxes. It is hence adding to the private sector's disposable income—what it has available for consumption expenditures. Further, since corresponding to a deficit is an increase in debt, the public deficit is adding to the private sector's perceived wealth in the form of its increased holdings of Treasury bills, notes, and bonds (or, if these are held by the Federal Reserve or banks, the money that they back). This increase in their perceived wealth leads private households to consume more.

Indeed, Pigou and Haberler had used a variant of this reasoning in an attempt to refute the argument by Keynes that without some government intervention an economy might be doomed to long-term, if not permanent, unemployment. They insisted that if wages and prices were freely flexible, unemployment—excess supply of labor—would generate lower wages and hence lower prices. This would raise the real value of the government money held by the public—but the argument applies all the more to the much larger amount of interest-bearing government debt held by the public. And this in turn would raise consumption, and keep raising it as long as unemployment continued and wages consequently fell, until total production to meet the greater consumer demand increased to such a point that all the unemployed were back at work.

There were many problems with this process as a solution for Keynesian unemployment, not the least of which was the failure of wages and prices to fall quickly and sufficiently.[5] But if increased wealth in the form of the government debt to the public does raise consumption, the result is achieved all the more readily by allowing a real budget deficit, rather than falling wages, to increase that wealth.

Thus, real budget deficits—that is, deficits that take into account the inflation tax—can be expected to be associated with subsequent increases

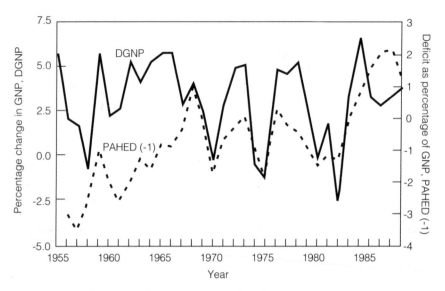

FIGURE 4-1 *Change in GNP and the Adjusted Deficit*

in consumption and hence increases in total output. The bigger those deficits, the bigger will be the increases in output. Surpluses, on the other hand, will tend to reduce output. And with surpluses reducing output, there will be reductions in employment and increases in unemployment.

All this is sensible theory. To test it on the facts, there is one further adjustment to introduce. Although deficits may affect the economy, the economy clearly affects deficits. A reduction in output and an increase in unemployment will raise the actual deficit as tax revenues decline with income and profits and as government expenditures rise with unemployment benefit payments. To analyze the independent effect of deficits on the economy, we have to abstract from these effects of the economy on the deficit. To do so, economists have utilized, as a measure of budget *policy*, what has been variously called the structural, cyclically adjusted, full-employment, or high-employment budget. This measure indicates what the budget expenditures and receipts, and hence surplus or deficit, would be if the economy were operating at some specified rate of economic activity or level of unemployment, such as 5 percent or 6 percent unemployment. The resultant measure of the deficit is then not itself affected by fluctuations in the economy.

When we match the high-employment, inflation-adjusted deficit against subsequent changes in real gross national product (GNP), both expressed as percentages of GNP over the years 1955 to 1988, the results are striking, as may be seen in Figure 4-1. It is very clear to the naked eye. Bigger deficits are associated with greater increases in GNP. Lesser deficits are associated with lesser increases. And those rare surpluses are associated with still smaller increases in GNP or with actual declines.

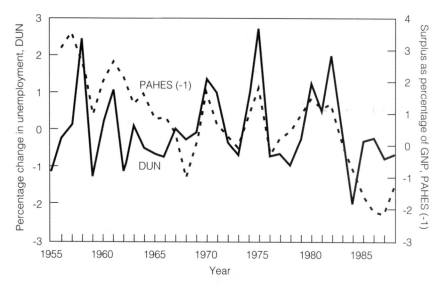

FIGURE 4-2 *Change in Unemployment and Adjusted Surplus*

Since slower growth in production implies slower growth of employment and, with a growing labor force, very possibly increases in unemployment, we may expect an analogous relation between the budget surplus—the inverse of the deficit—and increases in unemployment. And that is just what we see in Figure 4-2.

For those who need convincing with somewhat more rigorous presentation than eye-catching graphs, perusal of Table 4-3 will be in order. The regression results reported there confirm that deficits were associated with increases in GNP and decreases in unemployment. Looking at relations involving only the deficits, we see that each percentage point of deficit (expressed as a ratio of GNP) was associated with increases of from 1.2 to 1.8 percentage points of GNP and declines of from 0.56 to 0.85 percentage points in unemployment.

As can be seen in Figures 4-1 and 4-2, the good fits slip in the last few years. We have an explanation for that in terms of one of the (perhaps many) elements left out of the analysis. That is the effect of changes in foreign exchange rates. In fact, the Federal Reserve, in implicit if not explicit collaboration with other central banks, particularly those of Japan and Germany, followed policies which allowed the dollar to rise—or pushed it—to unprecedented heights. On a trade-weighted basis, that is, as an average of foreign exchange rates weighted by the shares of their nations in international trade of the United States, it rose some 55 percent from 1980 to 1985. As our dollars became more expensive to foreigners, so did the U.S. goods that could be purchased with them. Toyotas, Hondas, and Sonys on the other hand became relatively cheap. Eventually then, with the usual lag we have come to expect, we developed a substantial trade

TABLE 4-3

Real High-Employment Deficits, Changes in the Real Exchange Rate, and Changes in GNP and Unemployment

$$Y_t = b_{01} + b_{11}\text{PAHED}_{t-1} \qquad \text{for } t = 1956,...,1966$$
$$Y_t = b_{02} + b_{12}\text{PAHED}_{t-1} + b_{22}\text{DERR}_{t-4} \qquad \text{for } t = 1967,...,1988$$

| | Regression Coefficients* | | | | | | |
| | 1956–66 | | 1967–88 | | | | |
Dependent Variable (Y)	Constant (b_{01})	PAHED$_{t-1}$ (b_{11})	Constant (b_{02})	PAHED$_{t-1}$ (b_{12})	DERR$_{t-4}$ (b_{22})	$\hat{R}^2$	D-W
DGNP	7.214 (1.344)	1.805 (0.618)	2.884 (0.392)	1.206 (0.336)		0.386	1.79
			3.097 (0.420)	1.628 (0.462)	−0.131 (0.100)	0.401	1.82
DUN	−1.165 (0.639)	−0.561 (0.294)	0.013 (0.186)	−0.637 (0.160)		0.343	2.21
			−0.097 (0.199)	−0.854 (0.219)	0.067 (0.047)	0.366	2.22

SOURCE: Updated and revised (to include changes in the real exchange rate) from Eisner (1986), Table 9.1, p. 97.

*Ordinary least squares; standard errors are shown in parentheses.
    Y = dependent variable: DGNP or DUN
PAHED = price-adjusted, high-employment budget deficit as percentage of GNP
  DGNP = percentage change in gross national product
  DUN = percentage point change in unemployment
DERR = change in real exchange rate
    $\hat{R}^2$ = adjusted coefficient of determination (for 1956–88)
  D-W = Durbin–Watson ratio

deficit. This contributed to slowing the economy as against the pace it might have otherwise followed.

We therefore introduce into our relations a variable measuring the lagged change in the exchange rate. As expected, it is correlated negatively with changes in real GNP; increases in the cost of the dollar slowed our growth in output and contributed to more unemployment. Introduction of the exchange rate variable also points up the underlying separate contribution to economic growth, over the entire period, of real budget deficits. And as they contributed to increases in GNP they helped reduce unemployment.

I do not mean to argue that budget deficits can always contribute significantly, if at all, to increases in output and reductions in unemployment. They apparently did so contribute over the third of a century from

TABLE 4-4
Budget Deficits and Inflation

$$\text{DGNPDEF}_t = b_{01}X_1 + b_{02}X_2 + b_1\text{DGNPDEF}_{t-1} + b_2\text{U}_t + b_3\text{PAHED}_{t-1}$$
$$X_1 = 1, X_2 = 0 \qquad \text{for } t = 1956,....,1966$$
$$X_1 = 0, X_2 = 1 \qquad \text{for } t = 1967,....,1988$$

Variable or Statistic	Regression Coefficients and Standard Errors		Means and Standard Deviations
X_1 (1956–66)	2.231	0.011	4.670*
	(0.936)	(0.555)	(2.587)
X_2 (1967–88)	3.712	2.346	
	(0.976)	(0.940)	
DGNPDEF_{t-1}	0.856	0.588	4.675
	(0.170)	(0.157)	(2.584)
U_t	−0.464	—	5.883
	(0.165)		(1.584)
PAHED_{t-1}	−0.246	−0.485	−0.730
	(0.264)	(0.278)	(1.419)
$\hat{R}^2$	0.807	0.761	—
D-W	2.10	1.75	

SOURCE: Eisner (1989b).

*Dependent variable.
DGNPDEF = percentage change in GNP price deflator
    U = unemployment rate as percentage of labor force
PAHED = price-adjusted, high-employment deficit as percentage of GNP
    $\hat{R}^2$ = adjusted coefficient of determination (for 1956–88)
    D-W = Durbin–Watson ratio

1955–1988. That reflects the fact that over almost all of this period, except a couple of years at the height of the Vietnam War, our economy suffered varying degrees of unemployment—unemployment over that war-time minimum of 3 percent. If ever, hopefully without the benefit of war, we could get there again, further increases in deficits would be likely only to generate more inflation. Action by the monetary authorities to curb the inflation, by choking off investment, would then compound its cost.

The fact that we have generally had ample excess capacity is confirmed by the lack of evidence that the deficits have contributed to inflation over this period. Indeed, if anything, the data suggest that larger structural deficits have been associated with less, rather than more inflation, as may be seen in Table 4-4.

The deficits then have not been wolves. At no time, in no way, have they proved of immediate damage to our well-being. And despite my nomination to leadership of their school, we can truly hardly classify them as pussycats either, for it is not that they have quietly gone about their business, causing little damage but causing little note—except to a few feline lovers. In terms of immediate consequences, at least, they have generally been potent forces for good. There is every reason to believe that their reduction or elimination would have caused palpable current harm.

Solution

THE CASE FOR THE FUTURE

The most powerful and superficially credible argument that has been made against our federal budget deficits, particularly those of the 1980s, has been that they have reduced national saving, the vital provision that an economy makes for its future productivity. They have, by this scenario, been termites insidiously destroying the foundations of our tomorrows.

At the simplest—and most simplistic—level, the termite school points to an accounting identity. Gross saving must equal gross investment. Net saving must equal net investment. But national saving is the sum of private saving—personal saving and corporate saving (undistributed corporate profits)—and government saving, which last is the sum of federal, state, and local government budget surpluses. If that total of surpluses is negative, that is, amounts to a combined deficit, it hence reduces the total of saving, making national saving less than private saving. This in turn, following the logic of the identity, must mean that investment is less than private saving. Some of the private saving has gone to financing the government budget deficit and has not been available for private investment. For those who like to see identities, writing NS for national saving ("gross saving" in the official accounts), PS for private saving, GS for government saving, SD for the statistical discrepancy, GPDI for gross private domestic investment, and NFI for net foreign investment, we have:

$$NS \equiv PS + GS \equiv GPDI + NFI - SD, \text{ or}^6$$
$$701.6 \equiv 806.2 - 104.6 \equiv 773.4 - 96.2 + 24.4,$$

in the actual numbers in billions of dollars for 1989.

The figures show that despite the admitted fall in national saving, that coincided in part with the rise of the budget deficit, gross private domestic investment, that is, the acquisition by business of new plant, equipment, and inventories; investment in new housing; and nonprofit institution acquisition of fixed capital, has kept up very well.

But, the termite argument points out, this fortuitous strength of domestic investment (at $773.4 billion equalling 14.8 percent of GNP, and a higher 17.4 percent, virtually equal to the percentage a dozen years earlier, in real terms) has only been achieved with a substantial move into the red of our net foreign investment (-$96.2 billion). Foreigners have been using their saving to finance our investment. And the consequence of this, if it continues, is that we will have an increasing burden of foreign "debt" on which we will have to make payments. We may be able thus to maintain our own productivity by keeping up domestic investment despite the shortage of national saving, but growing portions of the fruits of that productivity will be going to foreigners and our own standard of living will increasingly suffer.

The first thing to be said about all this, and something unfortunately all too common, is that the numbers that are getting so much attention are not right or, to be fair and precise, not the right numbers.[7] This is not to assert that there are mistakes in the calculation, although inevitably there are these too, in that it is beyond the government's capability to get a record of all transactions. The difficulty is in what we are purporting to measure. The "net foreign investment" figures thus record the difference between the accrual of assets held by Americans in foreign countries and foreign assets in the United States. This, in principle, corresponds to the excess of foreign payments for our goods and services over our payments for theirs plus our net gifts and transfers and government interest payments to them. This measure of net foreign investment has been negative for the past half-dozen years, reflecting essentially our "unfavorable" balance of trade.

But the concern is about our increasing indebtedness to foreigners. We have even had a loud chorus of voices repeating again and again that we have become "the world's greatest debtor nation." In fact, the official "net foreign investment" figure offers only a very partial clue on that issue, because it does not take into account vast changes in actual market values of assets acquired by direct investment, whereby companies own all or part of firms in other countries. U.S. assets abroad, generally considerably older than foreign assets in the United States, have appreciated much more, calling into question the whole judgment of our "greatest debtor" status, if indeed we are a debtor at all. In calculations based on joint work with Paul Pieper,[8] I have estimated that the market value corrections alone add almost $250 billion to our net foreign investment figures over the years 1985–88. Another relevant correction would entail picking up the uncounted billions of assets, only a small proportion in Swiss bank accounts, that in effect become U.S. assets when more foreigners come to reside in this land of immigrants.

Correcting these net foreign investment figures would entail corresponding corrections of the saving figures so that saving would measure properly the additions to national wealth.[9] Correct measures would also point up the full effect of changing exchange rates and the benefits of allowing exchange rate fluctuations to balance the dollar values of our capital claims along with our current accounts.

But aside from the measurement issue, those who use the saving-investment identity to conclude that encouraging private or public saving will increase investment fall into one huge trap. It is a trap that I thought was well marked by economists over the last half-century, but apparently some can only learn by repeating past errors. Of course, more saving must mean more investment. But that does not mean that efforts to raise one component of saving will raise the aggregate. To assert so without evidence is to confuse an identity with behavioral economic relations and, in this case, to fall victim to the fallacy of composition.

One person can indeed save more by cutting consumption, properly assuming that this does not affect income. But our consumption expenditures generally represent income to those who produce what we buy. We cannot all cut our consumption and expect aggregate income to remain unaffected. With total income less, we may well have less consumption *and* less saving.

In the case at issue, suppose the federal deficit is reduced by eliminating some or all of those $120 billion of grants to states. In the first instance, the state and local budgets will move into deficit by just as much as the federal budget moves out of it. The total government deficit and hence national saving will not be affected at all. What happens subsequently will depend upon resultant behavior of all concerned, including governments, private business, and households.

Or suppose the federal deficit is reduced by an increase in taxes or a cut in social security benefits. Private income after taxes will then be reduced. Private consumption will hence be reduced but private saving will certainly decline as well; the marginal propensities to consume and save are universally viewed as greater than zero but less than one. In the first instance now, one may reasonably conjecture that private saving will decline by less than public saving increases. This indeed follows from the acknowledgement that the marginal propensity to consume is greater than zero or that the marginal propensity to save is less than one.

But remember that for aggregate or national saving to rise, aggregate investment, the sum of domestic investment and net foreign investment, must rise. At this point in my discussions of this issue, I like to ask audiences what they think will happen if, as a result of their lower incomes, whether because of higher taxes *or* lower government benefit payments, they decide not to buy that new Chrysler. Will that lead Mr. Iacocca to decide to invest more in new plants—or more likely, less?

In general, or whenever more productive capacity exists or can be created, which seems in our history to have been almost always, there is a positive relation between consumption and investment.[10] More consumption has not generally reduced or "crowded out" investment. It has rather induced more investment—or crowded it in. This is confirmed for budget deficits over more than a quarter-century, as shown in Table 4-5. There we see the results of regressions indicating that bigger adjusted, structural deficits have been associated not only with bigger subsequent increases in consumption and GNP, but also with bigger increases in gross private domestic investment. Each percentage point of deficit has been followed on the average, at least after adjustment for changes in the real exchange rate, by well over a percentage point *more* of domestic investment, both expressed as percentages of GNP.

It may also be noted, though, that along with more domestic investment have come less net exports,[11] the major component of net foreign investment. The verdict on total investment is yet to be rendered. Do budget deficits reduce net foreign investment by more than they raise domestic

TABLE 4-5

Real High-Employment Deficits, Changes in the Real Exchange Rate, and Changes in Components of GNP*

$$\text{DCOM}_t = b_{01} + b_{11}\text{PAHED}_{t-1} \qquad \text{for } t = 1957,...,1966$$
$$\text{DCOM}_t = b_{02} + b_{12}\text{PAHED}_{t-1} + b_{13}\text{DERR}_{t-4} \qquad \text{for } t = 1967,...,1988$$

Regression Coefficients

	1957–66		1967–88					
Dependent Variable (DCOM$_t$)	Constant (b_{01})	PAHED$_{t-1}$ (b_{11})	Constant (b_{02})	PAHED$_{t-1}$ (b_{12})	DERR$_{t-4}$ (b_{13})	$\hat{R}^2$	D-W	rho
Consumption	3.744 (0.706)	0.812 (0.342)	2.092 (0.238)	0.562 (0.194)		0.325	1.87	0.235
	3.757 (0.708)	0.818 (0.343)	2.150 (0.248)	0.651 (0.239)	−0.032 (0.046)	0.312	1.90	0.215
Investment	3.072 (1.216)	1.259 (0.588)	0.629 (0.344)	0.721 (0.311)		0.168	2.03	−0.032
	3.131 (1.191)	1.291 (0.577)	0.902 (0.376)	1.252 (0.420)	−0.154 (0.086)	0.230	2.00	0.009
Government	0.208 (0.483)	−0.523 (0.211)	0.344 (0.235)	0.146 (0.141)		0.443	1.47	0.573
	0.201 (0.496)	−0.535 (0.212)	0.300 (0.250)	0.102 (0.146)	0.022 (0.024)	0.440	1.42	0.595
Net Exports	−0.455 (0.635)	−0.167 (0.308)	−0.124 (0.280)	−0.350 (0.199)		0.184	1.55	0.457
	−0.486 (0.595)	−0.173 (0.290)	−0.254 (0.267)	−0.513 (0.215)	0.075 (0.034)	0.283	1.50	0.462
GNP	7.185 (1.507)	1.816 (0.730)	2.966 (0.456)	1.283 (0.395)		0.340	1.93	0.104
	7.204 (1.507)	1.825 (0.730)	3.152 (0.491)	1.617 (0.512)	−0.106 (0.104)	0.341	1.94	0.104

*Least squares with Cochrane–Orcutt, first-order autoregressive corrections; standard errors are shown in parentheses.

DCOM = change in component as percentage of GNP
PAHED = price-adjusted, high-employment deficit as percentage of GNP
DERR = change in real exchange rate
$\hat{R}^2$ = adjusted coefficient of determination
D-W = Durbin–Watson ratio
rho = AR(1) autoregressive coefficient

investment, thus reducing national saving? I have some at least tentative answers on that. Dealing with the conventional measure of national saving as taken from the national income and product accounts of the Bureau of Economic Analysis, we can see in Figure 4-3 and in Table 4-6 that budget ·deficits have generally had a positive effect. Greater adjusted structural

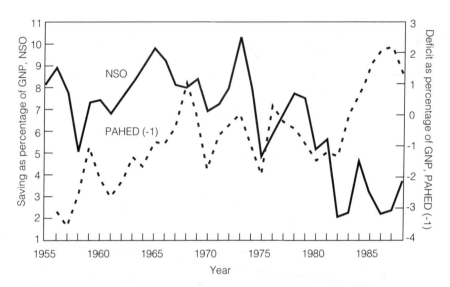

FIGURE 4-3   *Conventional Measure of National Saving and the Adjusted Deficit*

deficits have been associated with more, not less, national saving although, admittedly, that relation is not highly significant statistically and may not then prove that robust. The contrary case though, so usually argued, that the deficits are *reducing* national saving, is clearly not sustained.

Yet, we still have not come to the heart of the issue. A nation's investment consists of far more than what is usually counted in gross private domestic investment. Most countries other than the United States include public or government investment in reproducible tangible capital (that is, roads, structures and equipment). But what about personal or household investment in durable goods? Does it make sense to count as investment the acquisition of cars by Hertz or Avis and taxi companies and not count the cars purchased by individuals or government? They are, after all, investment in future transportation services. Does it make sense to count construction of new movie theaters or projectors as investment but not count purchases of television sets and VCRs that may be used to see the very films shown in the theaters?

What then is the relation between budget deficits and this broader, economically relevant measure of saving, comprising all investment in tangible capital, by business, nonprofit institutions, government, and households? Here, as might have been anticipated, the relation is all the clearer, as may be seen in Table 4-7 and in Figure 4-4. Budget deficits have been associated with more investment by consumers and government and hence with more total saving and investment.

For those concerned that public investment may somehow be wasteful while private investment is uniformly productive, I might point to accumulating evidence[12] that public investment, nonmilitary

TABLE 4-6
*Adjusted Budget Deficits, Changes in Monetary Base, and
Conventional National Saving*

| Variable or Parameter | Regression Coefficients and Standard Errors | | |
	1957–88 Without DMB	1962–88 Without DMB	With DMB
C	5.407*	4.825	3.500
	(2.178)	(3.326)	(4.970)
PAHED(-1)	0.508	0.568	0.324
	(0.317)	(0.341)	(0.319)
DMB(-1)	—	—	4.575*
			(1.814)
AR(1)	0.854*	0.897*	0.917*
	(0.105)	(0.105)	(0.098)
$\hat{R}^2$	0.633	0.687	0.755
D-W	1.843	1.777	1.953
n	32	27	27

*Significant at 0.05 probability level.
NSO = Conventional national saving in 1982 dollars (net private domestic investment plus statistical discrepancy in 1982 dollars plus current dollar net foreign investment divided by GNP implicit price deflator) as percentage of GNP in 1982 dollars: dependent variable
C = Constant term
PAHED(-1) = Lagged price-adjusted, high-employment budget deficit as percentage of GNP
DMB(-1) = Lagged real change in monetary base as percentage of GNP
AR(1) = First-order autoregressive coefficient
D-W = Durbin–Watson coefficient
$\hat{R}^2$ = Adjusted coefficient of determination
n = Number of observations

investment at least, contributes much more to productivity than does private investment. Those noting the losses ascribable to our crumbling infrastructure of roads and bridges and our general needs in public services may not be surprised. And for those who think consumers are investing too much in their future well-being, isn't that what it is all supposed to be about? Who are we to quarrel with individual preferences revealed in the market place?

We are still some distance from the complete story! We must by now all have read or heard of those tests of 13-year-olds in math and science in the United States, Canada, and a number of Asian and European countries. May we recall where our youngsters came out? Last, dead last! And with tests like these reflecting unfavorably on our students in relatively affluent neighborhoods and presumably better schools, what are we to say of the generation growing up in inner-city ghettos, where survival in school is a hurdle that must be passed in the effort to achieve even barely functional

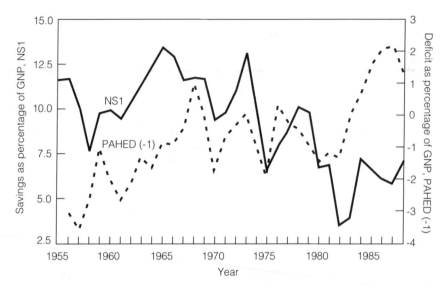

FIGURE 4-4   *Expanded Measure of National Saving and the Adjusted Deficit*

literacy? We have a leader who says he wants to be known as the "education president," but who can't seem to find the money—or who advises that
after all we cannot improve education, apparently unlike the military, by
"throwing money at it." While the very word "economics" is associated
with the striving for efficiency, few economists doubt that more output in
general can be gotten with more resources. There is every reason to believe
that this is true as well for the vast investment in human and intangible
capital that forms the major foundation for our future well-being.[13]

Fully one-half of saving and investment, broadly and appropriately
defined, is constituted by intangible investment—in research, in education
and training, and in health.[14] A very great deal of that is supported by
government, most of it, of course, out of tax revenues. But as with private
investment generally, whether in personal borrowing for housing or durable goods, business spending for plant and equipment, or paying for
higher education, expenditures with expected payoffs over a substantial
future period generally are financed in considerable part by going into debt.
If such debt (or deficit) financing were prohibited, there would almost
certainly be less investment. Why should it be otherwise for public investment expenditures?

It is therefore important that we relate the adjusted, structural deficit
to our most comprehensive measures of saving and investment. These
would include net foreign investment corrected to include the changing
value of foreign and domestic claims, due to both changing market values
and changing exchange rates. They would also include all domestic investment,
in tangible and intangible capital, by government, nonprofit institutions,
households, and business. With these comprehensive measures, we find, as

TABLE 4-7
Adjusted Budget Deficits, Changes in Monetary Base and Real National Saving (NS1), Including Saving in Public and Household Reproducible Capital

Variable or Parameter	Regression Coefficients and Standard Errors		
	1957–88 Without DMB	1962–88 Without DMB	With DMB
C	8.113	7.514	6.211
	(2.284)	(3.526)	(4.327)
PAHED (-1)	0.770*	0.876*	0.588
	(0.332)	(0.367)	(0.339)
DMB(-1)	—	—	5.280*
			(1.932)
AR(1)	0.861	0.897	0.911
	(0.096)	(0.099)	(0.092)
$\hat{R}^2$	0.668	0.711	0.782
D-W	1.677	1.689	1.916
n	32	27	27

*Significant at 0.05 probability level.
NS1 = Change in total fixed reproducible capital plus net foreign investment minus statistical discrepancy, as percentage of GNP.
$\hat{R}^2$ = Adjusted coefficient of determination
D-W = Durbin–Watson coefficient
n = Number of observations

shown in Table 4-8, the sharpest confirmation yet that budget deficits have been associated with more, not less national saving. Data for all of the relevant variables are only available for the years 1972 to 1981, but over this period each percentage point more of deficit was on the average followed by some four percentage points more of total saving (exclusive, I might add, of domestic capital gains). Easier monetary policy, as measured by real increases in the monetary base, was also associated with more saving. Monetary policy aside, though, one may infer, as might any political scientist, that insisting on reducing federal budget deficits can only retard comprehensive saving and block our vital investment in the future.[15]

IMPLICATIONS AND CONCLUSIONS

All of this should shed some new light on a number of issues that have been in the forefront of discussion by economists and policy-makers. Take the matter of social security and its financing, for one.

TABLE 4-8

Adjusted Budget Deficits, Changes in Monetary Base and Alternate Measure of Real National Saving (NS2), Including All Tangible and Intangible Capital and Adjusted Net Foreign Investment, 1972–81

Variable or Parameter	Regression Coefficients and Standard Errors	
	Without DMB	With DMB
C	41.117	39.537
	(3.659)	(2.565)
PAHED(-1)	9.819*	9.261*
	(3.817)	(2.576)
DMB(-1)	—	32.518*
		(13.555)
AR(1)	0.248	0.118
	(0.521)	(0.466)
$\hat{R}^2$	0.644	0.817
D-W	1.369	1.808
n	10	10

*Significant at 0.05 probability level.

NS2 = Change in total fixed reproducible capital plus adjusted net foreign investment minus statistical discrepancy plus change in real value of land plus investment in intangible capital and in government and household inventories and semidurables plus net revaluations exclusive of net revaluations on land, as percentage of GNP.

Social Security *Another*

Much concern has been expressed for the responsibility of the nation to provide decently for the retirement years of the baby-boom generation well into the twenty-first century. By current estimates, we would have some $12 trillion "in" the trust funds by the year 2030. This, some think, could be used to pay for the needs of those then no longer working.

With this premise, many express concern and even anger that the federal government is using the funds now being accumulated to finance other government expenditures in excess of tax revenues. We are told that this is masking the "true" deficit. Further, and more to the point, use of the growing social security surplus to finance the operational deficit elsewhere in the budget is said to be depriving the economy of saving that would constitute essential investment to provide for future needs.

First, I must assert that the claim that the social security surplus, more accurately, the excess of earmarked payroll taxes over social security benefit payments, is masking the true deficit is nonsense. Taken on a cash basis, as the budget is taken, it makes no difference to the aggregate how we compartmentalize our accounts. The deficit is the excess of what is currently paid to the public over what is taken from it in taxes. This is then the public borrowing requirement. Its economic significance in the aggregate is its contribution to the current flow of purchasing power and to the perceived wealth of households and business and hence, on both counts, to their expenditures. It is true, as Lawrence Kotlikoff (1986 and 1988) has pointed out, that one can change the measure of the deficit by classifying payroll taxes for social security as loans to the government and social security receipts as repayment of those loans with interest. There may indeed be some merit in that and in taking account of all likely future or contingency payments by the government—and all prospective receipts. The difficulty in taking this too seriously is that these future events are sufficiently uncertain and liable to changing expectations that it is doubtful that many people take them seriously and let them influence their current behavior. Until the social security reforms of a few years ago, which gave rise to the current and prospective surpluses in the social security retirement fund, it was argued that we really were incurring huge deficits in that the unrecorded liabilities to future retirees were accruing much more rapidly than the expected tax receipts to cover them. We had a huge implicit social security debt, far in excess of the official explicit debt. Martin Feldstein indeed argued that the social security deficit and debt had reduced private saving and the private capital stock by a fantastic 38 percent.[16]

Then, in one bit of legislation, all this net debt was wiped out. The combination of changing schedules for both tax contributions and benefits put the system in the black, with a vengeance. Had we included the present values of all these legislated changes in our current budget we would have suddenly showed a huge move to surplus. But could this really have been expected to have any immediate impact on the economy, as might, for example, a $300 billion increase in current taxes? It of course did not. It is doubtful whether those few who read the accounts of the changes recognized any difference in their current wealth positions. And if they behaved rationally they would well have concluded that between then and their retirement 20, 30, or 40 years in the future there would be other changes in social security laws or the economic situation so that there was not much sense to paying a lot of attention to what was said now about that future. And, I may add, I have not seen Feldstein or anyone else indicate that the consequence of the newly legislated social security surpluses of the future brought a reversal of the alleged decline in saving brought on by the original "deficits."

There are many changes I would make in the way we construct the federal budget and measure the deficit—changes that are pretty much anticipated in this chapter, but incorporating contingent future payments and taxes directly, rather than perhaps as footnotes, is not one of them. It appears likely to get us further from economic relevance rather than closer to it.

But back to the issue of providing for retirees of the future, what we declare to be in any trust fund—pieces of paper or accounting or computer entries—has nothing to do with what the economy will be able to provide them and, except possibly for its political ramifications, nothing to do with what they will actually get. Both will depend rather on the production of goods and services at the time they are retired, production by those then working, and on how much, of that total, society will then decide to give them. The total will depend on the number of people working, how much they work, and how productive they are.

One way to improve the prospects of retirees of the future is to increase current birth rates, or let in more young, working immigrants. Another is to see to it that those working are equipped with ample, technologically advanced physical capital, both public and private. And perhaps most important, we must ensure that all of the workers of the future are well educated and well trained. They should be productive workers, equipped for productive employment in a technologically advanced economy. And we should be following policies that offer jobs to all those willing and able to work. By now, we should all see that reducing conventionally measured budget deficits has little to do with achieving these objectives. It is most likely rather to stand in the way.

Payroll Taxes and Capital Gains Taxes

Two proposed changes in our tax structure currently in the news merit comment. One is the cancellation of the increases in payroll taxes giving rise to the current and prospective social security fund surpluses. The other is the proposed cut in capital gains taxes. Both will increase the deficit, although the capital gains tax cut, if it applies retroactively to past invest–ments, may bring a short-term bulge in revenues. I would not at this time, however, recommend increases in the deficit except to increase investment.

The notion that capital gains tax cuts will increase tangible investment seems fairly clearly to be based on fanciful self-interest of its protagonists rather than any empirical evidence or relevant economic theory.[17] The proposed rollbacks in social security taxes will not increase investment either, except possibly to the extent that resultant hugely greater deficits, if not counterbalanced by other tax increases, might increase aggregate demand and output and business investment along with it. But the better way to increase business investment at this time would be through an easier monetary policy. Social security tax cuts have a good bit to recommend them in terms of counteracting the moves away from progressivity in the tax system stemming from the combination of sharp cuts in personal income rates for the rich and increasing reliance on revenues from flat payroll taxes on lower and middle income workers. They may thus be supported on equity grounds but not directly in terms of investing in the future.

The Peace Dividend

There is, as there should be, much consideration now to the prospective peace dividend as the presumed adversary forces which appeared to justify our huge military expenditures are transformed or crumble before our eyes.

Much of those military expenditures could properly be qualified as invest-ment. Star wars programs, MX missiles, and B2 bombers may well be worthless—except in terms of the profits, salaries, and wages received by those involved—but they could clearly be expected to have payoffs, if at all, only in the future. The peace dividend cries for application now to all the public, nonmilitary investment in infrastructure, basic research, education, and health that our economy needs. Its use to reduce the deficit is exactly the wrong way to go.

The Policy Mix and the Issue of Full Employment

Convinced as I hope readers may be by now that our deficits are not the monsters so frequently portrayed, they may wonder why so many distin-guished economists—including some contributing to this volume—fail to come to my conclusions. The fundamental reason, I believe, is to be found in at least implicit, and frequently explicit, differences in the degrees of our commitment to full employment and faith that it can be approached by macroeconomic policy. Associated with this are differences in views as to the probable dangers and gravity of inflation.

Over the last two decades, since Milton Friedman's remarks (1968) on the subject in his presidential address to the American Economic Association at the end of 1967, the unfortunate concept of a "natural rate of unemploy-ment" came to dominate much of macroeconomic analysis and research. Despite some objection and eloquent criticism, for example, by fellow Nobel Laureates James Tobin (1972) and Franco Modigliani (1977) in their presi-dential addresses of 1971 and 1976, the debate seemed to move on from whether the concept—of a less than full employment rate from which the economy could not be moved without accelerating inflation or deflation—made sense or was supported by the facts. Rather, it turned on what that "natural" rate or "non-accelerating-inflation-rate-of-unemployment," the infamous "NAIRU," actually was. Papers presented at the Brookings Institution and elsewhere seemed to turn up "conservative" numbers as high as 6.5 and 7 percent. To some "liberals," a figure of 6 percent seemed more acceptable. The numbers seemed to move with the political and economic winds. One perhaps apocryphal story I picked up from Tobin was of the Stanford graduate student who declared in January of 1983, "The Bureau of Labor Statistics has just reported that the natural rate of unemployment last month was 10.7 percent"—the recession-high actual rate at that time.

The significance of all this was simply that if the economy were viewed as generally at its "natural" rate, stimulatory budget or monetary policies that might have been thought to reduce unemployment could have no useful result. They might at best offer some temporary condition of excess employment and GNP above "natural" output, although more extreme members of the rational expectations school denied even that possibility. Since we all "knew" that such stimulation would increase inflation, prices would be bid up immediately and the measures would die aborning in an instantaneous jump of prices and costs. In fact, as indicated above, one is hard pressed to find any evidence that structural budget deficits over our recent history were positively related to inflation. For whatever reason, what correlation there was would appear to be negative.[18]

But by the counterfactual logic that appeared to be current, to mitigate presumably deficit-induced inflation, the Federal Reserve was expected, and was indeed given license, to undertake counterbalancing monetary restraint. Thus, either from the original natural causes, or as a result of Central Bank reaction, budget deficits could bring no increase in employment or output. They could only change the allocation of that output. If the deficits came about as a result of increased government expenditures for goods and services, they would have to "crowd out" the output, for investment or consumption, available for private use, or force us to borrow from abroad to finance increased imports. If the deficits came from cuts in taxes or increases in "welfare" payments, the consequence would be a "consumption binge" that impinged entirely on private investment, either domestic or foreign.

I depart fundamentally from this reasoning in insisting that the "natural" rate of unemployment and the "NAIRU" are unsound theory, amply contradicted by the facts. Higher rates of employment may be associated with greater pressure on capacity and some upward movement in prices. How much upward movement will certainly be affected by institutional arrangements and government policies. Regulatory policies and price supports, tariffs and quotas, and general tolerance or encouragement of anticompetitive practices may well tend to keep prices from declining so that shocks to relative prices generally imply rises in the general level of prices; if some go up and all are protected against going down, the average clearly must rise. But if this is a prime explanation of recent inflation—and I challenge anyone to find evidence of a truly excess-demand inflation in this country at least in this century, aside from during wars or their immediate aftermaths—then there too is to be found the antidote, not in accepting or inviting excess unemployment.

And excess unemployment is what I insist we have almost always had, and have to this day. We clearly had it when unemployment hit that 10.7 percent in 1982, a level from which large deficits then contributed mightily to rescue us. We had it in 1985 and 1986 when we hovered around that "conservative" 7 percent rate. We had it in the beginning of 1987, as we hit 6.5 percent and then on down to the "liberal" 6 percent. And we have had it for the last two years as unemployment below 5.5 percent, without "accelerating" inflation, should have made sober economists reconsider the whole concept.

I am pleased to say that a number of outstanding economists have now done so. Olivier Blanchard and Lawrence Summers, for example, looking at the considerably higher rates of "natural" unemployment in Western Europe, have put forth the hypothesis of "hysteresis," suggesting that the "natural" rate in fact adjusts to the actual rate of unemployment.[19] Stimulus to the economy can then lower the natural rate as the economy adjusts to the lower rates of unemployment. If there is any acceleration of inflation, it need not prove permanent.

There is nothing natural about involuntary unemployment. It has varied greatly over time in our country. It has differed greatly from country to country. It is today decidedly less—in the 3 percent range—in Japan and Sweden than in the United States. We should not have given up on the 4 percent initial target long accepted as the full employment goal in the United States. There is no good reason why we should not be aiming at the 3 percent figure we now see elsewhere and that we ourselves obtained during the Vietnam War. We will certainly make attainment of that goal easier with the kind of public investment that will educate and train our labor force so that all are readily employable at wages that offer an inducement for efficient labor. But additional workers will not be hired if there is not purchasing power or demand for the products that they would produce.

Conceivably, additional purchasing power could come from *in*creases in our current federal budget deficit. I submit that this would be no calamity. I am, however, in agreement with those who argue that the combination of fiscal stimulus and relative monetary restraint into which we drifted in the past decade is far from optimum. It has resulted in *real* interest rates (that is, nominal rates minus the rate of inflation) that have been very high by historical standards. This has probably had some effect in holding down domestic investment—although my own research suggests that effect may have been less than some would argue. It has also, by keeping the dollar scarce and the return on dollar investment high, kept up the value of the dollar. It is this, I suspect, as much as or more than the budget deficits, that has contributed to our trade deficits and hence our negative net foreign investment, exaggerated though that may be.

I would look then to easier money for the further stimulus to reduce unemployment and increase real output. This would have some beneficial effect on domestic investment, perhaps particularly in housing and in consumer durables and in public investment by interest-conscious state and municipal governments, as well as by private business. It would also stimulate our exports as the dollar becomes less costly to foreigners. This would not only raise employment and output in our export industries, it would also reduce protectionist pressures that threaten to bring on further efficiency-reducing restrictions on our international economic relations. By increasing the foreign demand for our agricultural output, we might then permit easy reduction of costly interventions in the farm economy. And finally, both by reducing interest costs and increasing tax revenues in a more prosperous economy, easier money would actually reduce the deficit, and do it in the one way that would cause us no pain.

Some have argued that we should get these benefits of less restrictive monetary policy by changing the mix, that is, by reducing the federal deficit to tighten fiscal policy and then having easier money. By one view, reducing the budget deficit will itself bring lower interest rates. To the extent this would occur, I would counter, it would stem precisely from a slowing of the economy that would lower the demand for money. This implies then an actual decrease in output and increase in unemployment.

A more positive approach argues that we can expect—and that Alan Greenspan and his Federal Reserve have signalled—an active easing of monetary policy if the budget deficit is reduced. But I have two objections here. First, I should want more than a vague signal of monetary ease to match fiscal tightening. The Fed and banking circles generally have traditionally been more concerned about inflation, even minor possibilities of increased inflation, than in achieving maximum employment. I do not see how those recognizing the primacy of our real targets of employment and output now and in the future can properly rest their confidence in what the Fed may do.

But second, there is good reason to doubt that, even with the best of intentions, reasonably attainable monetary stimulus can entirely counterbalance major fiscal constraint. I am not of the school, if there is one, that says that money does not matter. But the stock of money is not everything. If aggregate demand is sufficiently depressed by high taxes or government frugality, business investment may collapse regardless of interest rates. Further, if we bring the rest of the world down with us in recession, as we can do, we can expect little remedy from increased foreign demand. And I must finally repeat that budgetary restraint will almost certainly make it all the more difficult to undertake sufficient public investment and accumulation of human capital.

I come then to the recommendation that we do change the monetary-fiscal mix. Monetary policy is too restrictive. But we should change the mix not by tightening fiscal policy but by easing monetary policy. This would have all of the advantages and none of the disadvantages. The one objection is that we are already at full employment, or so close to it that any monetary stimulus without fiscal restraint would only cause more inflation. This objection, I would argue, is a counsel of despair. It is a reflection of surrender in the struggle for full employment. It is a prophecy of gloom, if not doom, for the U.S. economy.

It is a continuation of a fight of the last war, indeed of World War II, the last occasion when we had really major, continuing excess demand. Inflation now is modest, at some 4 percent, less than in most of the rest of the world, and probably exaggerated at that by our failure to adjust adequately for quality improvements in services and throughout much of the economy. There are few signs of significant tightness in labor markets. What dangers there are of greater inflation would come mainly elsewhere, partly from such self-inflicted wounds as import restrictions and price supports. Or they may lurk in possible new supply shocks, such as the huge increases in petroleum prices in the 1970s, which should not, in any event, be countered by restricting demand.

I cannot guarantee that net stimulus to the economy now will not weight the probabilities somewhat higher for somewhat higher inflation.

TABLE 4-9
Deficit with Constant Debt–GNP Ratio

	Debt (Billions of Dollars)	GNP (Billions of Dollars)	Ratio
1988	$2,050	$4,927	0.416
7.029% Growth	144	346	0.416
1989	$2,194	$5,273	0.416
Deficit Increase in Debt = $144 (except for some accounting peculiarities)			
Actual Deficit $152 (Actual Increase in Debt = $139)			

But that is what we are talking about, uncertain and minor movements in minor probabilities of minor inflation. It is irresponsible and scientifically without foundation to frighten the public with forebodings of accelerating inflation—visions of interwar-German or current Latin American explosive hyperinflation—if we try to give more Americans what should be their birthright of decent jobs at decent pay.

A New Measure of Balance

I may finally offer a new rule of thumb for those interested in balanced budgets. Balance, we should now recognize, has nothing to do with Gramm–Rudman or the various ways conventional measures may describe balance. But, recognizing again that the deficit equals the increase in net debt, we can usefully define a balanced budget as one in which debt grows at the same percentage rate as income. In this case the debt–income ratio would be constant. We could proceed with balanced growth in the sense that the various components of asset portfolios could all grow in proportion.

As may be seen in Table 4-9, this rule has some intriguing implications for the current situation. With GNP growing at about 7 percent per year and the debt–GNP ratio currently just about three-sevenths, that debt–GNP ratio can stay constant with a deficit equal to three-sevenths of 7 percent, or 3 percent, of GNP. But with GNP likely to approach $5,600 billion in 1990, a deficit of some $168 billion would then leave that ratio constant. This would be a deficit somewhat larger than we had last year. We are currently in a state of balance! Reducing the deficit—and here we are ignoring state and local surpluses—would actually destroy that balance.

I must confess that there is nothing sacred about the particular debt–GNP ratio we enjoy now. As opposed to the current 42 percent, it was some 110 percent after World War II, and that brought no apparent disaster. It fell to just over 26 percent by 1980 and rose to its current value during the deficit decade of the 1980s. But the burden of proof might be put on those who would destroy the current balance rather than those who would leave it alone.

The real issues come back to those we have tried to highlight. What will be the consequences of budget changes for our current and future well-being? That is partly a question of the overall size of the deficit as conventionally measured. This will affect aggregate demand and hence our ability to maintain a high-employment, high-growth economy without undue inflation.

But it is also a matter of the composition of that budget and its effect on the utilization of our resources. If its effect is to direct resources to unnecessary and counterproductive uses, such as unneeded and even dangerous weapons of mass destruction, we are left far from an optimum. Objections may also be levelled at billions of dollars spent to restrict farm output or increase its price and reduce its availability to us and the rest of the world.

But if the budget is directed to necessary and productive investment in the tangible and intangible, human and nonhuman capital, public and private, on which our well-being and security ultimately and critically depend, it will be a good budget. And if that entails, as I believe it does, a "deficit" such as we have now, or even a larger one, so be it. It will then be contributing to elimination of many of the real deficits in the economy and in our nation.

NOTES

I have enjoyed the assistance of John Applegate, Sang-In Hwang, Craig Safir, Marc Sokol, and Stacey M. Tevlin, and the support of the National Science Foundation, currently through grant #SES-8909600, for research findings contributing to this paper, but I alone am of course responsible for its contents.

1. See U.S. Office of Management and Budget (1988), for example.

2. See the seminal Barro (1974), Barro (1989) and, of course, his chapter in this volume. Barro's argument is that a deficit, which adds to public debt, will not lead rational individuals to spend more because they will reason that they, or their descendants, will have to pay taxes in the future to pay the interest and principal on that increased debt. Since the deficit causes no change in the total of individuals' current and expected future after-tax incomes, it will, except for certain presumably minor complicating factors, cause no change in their current spending and hence have no overall impact on the economy. Government deficit spending, which is financed by borrowing, is thus equivalent in its effects to government spending financed by current taxes. Individuals simply save the amount they would, but for the deficit, have paid in current taxes, in order to pay their future taxes without reducing their future consumption.

There are many serious and valid objections to this "equivalence theorem" that have been addressed in this volume and elsewhere, but to these my analysis suggests another. Does not the equivalence theorem depend like so much else on the assumption of "natural" employment and unemployment, so that budget deficits can do nothing to increase real output and income? If they can increase output and investment, as indicated in the pages below, there is no reason rational individuals cannot spend more now and anticipate having more in the future as well.

3. Beginning essentially with Modigliani and Brumberg (1954).

4. Well reviewed in Patinkin (1948 and 1951).

5. See Patinkin (1951) on all of this.

6. Except for the trivial difference due to rounding.

7. For a general discussion of this issue, see Eisner (1989a).

8. Eisner and Pieper (1990). See also Stekler (1988) and Ulan and Dewald (1989).

9. See Eisner (1989d) for a comprehensive presentation of adjustments to our measures of saving. These stem generally from work reported in Eisner (1986, 1988, and 1989c) and Eisner and Pieper (1984 and 1988).

10. One might have thought that this possibility was clearly established half a century ago in Lange (1938 and 1944). Investment is a function of interest rates and output. Increasing consumption, with a given money supply, on the one hand raises interest rates and reduces investment but on the other hand increases output and raises investment. It is only as full employment is approached and there is little scope for increased output that one might expect the interest effect to dominate and investment to be reduced.

11. Somewhat inexplicably, not explained directly by the lagged change in the exchange rate. The sign of the DERR variable in Table 4-5 was "wrong."

12. See David Aschauer (1989), for example, as well as Eisner (1988 and 1989c).

13. See, of course, Nobel Laureate Schultz (1961) and Becker (1975) for classic works on human capital.

14. See Eisner (1989c) for detailed data.

15. For further treatment of the relation between budget deficits and saving, see Eisner (1990a) and (1990b).

16. See Feldstein (1974) and, in a response to criticism (1982). See also Eisner (1983).

17. Some of my own views, and evidence, on determinants of investment may be found, *inter alia*, in Eisner (1978), Eisner and Nadiri (1968), and Chirinko and Eisner (1983). See also Chirinko (1987).

18. As reported originally in Eisner (1989b).

19. See Blanchard and Summers (1986).

5   The Relationship Between Budget Deficits and the Saving/Investment Imbalance in the United States: Facts, Fancies, and Prescriptions

PETER L. BERNSTEIN AND ROBERT L. HEILBRONER

The most important issue in the debate over the debt and the deficit is whether the large budget deficits of the 1980s have been somehow "absorbing" saving that would otherwise be put to more productive use. The relationship between the deficit and saving and investment, therefore, is the focal point of this chapter.

By attacking the deficit problem from this viewpoint, the analysis can skip over many peripheral issues and come to grips with the questions that most deeply concern all serious citizens and economists: Is the deficit larger than Americans can afford? Is it a burden today? Are we bequeathing an intolerable burden to the next generation?

This last question is perhaps the most critical of all, for the economy appears to have at least survived and perhaps benefited from the deficits that have accrued so far. Therefore, the crux of the argument between our position and the mainstream revolves around the impact of the deficit on the future: Is the deficit destined to leave the next generation poorer than it would otherwise have been?

Few professional economists worry about the financial aspects of this matter. They understand that Americans owe most of the national debt to themselves and that paying the interest on the debt or paying off each obligation as it comes due simply takes from Peter American to pay Paul American. On the other hand, the consequences for the real economy, in contrast to the financial sector, are less obvious. If the deficit does in fact inhibit the volume of private real capital accumulation in the United States—and perhaps even public sector investment as well—then we are irresponsibly putting our own comfort and welfare ahead of the well-being of our children and grandchildren.

A SUMMARY OF THE CASE

The discussion that follows seeks to highlight the dangers of swallowing whole the mainstream's profound pessimism that today's deficit is unquestionably leaving a burden on the next generation. The analysis begins with a look at the contradictions of the theoretical case on which that position rests, followed by an array of facts that raise serious questions as to the empirical validity of the mainstream's theoretical underpinnings. After making some observations about whether the deficit is properly defined, the chapter concludes with a set of recommendations for achieving the goal that all of us seek—a healthier and more stable U.S. economy.

We should state the central theme of our position at the outset. We are deeply skeptical of the manner in which the mainstream frames the problem around the depressed U.S. rate of saving, from which the mainstream concludes that Americans are saving too little to provide themselves with a future that will be both profitable and productive.[1] Acceptance of that proposition leads, in turn, to the conclusion that cutting the budget deficit is the only feasible method of raising the national rate of saving and investment.

The view that the national saving rate is an independent variable, that readily produces an accompanying increase in investment, is a proposition so widely held that one confronts it only with the greatest trepidation. It finds impressive empirical confirmation, in fact, in a recent study by Martin Feldstein and Phillipe Bacchetta (1989), notably their Table 4, which uses an international cross-sectional set of regressions to demonstrate that changes in national saving lead changes in domestic investment rather than vice versa.

Nevertheless, the dynamics that determine this result are obscure. Saving at the household level, after all, is not spending. At the corporate and public sector level, saving is the equivalent of withholding income from households and thereby restraining consumption. The critical question, then, is to define precisely how an independent reduction in consumer demand translates itself into a higher level of private investment instead of a higher level of unemployment.

Classical economics nominates the interest rate as the market-clearing variable that brings a disequilibrium between saving and investment into balance. Contemporary economists generally recognize the loss in demand occasioned by saving but then, following the lead provided by classical economics, go on to promise that easier monetary policies—also known as lower interest rates—will ensure either an offsetting rise in domestic investment or a lower foreign exchange rate accompanied by an improvement in net foreign investment. Thus, monetary policy will avoid the sustained increase in unemployment that would otherwise result from the shrinkage in spending decisions.

Here, too, the route is unclear. The record shows that neither investment nor foreign exchange rates respond to changes in interest rates in any kind of a regular or predictable manner. Furthermore, long-term interest rates will fail to follow suit when the monetary authorities lower short-term rates, if in so doing the authorities excite inflation expectations.[2]

Some of the obscurity in the process arises from the very real possibility that the mainstream's initial assumption is flawed. We take the position that their position is flawed: saving is not an independent variable. Rather, saving is only one part of a general equilibrium solution for an economy in which saving is simultaneously a consequence of economic forces as well as one of the determinants of economic forces. For example, how can we be sure that efforts to reduce public sector dissaving, such as raising taxes or cutting government expenditures, will not reduce private saving at the same time that it raises public saving?

Although this offsetting action is precisely what happened in response to the income tax surcharge of 1968, there is another and more dramatic example of how an increase in public sector saving through higher taxes can be associated with lower private sector saving. Social security taxes rose from 4.96 percent of disposable personal incomes—personal incomes after personal taxes—in 1984 to their high point so far of 5.71 percent in 1987, while personal saving as a percentage of disposable personal incomes fell from 6.46 percent to its low point so far of 3.18 percent over the same period of time. Thus, the increase of 0.75 percentage points in social security taxes appears to have accounted for just about one fourth of the drop of 3.28 percentage points in the personal saving rate. Measured out over the longer period from 1984 to 1989, the increase in social security taxes was equal to about 65 percent of the decline in the personal saving rate.

Finally, the whole matter is complicated by the limitations of the data themselves. Quite aside from measurement problems, where sufficient controversy exists to justify great caution in jumping to hasty conclusions about the state of thrift in the U.S. economy, the data that we see relate only to the measured saving rate. The amount saved is only a garbled hint of the propensity to save, because a decline in measured saving flows can tell us little or nothing about future intentions to save. The reported figures simply cannot reveal how many people responded to unexpected changes in after-tax income to go into debt or to reduce planned saving in order to cover current living expenses.

In short, efforts to raise the national saving rate will be successful only under conditions in which the unpleasant consequences of these efforts are excluded from the calculations while the salutory consequences are given free rein. The discussion that follows will therefore return frequently to the question of how unrealistic these assumptions are while an attack is mounted on the budget deficit. We cannot categorically deny, but simply do not share, the high conviction imbedded in the mainstream view on this central issue in the debate.

Our strong preference, therefore, is for measures that will create an economic environment so favorable that a higher domestic saving rate is its most positive result rather than its primary goal. This means focussing attention on all of the factors that relate to economic growth and rising real incomes. The final section of this chapter offers prescriptions that tackle the problem from a microeconomic viewpoint, rather than striking out at it with blunderbuss, macroeconomic reforms.

HOW SHOULD THE PROBLEM BE FRAMED?

The interesting question is why today's fiscal policies are so bitterly opposed by orthodox Keynesian economists, particularly by the economists who so enthusiastically supported and, in many instances, actually shaped the budget-deficit-creating policies of the Kennedy administration. The answer, we believe, stems from two other deficits whose performances in the 1980s represent a radical transformation from their performance in the 1960s.

The first of these two other deficits is the saving deficit—the degree to which domestic saving falls short of domestic investment. The second is the deficit in our international current accounts—the degree to which our payments from foreigners for our goods and services sold to them fall short of the payments we make to foreigners for the goods and services we buy from them. The current-account balance minus net services equals the trade or merchandise balance.

Whether we invest at home more than we save as a nation or whether we spend more abroad than we earn abroad, the differences between each of these sets of flows have to come from somewhere. By definition, they are not available at home. The inevitable result, therefore, is that we cover these shortfalls—the saving/investment shortfall and the international payments shortfall— by borrowings from foreigners or by increased foreign acquisitions of capital assets in the United States.

In contrast, this country enjoyed a sufficient surplus of domestic saving over domestic investment during the 1960s to be able to invest the difference abroad, much as the Japanese are using their excess saving in today's world to invest in other countries. The domestic production that Americans did not buy during the 1960s provided a modest but persistent surplus on current account throughout the decade.

The argument, then, boils down to how one views the interrelationships among these three deficits—budget, saving, and international current accounts. Are they in fact interrelated? If so, which is cause and which is effect? Are the arrows of causality stable, or do they change direction from time to time?

The theory on which the mainstream position depends sees the three deficits as inseparably intertwined with one another, but with the budget deficit as the cause and the international current-account and saving deficits as its inevitable consequences. Nevertheless, even though the arithmetic of national income accounting can put all three deficits into the same equation, this procedure is proof of nothing except of a statistical identity.

Statistical identities are silent on which is cause and which is effect and are incapable of describing reverse causalities. For example, $3 + 1 = 4$, but it is equally true that $3 = 4 - 1$, the only difference being which number is chosen for the left-hand side of the equation. Furthermore, $3 = 2 + 1$, which means that, if the equation's primary terms are broken down into subcomponents, an even more varied perspective on the matter is revealed.

But that is not the only problem with the mainstream view. The facts fail to support it. We shall see that the experience of other countries is clearly inconsistent with the theory. In addition, the empirical evidence is at odds with the dynamics that are supposed to explain how the budget deficit causes the other two deficits—or, indeed, how an exogenous increase in the propensity to save is guaranteed to provide a corresponding increase in domestic plus international investment.

If you frame the problem in mainstream terms, the answer is simple. The saving shortfall and the excess of imports are sapping our long-run economic strength. Both are the result of the budget deficit. Cut the budget deficit, and, even though that may cause some short-run pain, our long-run health will be assured.

If you are less certain about cause and effect and if the facts leave you skeptical about the essential concept, concerns about counterproductive consequences will make you less hasty about raising taxes or reducing government spending. You will seek to discover whether the deficits are properly specified. You will also search for methods that will independently attack the saving and current-account deficits, with the expectation, resting on reverse causalities, that those measures may well tend to close the gap between government spending and revenue.

Indeed, the primary difference between our position and the mainstream position is one of degree. The mainstream position leaves no margin of doubt that cutting the budget deficit and easing monetary policy will result in both a higher level of saving and investment and a smaller deficit in our dealings with foreigners. We do not exclude that possibility, but we cannot accept it with the assurance with which so many others accept it. Rather, the many inconsistencies in the facts and the profound uncertainties in the theories have persuaded us to take a less rigid stand on the issue.

THE BUDGET DEFICIT AND THE CURRENT-ACCOUNT DEFICIT

The analysis begins with the deficit on international current account, because the mainstream view sees it as the ultimate consequence of the budget deficit. By starting here, we can work our way back to the budget deficit. Furthermore, by starting here, the issue of cause and effect can be confronted immediately.

The United States in 1989 imported goods and services worth $568 billion and paid over to foreigners an additional $124 billion as interest and dividends on the investments that foreigners made in the United States. At the same time, we sold abroad goods and services worth $475 billion and also earned $125 billion on our investments in foreign countries. In addition, we transferred to foreigners $19 billion in the form of unilateral government grants and remittances to friends and relatives living abroad. On balance, we had to pay foreigners just about $106 billion more than they paid over to us for the year's current business transactions.

Or, to put the same thing in different words, Americans bought goods and services of all kinds that ran to $106 billion more than the goods and services that they produced themselves. The difference had to be borrowed from foreigners or financed by selling off assets to them. Had our total spending been less, therefore—all other things being equal—the international deficit would have been smaller. And, had we spent less—all other things still being equal—we would have saved more. As spending for investment and other types of growth-creating purposes is essential for our future, the implication here is that Americans should have consumed less, unless in fact all other things did not remain equal.

There is considerable doubt that other things would have obliged Americans by remaining equal. For example:

1. How certain can we be that the incentives of business management to invest in new plant and equipment would have been buoyant at the same time that consumers were cutting back?

2. Given our importance in world trade and the importance of the U.S. market to our trading partners, how certain can we be that U.S. export trade would have flourished at a time that U.S. imports from abroad were falling off?

Nevertheless, by holding tenaciously to the assumption that all other things must remain equal, the mainstream goes on to argue that more frugality on the part of U.S. households would be welcome, but even that will be insufficient. A cure for the current-account deficit is impossible without a substantial reduction in the big hemorrhage of dissaving in the form of the federal government's excess of expenditure over tax revenues.

Although the underlying assumptions provide this argument with an attractive logic, how does it look when stood on its head? Let us consider the possibility that the budget deficit is not a cause but a consequence of the deficit on international account.

The goods and services that Americans import create incomes for citizens of other countries and, in the process, provide tax revenues for the governments of other countries. Competition from imports also tends to hold prices and wages down in the importing country, thereby depressing the flow of nominal incomes. Taken together, these forces tend to reduce our government's tax receipts and to make the budget deficit bigger than it would be otherwise—all other things once again being equal.

It has not only been imports that have cut into the flow of nominal incomes in the United States. Our exports have been held down by forces beyond our control, but the result has been slower economic growth and a further reduction in government revenues. Our prime trading partners— Europe and Japan—grew at a painfully slow pace during the first five years after the worldwide recession of 1982, as phobias about inflation were even more intense abroad than they were here. At the same time, the United States lost large export markets because major customers among the developing countries, especially in Latin America, simply did not have the wherewithal to buy from us. Finally, the sharp decline in oil prices in 1986, while helpful from other viewpoints, brought the OPEC importing spree to a sudden halt.

It would be difficult to argue that the entire budget deficit was a consequence of the current-account deficit. On the other hand, it would be difficult to argue that more success in the area of foreign trade would not have meant higher domestic incomes and a smaller government deficit.

The mainstream states flatly that the current-account deficit is going to plague us forever unless we cut the budget deficit and that even efforts to improve U.S. competitiveness are never going to help without a fundamental shift in fiscal policy. The logic is impeccable if we accept the assumption that the budget deficit is the independent variable that causes us to buy more than we produce. The logic falls apart if one asks why that is the way the world has to work. There is good reason to believe that that is not the way the world works.

Furthermore, the world is a complicated place. David H. Howard emphasizes that:

> The U.S. current-account balance is a general equilibrium phenomenon: it is jointly determined with other endogenous variables in the world economy. . . . [T]he general equilibrium nature of the problem is not just a theoretical fine point. . . . The current account . . . and the saving-investment balance . . . are actually functions of many variables, including importantly income, the exchange rate, and the interest rate. . . . Thus, the actual external balance can reflect changes in export and import behavior as well as changes in domestic saving and investment. (1989, pp. 155–56)

Albert Sommers provides another apt view of the matter:

A developed economy such as the U.S. economy contains an unimag-inable number of internal interactions, feedbacks, and reversible causalities; the logic by which it can be described is frustratingly circular.... [I]t doesn't much matter where in the circle the exploration begins. But it matters very much where it ends—that is, where the analyst stops, leaves the circle, and announces his conclusions. (1990, p. 2)

Possible confusions between cause and effect are not the only difficulty with the theoretical arguments in the conventional view. There is also the problem that arises from an oversimplified use of a statistical identity.

The mainstream is correct in pointing out that our current-account deficit, which is the excess of what we pay foreigners for goods and services over what they pay us, is identical in size to the saving deficit, which is the amount by which our domestic saving falls short of what we invest domes-tically. This is simply another way of saying that a nation that uses more goods and services than it produces will have to obtain the difference from abroad.

Yet, the statistical identity between the national investment and saving flows, on the one hand, and the international current-account deficit, on the other hand, is nothing more than that: a statistical identity. The arrangement of the statistics in this fashion reveals nothing about the process by which the budget deficit at home leads to an excess of imports from abroad.

The usual explanation is that the saving shortfall induced by the budget deficit leads to higher real interest rates in the United States—"real" meaning the difference between the market rate actually paid on debt instruments and the rate of inflation that eats into the purchasing power of those nominal interest payments. The high real interest rates, in turn, attract foreign funds that bid up the exchange rate of the dollar. The higher dollar, in turn, encourages imports and puts our exports at a competitive disadvantage.

This explanation is shaky, because it rests uniquely on still another assumption, namely, that the saving shortfall and the real interest rate are perfectly correlated. This case does not hold water at all when examined in terms of the empirical evidence presented below. The movement of real interest rates fails to correlate with the budget deficit in any meaningful fashion. Worse yet, the movement of real interest rates shows no systematic relationship to the balance between overall saving and investment flows in the U.S. economy. The linkage between the budget deficit, the interest rate, and the exchange value of the dollar therefore becomes much too amor-phous to justify anchoring policy decisions upon it.

The next step, therefore, is to look at the empirical evidence of the relationship among budget deficits, interest rates, and trade imbalances.

TABLE 5-1

	Ranking based on	
Change in general government debt/GDP,* 1980–86	Change in real long-term interest rates, 1980–86	
Canada	United Kingdom	
France	Italy	
Italy	France	
Germany	United States	
Japan	Canada	
United States	Germany	
United Kingdom	Japan	

SOURCE: Roubini and Sachs (1988) and *International Monetary Fund Yearbook* (1989).

*Gross domestic poduct (GDP) is gross national product less net foreign interest income.

THE EMPIRICAL EVIDENCE AGAINST THE MAINSTREAM VIEW

If a theory is valid, it should hold in all free market economies. For example, fundamental economic theorems like the law of supply and demand and the correlation between nominal interest rates and inflation work about as well in western Europe and Japan as they work in the United States—not perfectly but nevertheless visibly. If the theory that government deficits cause real interest rates to rise is valid, that relationship should be valid in other countries as well as in the United States.

The left-hand column of Table 5-1 lists seven major industrial countries, including the United States, in order of the increase from 1980 to 1986 in the growth in their general government debts relative to their gross domestic product (GDP). The growth in the government debt is the equivalent of the cumulative total of budget deficits during the period under review. Note, too, the use of the words "general government." As the internal political structure of a nation has unique features, the fairest comparison from an international point of view is one that considers all government together—federal as well as local—which is what the table shows. The right-hand column of the table lists the same countries in order of the increase in their real long-term interest rates—the difference between the nominal rate on long-term government bonds and the year-over-year change in the price level.

The table shows no systematic relationship at all between the growth in budget deficits and the real rate of interest. For example, the United

TABLE 5-2

	Ranking based on	
Change in general government debt/GDP,* 1980–86		Deterioration in international current accounts/GDP,* 1980–86
Canada		United States
France		Italy
Italy		France
Germany		Canada
Japan		Germany
United States		United Kingdom
United Kingdom		Japan

SOURCE: Roubini and Sachs (1988) and *International Monetary Fund Yearbook* (1989).

*Gross domestic product (GDP) is gross national product less net foreign interest income.

Kingdom had the smallest growth in budget deficit—in fact, the United Kingdom ran a budget surplus from 1980 to 1986—but they had the largest rise in their real rate notwithstanding. Canada shows the opposite situation. Not one country has the same ranking on the left-hand side of the table as on the right.

The theory that budget deficits contribute to deficits in international accounts should also work in other countries about the same as it appears to work in the United States. Nevertheless, a further look at these seven countries fails to reveal any relationship between the growth in government debt and trends in the international current accounts. Table 5-2 shows the seven countries from Table 5-1, ranked again by their cumulative deficits in the left-hand column, together with the change in their international current accounts in the right-hand column.

The relationship between deficits and international accounts shown in Table 5-2 has a little more consistency than the evidence in Table 5-1. Nevertheless, the serious deterioration in U.S. international accounts contrasts with the relatively modest growth in U.S. general government debt. Canada is three places out of order, Japan is two places out of order, and not one country is ranked the same in both columns.

The evidence presented up to this point has failed to show any consistent relationships between budget deficits and current accounts or between budget deficits and real interest rates. Notwithstanding that evidence, the mainstream position asserts that the budget deficit has reduced national saving below the rate of national investment, thereby raising real interest rates in the United States. Therefore, let us look at the association between real interest rates and the flows of saving and investment.

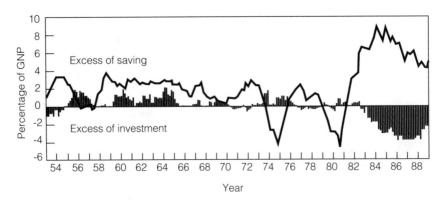

FIGURE 5-1   *National Saving Minus Private Investment Versus the Real Government Bond Rate (Quarterly, 1954:1–1988:4)*

Figure 5-1 shows what has actually happened in the U.S. economy since 1954. The line shows the real long-term interest rate, defined as the nominal interest rate on long-term government bonds minus the year-over-year rate of change in the Consumer Price Index (CPI). The bars show the difference between total real national saving and real private domestic investment; the bars are above the line when saving exceeded investment and fall below the line when investment exceeded saving. All data have been calculated as percentages of nominal gross national product (GNP).

Theory would tell us that the line showing real interest rates should be higher when the bars are below zero, indicating that saving is falling short of investment, than when the bars lie above zero, indicating that saving exceeds investment. Figure 5-1 shows that in fact no systematic relationship is apparent.

The facts fit the theory only during the 1950s and the second half of the 1970s. On the other hand, real rates were high in the early 1960s despite a large excess of saving and then fell as the excess of saving diminished! Real rates zoomed upward during 1980–82 while saving and investment were in rough balance; then real rates declined even as the saving shortfall reached nearly 4 percent of nominal GNP. In statistical terms, the coefficient of correlation between the two series was indistinguishable from zero up to 1981 and slightly positive instead of negative since then.

But what about short-term rates? As short-term obligations come due so frequently that they carry only negligible risk of loss of purchasing power, in theory their real rate should be approximately zero. Contrary to this expectation, the real Treasury bill rate was positive during much of the 1980s, suggesting that something was indeed amiss. Benjamin Friedman, an eloquent and authoritative spokesman for the mainstream view, cites the persistently positive real rate on short-term paper after 1980 as indisputable proof of the deleterious impact of the federal deficit on the U.S. economy:

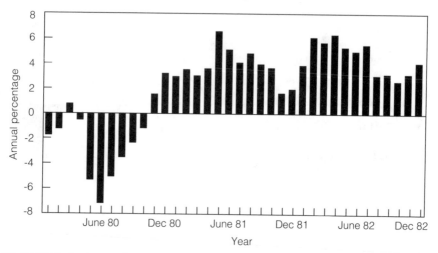

FIGURE 5-2   *Real Interest Rates on Treasury Bills (Monthly, January 1980–*
December 1982)

[T]he influence of deficits on real interest rates that was at best difficult to disentangle earlier on has been unusually clear. The connection is easiest to draw for short-term interest rates, simply because of the inevitable uncertainty about how much inflation borrowers expect over long time horizons. . . . In America during the 1980s, short-term real interest rates . . . reflected the extraordinary monetary policy that began the decade and the extraordinary fiscal policy that followed. . . . The change from the prior thirty years is startling. . . . Our new fiscal policy, generating ever larger deficits even in a fully employed economy, had long since replaced tight monetary policy as the reason for high real interest rates. (1988, pp. 171, 172, 174)

Figure 5-2 shows the path of the real interest rate on Treasury bills monthly, from January 1980 to December 1982. Note that the real Treasury bill rate (the nominal rate for each month minus the change in the CPI over the same month of the preceding year) touched its maximum negative point in June 1980, before anyone knew who the next president would be—even before anyone knew who the next candidates would be—and therefore before anyone knew what the future fiscal position of the U.S. government was going to be. The real Treasury bill rate did turn positive in December 1980, right after the election, but this was still some months before anyone would have any precise knowledge of future fiscal policies. Finally, the real bill rate peaked in June 1981, even though only a few weeks had passed since the administration had promised both tax cuts and increased spending on defense. As the new, deficit-creating fiscal policies worked their way through Congress, the real bill rate fluctuated but it clearly failed to rise to new heights. In fact, Figure 5-3 shows that the real

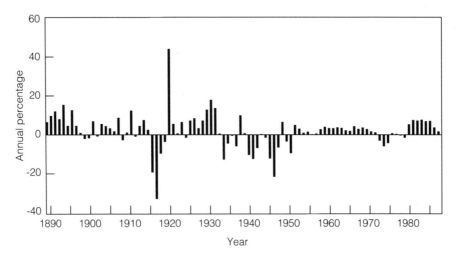

FIGURE 5-3   *Real Interest Rates on Commercial Paper (1890–1988)*

rate never surpassed the mid-1981 peak and subsequently declined as the federal deficit rose from 2.1 percent of GNP in 1981 to 4.9 percent in 1986.

This analysis reveals that fiscal policy and real rates of interest have little or nothing to do with each other. Many experts believe that monetary policy, rather than fiscal policy, explains most of the variations in real interest rates.

Our own position arrives at a simpler explanation, based on a careful look at the historical record. This record demonstrates that nominal interest rates—short-term as well as long—are less variable than the rate of inflation. In technical terms, the coefficient of variation on nominal commercial paper rates since 1890 has been only 0.26 percent per year; the coefficient of variation on the CPI has been 3.95 percent over the same period.

As a result, real interest rates will rise as inflation diminishes and will fall as inflation heats up. These tendencies are dramatically clear in the case of long-term interest rates, but, in the interest of confronting the emphasis that Friedman places on the short-term rate, Figure 5-3 provides a look at nearly 100 years of real interest rates on commercial paper.

Figure 5-3 reveals that real rates on short-term paper have averaged well over zero for most of history. Furthermore, the experience of the 1980s is by no means unique. Real short rates were even higher in other periods when the inflation rate was falling, such as the 1890s and 1920s—neither of which was troubled by budget deficits.

Thus, the theoretical support for the mainstream view of the source of the current-account deficit finds no empirical verification in an international comparison, while the history of interest rates fails to explain how the budget deficit translates into a current-account deficit. But what about the argument that the budget deficit has contributed to the depressed saving rate by encouraging an excessive growth rate in personal consumption expenditures?

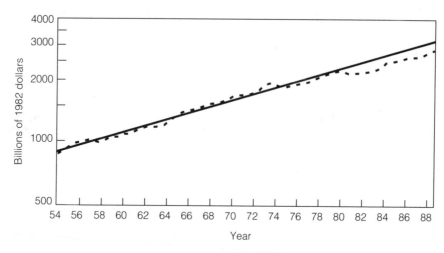

FIGURE 5-4   *Disposable Personal Income and Long-Term Trend (Quarterly, 1954:1–1988:4)*

ARE AMERICANS OVERCONSUMING?

Although many people complain with monotonous frequency that Americans consume too much, the evidence here is also open to serious question. Remember that the ratio of consumption to income, as with all ratios, is composed of two variables. Like the argument over whether a glass is half full or half empty, one should consider whether the recent jump in the ratio of consumption to income is the result of too high a level of consumption or too low a level of income.

Figures 5-4 and 5-5 show the paths of real disposable personal income and real personal consumption expenditures, quarterly, from 1954 to 1988, together with trend lines based on the experience from 1954 to 1980, prior to the onset of major budget deficits. Figure 5-6 shows the deviation of each series from those trend lines.

While it is clear that consumer spending has been high relative to income during the 1980s, Figures 5-5 and 5-6 show that this shift has not come about because consumers have been in an unusually spendthrift mood. On the contrary, real spending has been running at an annual rate of some $200 billion, or about 8 percent, below the trend rate of growth established over the two and one-half decades preceding the 1980s. *The reason that the saving rate has been so low, therefore, is not because consumption has been out of control but, rather, because real income growth has been so dismal.*

The patterns shown here suggest that efforts to restrain consumption are aiming at the wrong objective. The problem in the U.S. economy has been insufficient growth in real incomes—a consequence of poor productivity performance, the preference for goods and services produced outside the United States, and a bias in monetary policy in favor of suppressing inflation rather than encouraging real growth.

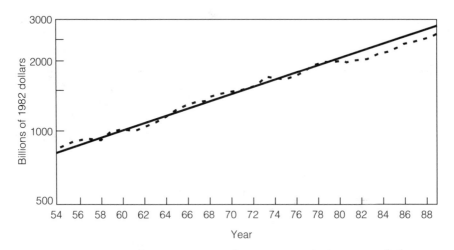

FIGURE 5–5 *Personal Consumption Expenditures and Long-Term Trend (Quarterly, 1954:1–1988:4)*

The ultimate source of the problem is the unsatisfactory rate of growth of *potential* GNP—the volume of goods and services that the economy can produce without igniting inflationary pressures. In this connection, it is important to recognize that high levels of investment are no guarantee that potential output will grow at an acceptable rate. Despite the sustained investment booms of the 1960s and 1970s, the huge wave of corporate restructuring in recent years is eloquent testimony to the probability that errors in private sector investment decisions during those investment booms must have been rampant.

It is a sad commentary on our productivity that inflation and interest rates were rising and the Federal Reserve was trying to hold the economy in check when the peak in manufacturing capacity utilization in the expansion that began in 1982 was only 84.7 percent, the lowest utilization peak in any postwar expansion and three percentage points below the average of the previous peaks. Nor is it reassuring that the low point in the civilian unemployment rate in this expansion has been 5.2 percent, only 0.2 percentage points below the average unemployment rate from 1954 to 1979.

Henry Aaron of The Brookings Institution recently provided some statistical support for the proposition that the essence of our problem is too little growth rather than too much expenditure—and, indeed, that *this disorder goes far to explain the budget deficit itself.* In his Richard T. Ely lecture to the American Economic Association, Aaron declared:

> Had gross output per hour in the United States grown from 1973 to 1988 as fast as it did from 1950 through 1973, output would be one-fifth larger than it is today. Government revenues at current average tax rates would be a bit under $200 billion larger in 1988 than they turned out to be. Outlays would be smaller by some tens of billions of dollars because of reduced interest on a smaller debt. Given other

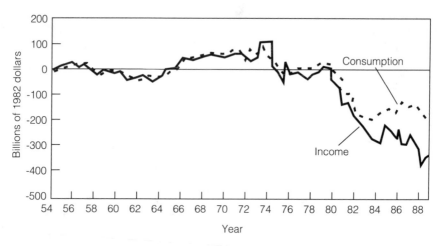

FIGURE 5-6 *Personal Income and Expenditure, Deviations from Trends of 1954–80 (Quarterly 1954:1–1988:4)*

expenditures as they are, the United States in 1988 would have been facing a budget surplus in the vicinity of $100 billion, rather than a deficit of $155 billion. (1989, p. 2)

Finally, there is little justification for the moral tone with which American households are accused of being spendthrifts and failing to save for the future. Americans are not alone! With the exception of Japan, the personal saving rate of every major nation today is well below earlier peak levels. The West German rate is five percentage points below 1975; the rate in the United Kingdom has fallen from 14 percent at the start of this decade to only about 5 percent at present; Canada's rate has dropped to little more than one-half its level in 1982; and the rate in France has been falling for more than 10 years.

Despite these roughly similar developments in saving ratios, real interest rates, national accounts, and fiscal policies in these countries have followed trends that are markedly different from ours. The easy generalizations about the depressed American flow of saving, therefore, fail to stand up to careful scrutiny.

THE DEFICIT AND INVESTMENT

So far, the discussion has considered whether the budget deficit is the cause of the current-account deficit and high real interest rates, as well as examining the supposedly sad record of personal saving. On all scores, the data fail to support the theoretical hypotheses of the mainstream position.

One further aspect of the matter merits analysis: the relationship between government deficits and the rate of investment or capital formation.

TABLE 5-3

	Government saving as percentage of GDP*		Gross private capital formation** as percentage of GDP	
	1980	1986	1980	1986
United States	−1.26	−3.41	16.47	12.36
Canada	−1.58	−4.54	19.87	15.72
Japan	+2.58	+4.15	21.63	25.76
France	+3.75	+0.61	20.47	17.88
United Kingdom	−0.52	−0.55	18.61	15.72

SOURCE: Organization for Economic Cooperation and Development (OECD) (1989)
*Gross domestic product (GDP) is gross national product less net foreign interest income.
**Includes net foreign investment.

This issue is perhaps the most important of all, because the mainstream argues that deficits "crowd-out" investment by absorbing saving flows that would otherwise bring about higher rates of investment.

Some of the empirical evidence on budget deficits and investment gives just a bit more credence to the mainstream view than we have seen up to this point. Even here, however, that credence is limited.

Table 5-3 compares the change in government deficits with the change in total private capital formation from 1980 to 1986, as percentages of GDP, in the United States and four major industrial countries for which good data are available. The capital formation figure reflects gross private domestic investment plus net foreign investment (roughly, the current-account balance on goods and services).

With the exception of Japan, all four countries show a deterioration in their fiscal position from 1980 to 1986. Japan shows a rise in capital formation as a share of GDP; the other four show a decline. These trends are all in accordance with theory. Note, however, that the French fiscal position deteriorated by the most, but the decline in their capital formation ratio was only 60 percent of the decline in Canada and the United States. The United Kingdom, whose fiscal position was just about unchanged, saw its capital formation ratio shrink by the same amount as the shrinkage in the French ratio. Note, further, that each year's capital formation ratios themselves are roughly equal for Canada, France, and the United Kingdom, despite radically different fiscal situations.

An even wider discrepancy in the relationship between deficits and investment appears in data provided by Feldstein and Bacchetta (1989). We refer in particular to their Table 3, which lists the average levels of general government deficits, private saving, and investment—all as a percentage of

GDP—for 13 industrial countries, including the United States, for the periods 1970–79 and 1980–84.

It should be noted at the outset that all 13 countries show a deterioration in their governmental fiscal position between the two time periods, accompanied by an equally unanimous decline in their investment/GDP ratios. Nevertheless, seven, or slightly more than one-half, of the 13 countries show increases in their saving ratios.

It is fair to ask, however, whether any systematic relationships existed between the deterioration in fiscal position and variations in the rates of saving and investment. Was there systematic evidence that the negative fiscal shifts were crowding out investment or absorbing saving?

To this end, we first regressed the change in investment rates on the change in the deficits from the earlier period to the later and produced an R^2 of only 0.16 with a hefty standard error of 1.5 percentage points. The coefficient on the change in the deficits of -0.30 is predictably negative with a standard error of 0.21; however, it is statistically indistinguishable from zero.

We also regressed the change in private saving rates on the change in the deficits to determine whether we could find evidence of deficits absorbing private saving. Here the relationship was even weaker than in the case of investment: The R^2 is zero, and the coefficient on the change in the deficits is only -0.02 with a standard error of 0.37.

One problem with these calculations is that Feldstein and Bacchetta carry out their calculations of the ratios to only two decimal places, while the changes in the ratios are all less than 10 percentage points in size. This limitation means that the inputs to the regressions are only single-digit numbers that could be as much as one-half a percentage point away from the actual number. In addition, our analysis shares with Feldstein and Bacchetta the difficulty that their sample includes only 13 observations. As a result, the regressions themselves do not necessarily carry high statistical significance. On the other hand, the regressions so clearly show the absence of any systematic relationships that greater accuracy or a larger sample would be most unlikely to lead to materially different conclusions.

In short, the world economy appears to be far too noisy to provide unambiguous support to the widely held hypothesis that budget deficits have a negative impact on private investment, saving, and trade flows. The patterns are so irregular that many other forces must have been at work to produce these particular results.[3]

DEFINING "DEFICITS"

We have seen that the budget deficit is not necessarily or systematically a cause of the current-account deficit and that, in fact, the opposite may be closer to the truth. We have also noted that the saving shortfall is something quite different in character from the way it is usually presented and can hardly be a consequence of the budget deficit. Finally, we have observed that the relationship between budget deficits and private capital formation finds only modest and inconsistent support from the empirical evidence.

Now it is appropriate to ask an even more telling question: To what extent is the budget "deficit" a consequence of the budget deficit? This is not a play on words.

A proper solution to a problem must depend upon a proper understanding of what the problem is. Hence, there are dangerous consequences stemming from the broad use of the word "deficit" as it is applied to the excess of government expenditure over government revenue and to the excess of imports over exports. No one applies this word to corporations that make growth-related investments in new plant and equipment, even though such outlays usually exceed revenues from the normal cost of business, nor does anyone accuse a household of running a deficit when the family takes out a mortgage to purchase a new home.

Growth-related capital expenditures, in other words, deserve separate treatment from operating expenditures, because these expenditures pay for something that will provide services over a period of years, not just at the moment that the checks are written. They contribute toward tomorrow's production, rather than to today's. This is the rationale that underlies business and household bookkeeping and that underlies the normal practice of financing these outlays by borrowing instead of paying for them out of current revenues.

The principle should apply equally well to government bookkeeping and to our international accounts. Growth-related outlays should be reported separately from operating outlays, and should normally be financed differently. Public investments are not properly part of a "deficit," which is the difference between current spending and current revenues and which prudent finance dictates keeping to a practical minimum.

In *The Debt and the Deficit* (1989), we estimate the federal government's growth-related outlays at some $40 billion at the least (see Table 6, page 83 of that document). State and municipal spending for these purposes exceeds $50 billion, most of which is essentially financed by Washington. As a result, this $90 billion of investment in the nation's future reduces the combined federal and state/local "deficit" for 1989 to only $15 billion.

The same distinction between outlays for investment and outlays for consumption is relevant to the current-account deficit. Imports of capital goods improve U.S. capacity to produce and our rate of productivity growth. It is one thing to finance the importation of Italian shoes and Japanese cars by selling to foreigners choice real estate, shares in the best corporations, and government bonds on which we will have to pay them interest. It is something else again to sell these assets to foreigners in exchange for assets that improve the productive base of the United States itself.

That is essentially what has been going on. Imports of machinery, aircraft, and other capital goods—excluding motor vehicles of all types, even trucks—amounted to about $113 billion in 1989, or approximately 20 percent of our total merchandise imports and almost precisely equal to our total merchandise trade deficit. In fact, the share of imports accounted for by capital goods has been rising steadily since 1980, when they accounted for only 13 percent of our total merchandise imports.

This means that our receipts from our export trade in merchandise are paying for all of our consumption-type imports, so that our trade "deficit" in goods, properly measured, is essentially zero, not $113 billion. The borrowings from foreigners and sales of assets to them are financing the purchase of capital goods that make our economy more productive.

In short, the terminology in use overstates both deficits, because some government spending and some outlays for imports pay for growth-related investments that will make our future output higher than it would be without them. Borrowing to finance such outlays is normal and prudent. There is no reason why it should elicit cries of alarm.

THE CASE IN RECAPITULATION

Before setting out a prescription for how to deal with the economic problems of the United States, a brief review of our case is in order. The argument centers on the essential underpinnings of the mainstream view that the budget deficit is absorbing saving that would otherwise go to more productive use and that the budget deficit is the cause of the current-account deficit. We have shown how cause and effect might well run in the opposite direction, while questioning the reality of the assumptions used to support the case for an attack on the national saving rate. Finally, we expressed doubts about the mainstream's description of the process whereby the budget deficit causes all these difficulties.

The theoretical case has been buttressed with empirical evidence showing that the mainstream's description of reality lacks consistency and historical validity. We found no systematic relationship between budget deficits and real interest rates or between budget deficits and changes in international current accounts. We also failed to find any systematic relationships between real interest rates and the balance between saving and investment or between real interest rates and the budget deficit. Although there does appear to be some negative correlation between budget deficits and private capital formation, even here the data are too erratic to provide any confidence that the deficit is the determining factor. The data also show that Americans are not consuming at a pace that exceeds historical ranges; on the contrary, the decline in personal saving appears to be primarily the result of sluggish growth in after-tax incomes rather than of a consumer spending spree.

Finally, we have shown that the deficit problem is usually specified in an unsatisfactory and deceptive fashion. Government spending in excess of tax revenue is a "deficit" only insofar as it excludes growth-promoting government expenditures. Imports in excess of exports reflect a "deficit" only insofar as they exclude imports of capital goods. After defining the budget and current-account deficits properly to reflect the capital formation activities of government and imports of capital goods, both deficits appear far smaller than they appear under conventional definitions.

WHAT TO DO?

Prescriptions to cure America's ills abound. Because they promise to cure ills diagnosed by oversimplifications and emotional exhortations, these prescriptions sound appealing, but many of them are high-risk in character and could easily be counterproductive. The more skeptical view presented here has demonstrated that these oversimplifications do not stand up under careful analysis. Our assessment of the matter leads to recommendations for different types of cures, because the analysis perceives the problem itself in different terms.

Measures whose primary focus is to raise the saving rate—and that includes hasty steps to push down the federal budget deficit—deserve a special dose of skepticism. To the extent that these measures result in less public or private spending, their immediate consequence will be loss of jobs, a loss of income, lower personal saving, and less revenue accruing to the federal government—without any sure offsets in the form of higher domestic or foreign investment.

In addition, the efficacy of easier monetary policies is open to question, although easy money is an integral part of the mainstream recommendations to offset the depressing impact of a higher propensity to save. For example, the U.S. nonfinancial corporate sector is now in a state of seriously depleted liquidity, with shrunken supplies of financial assets and bloated liabilities of all types. The financial sector itself is in deep trouble, leading to even more concern about higher costs of liquidity.

If the immediate effect of reducing the budget deficit is to squeeze corporate cash flows through lower sales and higher tax rates, more private borrowing will simply replace public borrowing in the capital markets and interest rates will fail to decline. In any case, business investment is not as sensitive to interest rates as it is to profit expectations—and profit expectations would be diminished by lower personal incomes and by the increased incentives for household saving.

A weaker dollar that might result from easy money also has inflationary implications and may not stimulate exports sufficiently unless other countries are expanding their economies more rapidly than ours at the same time. And there is no guarantee that the dollar will move downward under these circumstances, if foreigners take a favorable view of the apparent shift toward greater rectitude by the United States and decide to increase the already large inflow of capital to this country.

This examination of the limitations of monetary policy is not meant to imply that we oppose lower interest rates as an offset to more conservative fiscal policies and inducements to households to save more. On the contrary, our concern rather is that there is many a slip 'twixt cup and lip in efforts to find *effective* offsets to these measures.

The thrust of our own recommendations stems from the critical difference between our position and the mainstream view. The mainstream position is that the budget deficit and low saving are the cause of the current-account deficit and inadequate rates of investment. We see the budget deficit and the low saving rate as the consequence of an unsatisfactory environment consisting of low productivity, too little public investment, and little or no growth in real incomes.

Advocates of the mainstream position believe that the current-account deficit will persist, no matter what, so long as the budget deficit persists. We would argue that steps to improve U.S. competitiveness will lead to a lower budget deficit and to a higher personal saving rate as well. Hence, all measures designed to improve the productivity of the U.S. economy merit full support.

These measures should include public spending on education, infrastructure, and the environment, even if financed by borrowing. A recent study conducted by David Aschauer at the Chicago Federal Reserve Bank (1988) calculates that private profitability would rise by two percentage points if nondefense public investment were to expand from its present abysmal low of 0.3 percent of GNP to the 2.1 percent level of the early 1980s—which would still be less than one-half of what Japan spends for these purposes. The 1989 *Economic Report of the President* confirms the validity of this approach (see pages 80–81 of that report). Further convincing evidence of the relationship between productivity growth and public investment may be found in Alicia Munnell (1990), who supplies convincing evidence that:

> The drop in labor productivity [since the 1960s] has not been due to a decline in the growth of some mystical concept of multifactor productivity or technical progress. Rather, it has been due to a decline in the growth of public infrastructure. (p. 20)

While one can find good reasons to have doubts about tax-related incentives for business investment and research—they are counter to tax simplification and may provide windfalls to those who would make such expenditures anyway—the urgent need to reduce the cost of capital in the United States may outweigh these disadvantages.

Indeed, measures that are likely to raise the price/earnings ratios of U.S. common stocks are essential for improving our international competitiveness. As the recent wave of equity issuance in Japan has demonstrated, higher price/earnings ratios are not only the best way to reverse the recent distressing trend to substitute equity with debt. They simultaneously discourage the takeover frenzy by making it more attractive to raise money to create new assets than to raise money by gobbling up the old.

In short, economists must cease looking at the budget deficit and the personal saving ratio as independent variables that can be manipulated at will without any second order and counterproductive effects. Rather, the budget deficit and the low saving rate should be recognized as symptoms that are the consequence of disappointing productivity and misallocation of resources. From that fresh perspective, an exciting path opens up that can extricate the United States from the dead weight of debt and that can give us the bright future that our talents, hard work, and natural resources can provide.

NOTES

The authors wish to express their gratitude for helpful criticisms from Robert Eisner and members of the staff of the Secretary of the Treasury.

1. In the interests of space and minimizing monotony, we resist the temptation to recite examples of the mainstream view. They are legion in the literature, in the press, and in public documents.

2. Examples of this perverse reaction, when a lower rate on Federal Reserve Funds produces a rise in long-term bond yields, occurred in early 1969, late 1971, late 1975, early 1977, and during most of 1987.

3. Here is one "other" force that may have been at work. Budget deficits, by sustaining business activity, tend to reduce default risk on corporate bonds, thereby narrowing the spread between the yields on corporate and government bonds. Consequently, deficits may actually reduce the cost of capital to the private sector. See David Bowles et al. (1989).

6   The Ricardian Model of Budget Deficits

ROBERT J. BARRO

My wife was watching C-Span on television, and one of the economists from the Congressional Budget Office (CBO) was talking about the U.S. budget deficit. He said that the deficit was a major crisis, but people were being misled about the severity because most of the usual indicators—such as prices of financial assets, inflation, and real economic activity—were giving off reasonably rosy, but false, signals. My wife was justifiably skeptical; could it not be that these indicators were right and that the deficit was just not a big deal? Anyhow, my wife argued, where did this CBO economist get his information if not from all the data that gave different answers? Probably he was just a slave to some outmoded economic theory that predicted effects that had not shown up. Moreover, she recalled that David Ricardo had developed a theory that said that budget deficits were roughly equivalent to taxation, and she thought that this theory conformed pretty well with the evidence that the CBO economist said we should ignore.

Naturally, I agreed with my wife, and said that the frequent expression of crisis was especially surprising because the ratio of privately held U.S. public debt to gross national product (GNP) has not been growing since 1987. Figure 6-1, which plots the data from 1790 to 1989, shows that the ratio fell from 0.39 at the end of 1987 to 0.38 at the end of 1989. As a related matter, Figure 6-2 shows that the ratio of the real budget deficit (measured here as the change in privately held real public debt) to real GNP declined from over 4 percent in 1983–85 to about 1 percent in 1989. I told my wife that, despite the virtual elimination of the budget deficit in 1988–89 and the absence of evidence that the deficits of prior years had any adverse consequences, it was hard to convince people that the U.S. budget deficit was not a major problem. But I promised to be convincing in this chapter.

THE STANDARD THEORY OF BUDGET DEFICITS

I will start with the standard theoretical model of budget deficits. Suppose that the government cuts current taxes and runs a budget deficit. The

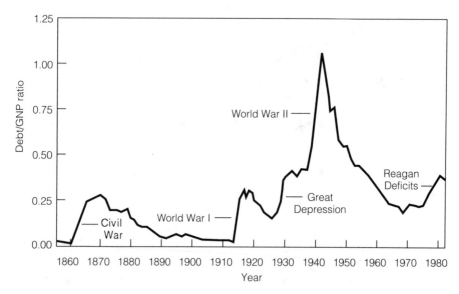

FIGURE 6-1   *Ratio of Privately Held U.S. Public Debt to GNP*

higher deficit implies, by definition, an equal decline in public saving. The standard analysis assumes that households respond to the increase in current disposable income, which equals the amount of the tax cut, partly with higher desired private saving and partly with higher consumer demand. Because desired private saving rises by only a fraction of the budget deficit, desired national saving (the sum of public and private saving) declines.

In a closed economy, accounting identities imply that national saving must end up equal to domestic investment. Therefore, the decline in desired national saving means that the real interest rate has to rise. (With the fall in desired national saving, there is an insufficient supply of funds to provide for the unchanged quantity of domestic investment demand.) The higher real interest rate restores an equilibrium by reducing investment demand and raising desired private saving. In particular, the new equilibrium features a smaller quantity of domestic investment. This "crowding out" of investment in the short run corresponds in the long run to a smaller stock of domestic capital. Thereby, in the language of Franco Modigliani (1961), the accumulation of public debt due to a budget deficit is a burden in that it leads to a smaller stock of productive capital for future generations. Similar reasoning applies to pay-as-you-go social security programs, as stressed by Martin Feldstein (1974). An increase in the scale of these programs raises aggregate demand and thereby leads to a higher real interest rate, a reduced flow of investment in the short run, and a smaller stock of capital in the long run.

The standard theory, as sketched above, implies a close association among budget deficits, real interest rates, and levels of investment. As I will argue later, these predictions do not accord well with evidence from the

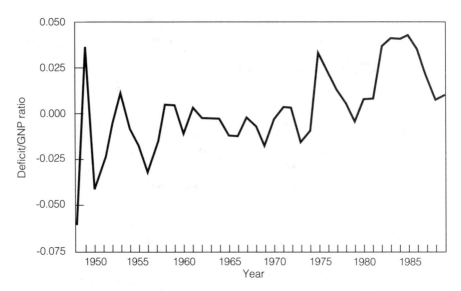

FIGURE 6-2   *Ratio of U.S. Real Budget Deficit to Real GNP*

United States or other industrialized countries. Because of this empirical failure and because of the increasing integration of the world economy, many economists have abandoned the framework of a closed economy when thinking about the effects of budget deficits.

In a setting of open economies, the standard analysis of budget deficits must be modified to allow for borrowing and lending across countries. A country's national saving now finances the total of domestic and net foreign investment. Net foreign investment equals the investments that the country pays for abroad less the amounts that foreigners pay for in this country. Hence, net foreign investment equals the current-account balance, which is the addition to this country's net claims on the rest of the world.

In an international economy with perfect markets for goods and credit, each country faces the same "world real interest rate," which is determined by the world aggregates of investment demand and desired saving. Therefore, if a single country's contribution to these world aggregates is small, the country's budget deficits and social security programs have negligible effects on the real interest rate that the country faces.

Given the assumptions about consumer behavior that we made before, a decision to finance government spending by a budget deficit rather than current taxes still leads in an open economy to an excess of domestic investment demand over desired national saving. But, instead of raising the real interest rate, this excess of investment demand is accommodated by borrowing from abroad. That is, a budget deficit leads to a current-account deficit or, equivalently, to a decline in net foreign investment. Real interest rates rise only to the extent that the country is large enough to influence the world economy, or to the extent that the increase in the country's national debt induces foreign lenders to demand higher real interest rates as a risk premium. (Because of past and prospective defaults, many Latin American countries would have to pay high real interest rates on their debt—if anyone would lend to them at all these days.)

The main new result for an open economy is the much weaker tendency for a single country's budget deficit to be associated with higher real interest rates or reduced domestic investment. On the other hand, if the whole world runs budget deficits (or expands the scale of social security programs), then real interest rates would rise on international capital markets and investment would be crowded out in each country. These effects for the world parallel those for a single closed economy, as discussed before.

THE RICARDIAN THEORY OF BUDGET DEFICITS

An alternative theory of budget deficits relates to the research of the nineteenth century British economist, David Ricardo (see Ricardo, 1951; Barro, 1989). (Despite some misinformed opinions and independently of whether he regarded the theory as empirically valid, Ricardo was the first to enunciate this view in a clear manner; see Gerald O'Driscoll, 1977.) The Ricardian analysis begins with the proposition that a deficit-financed cut in current taxes leads to higher future taxes that have the same present value as the initial tax cut. In particular, the total present value of taxes cannot change unless the government changes the present value of its expenditures.[1] (The working assumption here is that the path of expenditures is given; nothing in the Ricardian view rules out important effects from changes in current or prospective government spending.) The invariance of the total present value of taxes amounts to the economist's standard notion of the absence of a free lunch—government spending has to be paid for now or later, but not never.

The next step in the Ricardian argument is that consumer demand depends on the anticipated present value of taxes. That is, each person subtracts his or her share of this present value from the present value of income to determine a net wealth position, which then determines desired consumption. Recall that a budget deficit does not affect the present value of taxes. Therefore, a budget deficit also has no impact on aggregate consumer demand. Another way to express this result is that a decrease in public saving (implied by a larger budget deficit) leads to an exactly offsetting increase in desired private saving, and hence to no change in desired national saving.

Note that the constancy of desired national saving applies in the Ricardian analysis only if the budget deficit is not accompanied by a recession, which would alter the expected path of household income, or by a shift in the expected present value of government spending. Changes in anticipated income or government spending generally affect desired national saving;

that is, the response of desired private saving would no longer precisely offset the change in public saving. These caveats are important because budget deficits are, in practice, often associated with recessions or wartime expenditures. The Ricardian invariance of desired national saving applies only if the effects from recession and wartime spending are held constant.

Recall for a closed economy that desired national saving must be equated to domestic investment demand. The result that we just derived is that a budget deficit does not affect desired national saving. Therefore, the real interest rate does not have to change to maintain the equality between desired national saving and domestic investment demand, each of which has not changed. In other words, the Ricardian model implies that a budget deficit has no effect in a closed economy on the real interest rate or the quantity of investment. With investment unchanged, budget deficits also have no long-term implications for the capital stock; hence, there is no burden of the debt in the sense of Modigliani.

In an open economy, the current-account balance equals net foreign investment, which equals the excess of desired national saving over domestic investment demand. In the Ricardian model, a budget deficit does not affect desired national saving and therefore does not affect the current-account balance. That is, budget deficits do not lead to current-account deficits. There is no need to borrow from abroad because desired private saving from domestic residents rises enough to compensate for the decline in public saving.

To summarize, the Ricardian analysis implies that shifts between taxes and budget deficits do not matter for the real interest rate, the quantity of investment, or the current-account balance. These conclusions are sometimes referred to as the Ricardian Equivalence Theorem. That is, given the quantity of government spending, taxes and budget deficits have equivalent effects on the economy. Basically, the effects are equivalent because a higher current budget deficit (to finance a current tax cut) implies an increase by an equal amount in the present value of future taxes.

THEORETICAL OBJECTIONS TO THE RICARDIAN MODEL

I shall discuss four major theoretical criticisms that have been raised against the Ricardian approach. The first is that people do not live forever, and hence do not care about taxes that are levied after death. The second is that private capital markets are "imperfect," with the typical person's real discount rate exceeding the real interest rate paid by the government. The third is that future taxes and incomes are uncertain. The fourth is that the timing of taxes matters if taxes are not lump sum; specifically, if taxes apply to income, spending, wealth, and so on.

It turns out that each of the four types of criticisms may imply that budget deficits matter; that is, are nonneutral and hence not fully Ricardian.

Nevertheless, it is important to consider in each case first, whether the effects are likely to be quantitatively significant, and second, whether the particular point supports the standard model of budget deficits that was outlined before. There is an unfortunate tendency among macroeconomists to make an argument about why budget deficits are not fully neutral, and then use the standard approach, which usually is not supported by the argument.

Finite Lifetimes

I will, of course, accept the empirical proposition that people do not live forever. The question is the relevance of this fact for the Ricardian conclusions. The channel for overturning Ricardian equivalence is that, with finite lifetimes, people may consider only the future taxes that they expect to face before dying.

Suppose that a deficit-financed tax cut raises future taxes partly during the typical person's expected lifetime and partly afterwards. Then the present value of the first part must fall short of the initial tax cut because a balance occurs only if the second part is also included. Hence the net wealth of people currently alive rises. Households respond to the rise in wealth by raising consumption demand; that is, only a fraction of the extra disposable income goes into desired private saving. The increase in consumer demand implies an increase in aggregate demand, which was the starting point for the standard model that was sketched before. Therefore, the other conclusions from the standard analysis apply: A budget deficit leads in a closed economy to a higher real interest rate and lower investment, and in an open economy to a current-account deficit.

This analysis of the effects of finite lifetimes is valid only if the typical person feels wealthier when the government shifts a tax burden to his or her descendants. The reasoning fails if the typical person is already giving or planning to give to his or her children out of altruism, a situation that appears to be prevalent. In this case, people react to the government's imposed intergenerational transfers, which are implied by a budget deficit or social security, with a compensating increase in voluntary transfers (see Barro, 1974). For example, parents adjust their bequests or the amounts given to children while the parents are still living. Alternatively, if children provide support to aged parents, the amounts given respond inversely to budget deficits or social security.

The central idea is that a network of intergenerational transfers makes the typical individual part of an extended family that goes on indefinitely. In this setting, households consider the entire stream of expected future taxes, as assumed in the Ricardian analysis. In other words, the Ricardian results, which seemed to depend on people living forever, can remain valid in a model with finite lifetimes.

It is worth noting that the results do not require large intergenerational transfers; what is necessary is that transfers based on altruism be operative at the margin for most people. Also, the transfers do not have to show up as bequests at death. Other forms of intergenerational transfers, such as *inter vivos* gifts to children, support of children's education, and child support of aged parents, work in a similar manner. Therefore, the Ricardian results can hold even if many persons leave little in the way of formal bequests.

Imperfect Loan Markets

Many economists argue that the imperfection of private credit markets is central to analyses of budget deficits. The nature of credit markets arises in the computation of the present value of expected future taxes. The assumption in the Ricardian analysis is that the discount rate used to determine the present value is the same as the real interest rate that the government pays on its debts. More realistically, many borrowers have to pay interest rates that substantially exceed the government's rate. These high interest rates reflect the costs of evaluating, processing, and collecting loans.

The effects of credit-market imperfections can be studied satisfactorily by returning to the setting of a closed economy in which households effectively have infinite horizons. Suppose that some businesses and households, denoted as group I, have low interest rates—good access to credit markets—and are therefore willing to hold government bonds. A second group, denoted as group II, have high interest rates for borrowing and therefore do not want to hold government bonds.

Consider now the effect of a deficit-financed tax cut. We know from previous discussions that the present value of future taxes (discounted by the government's interest rate) goes up by as much as the tax cut. Assume that today's tax cut is divided evenly between group I and group II, and that the higher future taxes are also divided evenly between the two groups. Then the members of group I willingly hold 50 percent of the extra government bonds, as in previous analyses. The members of group II, however, do not want to hold government bonds; they use their tax cut instead to raise demand for consumption and investment. In the aggregate, therefore, desired national saving decreases (because private saving rises by less than the decline in public saving) and investment demand increases. Consequently, the real interest rate has to rise to restore equality between desired national saving and investment demand, or equivalently, the government has to pay a more attractive interest rate to induce the private sector to absorb its extra debt.

Because the members of group II are unwilling to hold government bonds, the interest rate must rise by enough to induce members of group I to hold the additional bonds. If the interest rate rises a lot, then some members of group II would start to hold government bonds; that is, some members of group II would become members of group I. But, in any event, the key result is that group I ends up holding more than 50 percent (and perhaps as much as 100 percent) of the additional public debt, whereas group II ends up holding less than 50 percent (and perhaps as little as 0 percent) of the debt.

Because group I and group II end up holding unequal shares of the new government bonds, the budget deficit turns out to improve the allocation of credit in the economy. In particular, by holding less than their share of the new bonds, the individuals and businesses with poor access to credit markets (group II) effectively receive loans from the individuals and businesses with good access to credit (group I). The government acts like a financial intermediary between the two groups; it collects taxes from members of group II and distributes the proceeds as interest payments to members of group I. The process works because the government guarantees repayment of loans through its tax collections and debt payments. Thus, loans between members of groups I and II effectively take place even though such loans were not viable privately because of the high costs of evaluation, processing, and collection.

The government may be relatively efficient at collecting funds from people with poor collateral (members of group II) because of compulsory taxation and police powers. Offsetting this force is the tendency for private organizations to be more efficient than government because choices in the public sector involve greater problems of incentives and information. If the government really were more efficient at the credit process, one wonders why it has such difficulty in collecting on loans from students!

If the government is more efficient than the private market in the loan process, then an expansion of public debt amounts to an improvement in financial intermediation. The main result is a better allocation of credit, in the sense that funds flow toward the higher-return investments or more urgent consumption expenditures for members of group II. (Because of high interest rates on loans, the members of group II were previously unable to exploit fully their opportunities for high-return investment or urgent consumption.) The effect on aggregate investment is unclear; the results depend on whether members of group II are more likely to spend their tax cut on investment or consumption and on whether members of group I are more likely to cut back on investment or consumption (in response to the rise in the interest rate). In any event, although budget deficits are nonneutral and hence non-Ricardian, the results do not resemble those from the standard model of budget deficits. In particular, budget deficits are basically a good idea in this model.

Another possibility is that the government is no more efficient than the private market in the loan process; that is, the provision of credit involves "transaction costs" and is therefore "imperfect" whether carried out publicly or privately. In this case, a budget deficit turns out not to affect the distribution of spending across groups or the aggregate levels of investment and consumption. The reason is that the intermediation implied by the government's deficit is now no different from the intermediation that can occur privately. Thus, in this case, the Ricardian equivalence result—that budget deficits do not matter—holds even though credit markets are imperfect.

Uncertainty about Future Taxes and Incomes

Uncertainty about an individual's future taxes does not imply that the expected level of these taxes counts for less than otherwise. In fact, with the introduction of uncertainty, it is possible to get an increase in desired national saving in response to a budget deficit. This possibility arises because people want to protect themselves against the chance of surprisingly high future taxes. The main counter force is that, with income taxes, the government shares the risks of income uncertainty with individuals. People pay more in taxes if they are lucky to have unexpectedly high income and vice versa. A budget deficit raises the extent of this sharing in the future (when taxes are higher), and may therefore motivate a reduction in current desired saving. Thus, the overall implications of uncertainty for the effects of budget deficits are ambiguous.

The Timing of Taxes

Budget deficits affect the timing of taxes; specifically, a larger deficit means less taxes today and more in the future. Unless the taxes are lump sum, household behavior would depend on when the taxes were levied. For example, with an income tax, a change in timing alters people's incentives to work and produce in various periods. It follows that a budget deficit is nonneutral; that is, the results are non-Ricardian. The conclusions tend, however, also to depart from the standard model of budget deficits.

Because a budget deficit lowers today's income tax rate relative to future rates, people tend to raise today's income (by increasing current labor supply and production) relative to future income. On the other hand, because the tax rates do not apply to consumption, households have no incentive to change the time pattern of consumer demand. It follows that desired national saving would rise; the result opposite to that in the standard analysis. The standard conclusion of a decline in desired national saving tends to hold, however, if the government uses the budget deficit to rearrange the timing of consumption taxes (such as sales taxes in the United States or value-added taxes in many other countries).

To go further, one can derive the path of tax rates and hence budget deficits that is optimal from the standpoint of an overall package of public finance. That is, in addition to choosing the types of taxes—such as levies on income, consumption, and wealth—the government would also choose when to collect each tax. The budget deficit would emerge as a by-product of this "optimal-tax" calculation.

One conclusion from this optimal-tax analysis is that budget deficits can be used advantageously to smooth tax rates over time, despite fluctuations in government expenditures and the tax base (see A.C. Pigou, 1928, Ch. 6; Barro, 1979). For example, budget deficits would be large during wars and recessions to avoid abnormally high tax rates during these emergencies. Furthermore, because the optimal-tax policy is framed in real terms, the nominal debt would rise along with expected increases in the price level. This behavior corresponds to the common practice of making inflation adjustments to the reported figures on budget deficits. For example, in Figure 6-2, these adjustments were made by computing the real deficit as the change over the year in the real quantity of outstanding debt. Pure inflation, which leads to corresponding growth of the nominal debt, would not affect this measure of the real budget deficit.

The tax-smoothing view of budget deficits accounts for much of the history of the public debt in the United States and other countries. In the long-term U.S. data, most of the movements in the ratio of the public debt to GNP, as shown in Figure 6-1, can be explained by war and recession. For example, the debt–GNP ratio rose during the Civil War from 0.01 in 1860 to 0.24 in 1865, during World War I from 0.02 in 1916 to 0.31 in 1919, and during World War II from 0.42 in 1941 to 1.07 in 1945.[2] With respect to economic contraction, the debt–GNP ratio rose from 0.14 in 1929 to 0.38 in 1933 (the period of the Great Depression), from 0.18 in 1974 to 0.23 in 1976 (with the 1974–75 recession), and from 0.22 in 1979 to 0.30 in 1983 (with the recessions from 1980 to 1983).

Aside from periods of war or major economic contraction, the typical behavior shown in Figure 6-1 is a declining ratio of the public debt to GNP. The major departure from this long-established pattern shows up during the Reagan administration, especially from 1984 to 1987. The debt–GNP ratio rose from 0.30 in 1983 to 0.39 in 1987 (before declining to 0.38 in 1989), despite the absence of war or recession. This behavior of the debt–GNP ratio corresponds to high ratios of real budget deficits to real GNP, which averaged 3.4 percent from 1984 to 1987, before declining to an average of less than 0.8 percent for 1988–89 (see Figure 6-2).

I should note that the measure of public debt used in these calculations is the privately held total; amounts held by the Federal Reserve and government trust funds, including social security, are netted out.[3] In particular, this definition effectively consolidates expenditures and receipts of the social security system with the rest of the federal government. In the past, economists agreed that this consolidation was a good idea; after all, social security expenditures (a type of transfer payment) are a form of federal spending and social security receipts amount to a federal payroll tax.

Recently—that is, since the social security system began to run a surplus—some people have argued that the federal government's deficit or surplus should be calculated independently of social security. One possible reason to think about social security separately is that, because of demographic trends, the ratio of social security benefit payments to GNP is expected to grow over time. If other components of federal spending were expected to maintain a constant ratio to GNP, then the tax-smoothing viewpoint would argue for a current budget surplus. That is, tax rates should be raised currently to match the higher anticipated future ratio of total government spending, including social security transfers, to GNP. Of course, this projection about social security expenditures may be incorrect.

In particular, forecasts for social security depend on whether changes occur in benefit formulas, on whether immigration upsets the demographic projections, and so on.

The general point, which is not special to social security, is that projections about future government spending would influence today's optimal fiscal policy. If the ratio to GNP of some component of spending—such as national defense—is projected to rise or fall over time, and if the rest of spending is expected to stay constant in relation to GNP, then tax smoothing calls, respectively, for a current budget surplus or deficit. For example, if we (or Ronald Reagan) somehow knew in the mid-1980s that future changes in Eastern Europe would allow for a peace dividend, then the appropriate response would have been to run a budget deficit. This deficit would be reasonable if we expected the decline in defense spending to result in a decrease in the ratio of total government spending to GNP.

In any event, the implications for desirable deficit policy involve forecasts of the overall level of federal spending, including social security, as a ratio to GNP. Thus, it would surely be inappropriate to follow the suggestion of omitting social security in a consideration of federal spending, taxes, and budget deficits.

I have seen three possible explanations for the excessive real budget deficits of 1984–87. First, they may simply be mistakes.[4] The cost of these mistakes involves the future tax rates that are higher than otherwise because of the financing required for the higher stock of accumulated public debt. The alternative would have been a smoother pattern in which tax rates were above the actual values at the beginning (that is, in the mid-1980s) and below the actual values later on.

Second, people may believe that the "Reagan Revolution" portends a declining share of federal spending in GNP. In that case, current spending would be temporarily high in relation to GNP. Then, as in wartime, it would be sensible to run a budget deficit instead of maintaining temporarily high tax rates. I thought until recently that this argument was implausible, but—as suggested before—the possibility of a peace dividend may make it correct after all. (Could Reagan have anticipated this peace dividend?)

The third argument is that the buildup of federal debt is a device to make it harder for subsequent administrations (maybe even Democrats) to raise spending on other programs. If a president who favors a smaller federal government, such as Ronald Reagan, leaves office with a large stock of accumulated public debt, then the interest payments on this debt would absorb a large amount of future tax revenues. If the next president and Congress want to fund some new or expanded social programs, such as day care, environmental protection, or education, then tax revenues would have to be raised still further. The difficulty of these tax increases makes it less likely that the social programs will be implemented.

Although this political argument has some appeal, the puzzle is why the device was first discovered in 1984. That is, previous periods do not seem to reveal the same kind of strategic political behavior. At least, one does not have to bring in these political arguments to explain most of the history of the U.S. public debt.

EMPIRICAL EVIDENCE ON THE ECONOMIC EFFECTS OF BUDGET DEFICITS

It is easy on theoretical grounds to raise points that invalidate strict Ricardian equivalence between budget deficits and taxes. Nevertheless, it may still be that the Ricardian view provides a useful framework for assessing the main effects of fiscal policy. Furthermore, it is unclear that the standard approach offers a more accurate guide. For these reasons, it is especially important to examine empirical evidence.

Interest Rates

The Ricardian model predicts that real interest rates will not respond to an increase in the budget deficit or the stock of public debt, whereas the standard view predicts that real interest rates will rise (at least in the context of a closed economy). Many economists have tested these propositions empirically for the United States and other countries (see, for example, Plosser [1982, 1987]; Evans [1987a, 1987b]; U.S. Treasury Department [1984]; Barro and Martin [1990]). Typical results show little relation of interest rates to budget deficits or the stock of public debt.

Although it is only a minor part of the overall statistical picture, the U.S. behavior since 1981 highlights the results about interest rates. Despite high and typically rising real budget deficits from 1981 to 1986, nominal interest rates fell dramatically until recently. Moreover, short-term expected real interest rates fell from 1984 to 1986, and rose in 1989 when the real budget deficit was relatively small.

Overall, the empirical evidence on interest rates supports the Ricardian view. Given these findings, it is remarkable that most people remain confident that budget deficits raise interest rates. Such confidence derives more from repetition of the story than from economic theory or empirical results.

Investment and Saving

The Ricardian model predicts that domestic investment and national saving will not react to an increase in the budget deficit or the stock of public debt. The standard model predicts that domestic investment and national saving will decline in a closed economy, and that national saving will decline in an open economy.

The evidence about the effects of budget deficits on investment and saving is less clear than it is for interest rates. Unfortunately, statistical issues and questions about how to measure investment and saving cause problems in getting definitive answers. For example, in the U.S. data since the mid-1980s, the ratio of a broad concept of real gross investment spending (including purchases of consumer durables) to real GNP is at a post-World War II high, whereas the ratio of the national accounts' concept of net national saving to GNP is low. Thus, the picture depends on issues such as the accuracy of the reported figures on depreciation, the inclusion of purchases of consumer durables as a component of investment and saving, and the distinction between real investment (relative to real GNP) versus nominal investment (relative to nominal GNP).

Because of these problems, I put a lot of weight on some special situations that look more like natural experiments. One such study, carried out by Chris Carroll and Lawrence Summers (1987), compares saving rates in Canada and the United States. They note that the private saving rates in the two countries were similar until the early 1970s, but have since diverged; for 1983–85, the Canadian rate was higher by about six percentage points. After holding fixed some macroeconomic variables and aspects of the tax systems that influence saving, the authors isolate a roughly one-to-one, positive effect of government budget deficits on private saving. That is, the rise in the private saving rate in Canada, relative to that in the United States, reflected the greater increase in the Canadian budget deficit as a ratio to GNP. Thus, as implied by the Ricardian view, the relative values of the national saving rates in the two countries appeared to be invariant with the relative values of the budget deficits.

Recent fiscal policy in Israel comes close to providing a natural experiment for studying the interplay between budget deficits and saving. In 1983, the gross national saving rate of 13 percent consisted of a private saving rate of 17 percent and a public saving rate of -4 percent. In 1984, a dramatic rise in the budget deficit led to a public saving rate of -11 percent. Interestingly, the private saving rate rose to 26 percent, so that the national saving rate changed little; actually rising from 13 to 15 percent. Then the Israeli stabilization program in 1985 eliminated the budget deficit, so that the public saving rate rose from -11 percent in 1984 to values close to 0 in 1985–87. Remarkably, the private saving rate decreased dramatically at the same time, going from 26 percent in 1984 to 19 percent in 1985 and 14 percent in 1986–87. Therefore, national saving rates were relatively stable, going from 15 percent in 1984 to 18 percent in 1985, 14 percent in 1986, and 12 percent in 1987. The main point is that this extreme experiment reveals the roughly one-to-one offset between public and private saving that the Ricardian model predicts.

Finally, Barro and Xavier Sala i Martin (1990) studied the determination of gross investment for 10 major industrialized countries. The overall production of these countries is large enough (about two-thirds of the gross domestic product for the world's market economies) that we can think of the 10-country aggregate of investment as determined in a closed economy that approximates the entire world. The empirical results pinpointed a number of variables that mattered for aggregate investment, including shifts in stock market prices (which reflect changes in the perceived profitability of investment) and movements in oil prices. However, fiscal variables—measured as 10-country aggregates of real budget deficits and stocks of public debt—were insignificantly related to investment (or to real interest rates).

Current-Account Deficits

The Ricardian approach predicts that the current-account deficit would not respond to an increase in the budget deficit, whereas the standard analysis predicts that the current-account deficit would increase. Thus, an advocate of the standard model would emphasize the coincidence of large current-account and budget deficits in the United States since 1983. A careful study of the U.S. time series is, however, less supportive of the standard view that budget deficits lead to current-account deficits. For example, U.S. budget and current-account deficits were virtually uncorrelated from 1948 to 1982. Moreover, the details of the timing after 1982 do not reveal a positive linkage from budget to current-account deficits.

One clue to the recent behavior of the U.S. current account comes from the performance of U.S. investment. As mentioned before, a broad concept of U.S. investment spending (including consumer durables) has been at a post-World War II high in relation to GNP since the mid-1980s. The standard theory of the current account, which stresses high U.S. budget deficits, would predict low, or at best average, U.S. domestic investment. An alternative view is that changes in regulatory and tax policies in the 1980s made investments in the United States more attractive relative to investments in other countries. Unlike the standard view, this approach can explain a high U.S. current-account deficit along with robust investment in the United States.

In a recent study, Paul Evans (1988) carried out an empirical investigation of the relation between budget and current-account deficits in five major industrialized countries (Canada, France, Germany, the United Kingdom, and the United States). His overall finding is that the current account is largely independent of budget deficits. Hence, these results are consistent with the Ricardian position. A priority item on the list of desirable research is more international evidence of this kind.

CONCLUDING OBSERVATIONS

The Ricardian approach to budget deficits amounts to the statement that the government's fiscal impact is summarized by the present value of its expenditures. Given this present value, rearrangements of the timing of taxes—as implied by budget deficits—have no first-order effect on the economy. Second-order effects arise for various reasons, which include the distorting effects of taxes, the uncertainties about individual incomes and tax obligations, the imperfections of credit markets, and the finiteness of life. To say that these effects are second order is not to say that they are uninteresting; in fact, the analysis of different kinds of taxes in the theory of public finance is second order in the same sense. Careful analysis of these second-order effects tends, however, to deliver predictions about budget deficits that usually depart from those of standard macroeconomic models.

I have argued that empirical findings on interest rates, investment and saving, and the current-account balance tend mainly to support the Ricardian viewpoint. However, this empirical analysis involves substantial problems about data and statistical technique, and the results are sometimes inconclusive. It would be useful to assemble additional evidence, especially in an international context.

Although the majority of economists still leans toward standard macroeconomic models of fiscal policy, it is remarkable how respectable the Ricardian approach has become in the last decade. Most macroeconomists now feel obligated to state the Ricardian position, even if they then argue that it is either theoretically or empirically wrong. I predict that this trend will continue and that the Ricardian approach will become the benchmark model for assessing fiscal policy.

Finally, given my view that U.S. budget deficits are not very important, I should comment about why I think the debate about these deficits is so intense and enduring. The likely reason is that the real controversy is about the size of the federal government, rather than the size of the federal deficit. That is, the key question is not whether the deficit will be reduced (as it was from 1987 to 1989), but whether the reduction will involve increases in taxes or cuts in expenditures. Those who argue that taxes must rise (and are dutifully applauded by most of the media as being realistic and courageous) are really saying that they want a larger federal government. Those who rule out tax increases are seeking to maintain or decrease the scope of the government. At least for people who like smaller government, it is these latter politicians who are candidates for heroism. In any event, unlike the budget deficit, the size of government is an important question, which does deserve a lot of attention. Perhaps it would be better if the debate were couched in these terms, rather than in terms of who is or is not realistic or courageous, and who is or is not a fiscal conservative.

NOTES

1. For this proposition to be exact, we have to include the revenue from money creation as a form of tax (the "inflation tax").

2. For a discussion of the behavior of the British public debt during wartime from 1700 to 1918, see Barro (1987).

3. The figures apply, however, to the federal government and not to total government. In particular, state and local governments are combined with the private sector. It would be preferable to look at consolidated government, but the data from the state and local sector are not as good, especially in earlier years.

4. In this case, they also constitute good scientific experiments, because budget deficits run for no good reason make it easier to figure out the consequences of these deficits. Thus, economists who dislike Reagan's fiscal policies on other grounds should at least applaud this contribution to scientific inquiry.

7

U.S. Fiscal Policy in the 1980s: Consequences of Large Budget Deficits at Full Employment

BENJAMIN M. FRIEDMAN

The high-deficit fiscal policy that the United States pursued during the 1980s—and, as of the time of writing, is maintaining into the 1990s—has been an increasingly costly failure. The large gap between the federal government's expenditures and its revenues, which first emerged during the 1981–82 business recession, has persisted long since the U.S. economy returned to approximately full employment. This continuing fiscal imbalance, despite the absence of either war or economic slack, is unprecedented in U.S. history. It has already more than doubled the national debt, even after allowance for inflation, just since 1980. More importantly, the economic consequences of this policy have by now damaged the nation's domestic economic well-being as well as its position in the global economy. If left unchecked, the current high-deficit fiscal policy will continue to erode the nation's long-run prospects both at home and abroad.

The heart of the problem is that, on average since 1980, the borrowing that the U.S. government has had to do in order to cover its unprecedented excess of spending over income has absorbed nearly three-fourths of all net saving done by U.S. individuals and businesses combined. The United States has always been a low-saving country compared with most of its international trading partners and competitors. But in the past, the bulk of what the economy's private sector did save was at least available to finance private investment—including productive new assets for business use, as well as housing for a growing population. By contrast, with so little of the economy's private saving left over for private use in the 1980s, net investment in business plant and machinery fell to a lower share of national income than in the 1950s, the 1960s, or the 1970s. As a result, productivity gains have continued to be disappointing, and wages have lagged, despite the cessation or even reversal of a variety of influences that had retarded U.S. productivity growth earlier on.

A further consequence of the federal deficit's absorbing so much of U.S. private saving since 1980 is that the United States has become dependent on saving provided from abroad. The huge capital inflows that now provide this additional wherewithal to the U.S. financial markets, however, are just the mirror image of U.S. producers' diminished ability to compete in product markets around the world, or even in the United States. The accumulation of such large capital inflows through most of a decade has converted the United States from the world's largest creditor country—providing its investment capital to support other economies around the world and enjoying the leadership position that has always gone along with that role—to the world's largest debtor. As a result, U.S. influence in world affairs has already begun to lessen. Given the nation's new net debtor status, this trend will probably continue even if the United States now somehow manages to balance its imports and its exports (a highly unlikely prospect any time soon, at least under a continuation of the current policy of large budget deficits at full employment).

These two sets of adverse developments were not surprises, but instead the predictable (and widely predicted) consequences of the high-deficit fiscal policy adopted beginning in 1981. The channel of influence running from large budget deficits at full employment to high real interest rates, and from high real interest rates to inadequate investment, sluggish productivity growth, and stagnant real wages, is hardly unfamiliar. Neither is the parallel channel running from high real interest rates to an overvalued currency, and from an overvalued currency to chronic trade deficits, capital inflows, and an ever larger international debt relative to the economy's ability to pay. The only real surprise in what has happened is that the U.S. economy turned out to be sufficiently open that the deterioration of the economy's international position was greater, and the deterioration of its domestic investment correspondingly smaller, than most prior predictions of what this policy would bring had anticipated.

The challenge now facing U.S. economic policy-makers is to adopt some combination of cuts in government spending (at least relative to trend) and increases in government revenues sufficient to place the United States once again on a trajectory consistent with fiscal stability, rising productivity, and international competitiveness. Doing so will not magically erase the damage done by a decade of underinvestment at home and excessive borrowing from abroad. But at least it will put fundamental indicators of the nation's economic health, such as its debt compared with its income, its production compared with its consumption, and its exports compared with its imports, back on a path that is both desirable and sustainable in the long run. The fact that achieving this end will require making choices that may be politically unpopular in the short run does not make doing so any less compelling.

TABLE 7-1

Private Saving, Federal Dissaving, and Private Investment, 1951–89
(Percentages of Gross National Product)

Years	Net Private Saving	Federal Governmental Budget Deficit	Net Investment in Plant and Equipment	Gross Investment in Plant and Equipment
1951–60	7.5	0.2	3.0	9.6
1961–70	8.2	0.5	3.5	9.9
1971–80	8.0	1.8	3.3	10.8
1981–89	5.4	3.9	2.0	10.7

SOURCE: U.S. Department of Commerce.

BUDGET DEFICITS, CAPITAL FORMATION, AND PRODUCTIVITY

The most basic cost of a high-deficit fiscal policy in a low-saving country is no more, and no less, than what any society pays for eating its seed corn rather than planting it. The federal deficit averaged 3.9 percent of U.S. national income during 1981–89, compared with the 5.4 percent of the nation's income that individuals and businesses together managed to save after spending for consumption and for the replacement of physical assets, like houses or machines, that wear out. As a result, the nation's net investment in business plant and equipment fell to a smaller share of national income than in any sustained period since World War II (see Table 7-1). Indeed, net investment spending declined during the 1980s not just compared with national income but absolutely. In 1989, U.S. businesses spent just $84 billion on net investment in new plant and equipment. That was 15 percent less than they spent in 1979. After allowance for inflation, it was 41 percent less than in 1979.

For some purposes, gross investment—that is, investment spending inclusive of the replacement of worn-out assets—may be the better measure of the capital formation that bears on an economy's productivity growth. (This is especially so at times of rapid technical progress, when new plants and machines are qualitatively superior to the old ones they replace.) On this scale too, however, the story of the 1980s is one of decline. Gross business fixed investment was relatively high on average in the 1980s (see again Table 7-1), but only because the starting point inherited from the past was so high. Gross investment in machinery and plant amounted to 12.1 percent of U.S. national income in 1981, but that turned out to be the

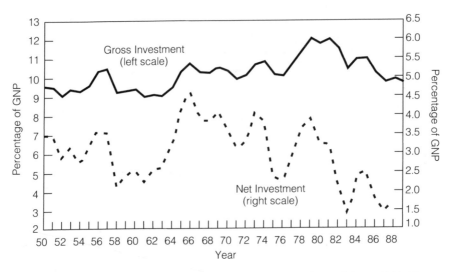

FIGURE 7-1 *Investment in Plant and Equipment as a Share of GNP, 1950–88*

postwar peak and the trend has been downhill ever since. By 1989, the gross investment rate had fallen to just 9.8 percent, a level not experienced since 1964 (see Figure 7-1).

The principal market mechanism that links declining investment to high government deficits at full employment is interest rates—more specifically, interest rates in relation to price inflation. The government's absorption of so much of the economy's available saving forces businesses seeking to finance capital spending, and families hoping to finance new houses, to compete all the harder for the remainder. The result of this heightened competition in the financial markets is that interest rates rise to levels sufficient to discourage enough would-be builders of new facilities or purchasers of new machines, or enough would-be homebuyers, that the amount of investment activity actually undertaken turns out to be no more than what the remaining available saving can finance.

Although many people think of the 1980s as a period of low (or at least declining) interest rates in the United States, this attitude mostly reflects a confusion due to the sharp slowing of inflation. Market interest rates less inflation—that is, the real interest rates that presumably matter for most kinds of investment spending—stood at record highs throughout the decade (see Table 7-2). The market interest rate on short-term borrowing by investment-grade business corporations averaged only 0.85 percent above the ongoing inflation rate during 1951–80. During 1981–89 the average real interest rate for these borrowers was 4.99 percent.

The link between government deficits and real interest rates has been notoriously difficult to document in any irrefutable way. Before the 1980s, U.S. deficits in peacetime had mostly been small and short-lived anyway. Moreover, what few large peacetime deficits there were had typically

TABLE 7-2
Nominal and Real Interest Rates, 1951–89
(Average Percentages per Year)

Years	Commercial Paper Rate	Rate of Price Inflation*	Resulting Real Interest Rate
1951–60	2.87	2.06	0.80
1961–70	5.02	3.28	1.74
1971–80	7.63	7.74	-0.11
1981–89	9.09	4.10	4.99

SOURCE: Board of Governors of the Federal Reserve Board, U.S. Department of Commerce.
*Inflation rate is for the GNP implicit deflator.

occurred either during or immediately after economic downturns (the pre-1981 peak was in 1975), when interest rates were likely to be not higher than usual but lower because of both the sluggish economy and the resulting easy monetary policy. Since 1980, however, the government's deficit has been neither small nor short-lived. More importantly, at least since 1985, the budget has been out of balance not because a slack economy has depressed tax revenues and also boosted some kinds of government spending like unemployment benefits, but simply because of the fundamental imbalance between revenues and expenditures even at full employment (see Figure 7-2).

To be sure, no one can read the experience of the 1980s as evidence that government deficits are all that matters for real interest rates. (Nor would such a claim be consistent with standard economic thinking anyway.) For example, real interest rates rose to what were then record levels for the post-war period in 1980, and again in 1981, before the high-deficit fiscal policy had even begun. Presumably the cause then was monetary policy, which most economists (though surely not all) believe can affect not just nominal interest rates but real rates also, over periods of up to several years. By contrast, the persistence of historically high real interest rates throughout an entire decade (see again Figure 7-2) is unlikely to be a monetary phenomenon.

Given the large deficits, and hence high real interest rates and depressed investment of the 1980s, it is not surprising that the productivity gains achieved by U.S. firms have continued to lag behind those of other major industrialized countries, as well as behind the results achieved by the United States itself in most earlier periods (see Table 7-3). This outcome is all the more disappointing in that several of the other forces that typically affect business performance improved sharply in the 1980s. During the late 1960s and most of the 1970s, for example, the coming of age of the post-war baby-boom generation had swelled the labor force with new workers,

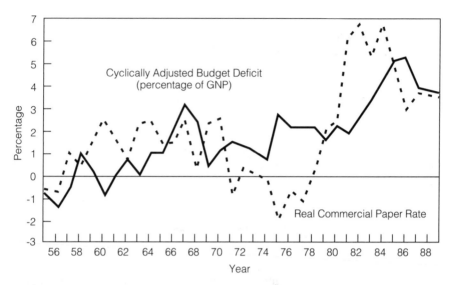

FIGURE 7-2 *Budget Deficits and Real Interest Rates, 1955–89*

so that the average age and experience level of workers on the job was declining. The inflow of new workers subsided in the 1980s, and today U.S. workers on average are older and more experienced than they were a decade ago. Similarly, energy prices rose rapidly in the mid- and late 1970s, discouraging many forms of labor-saving investment. In the 1980s, energy prices fell sharply. Business spending on research and development slowed in the 1970s, but regained strength in the 1980s. The capital investment needed to meet environmental regulations was a major drain on many industries in the 1970s, but much less so in the 1980s.

But the weakness in business investment has simply overwhelmed these favorable developments. In contrast to the record of prior decades, the amount of capital at the disposal of the average worker in the private sector of the U.S. economy has shown little increase since 1980 (see again Table 7-3) despite the fact that, with slower labor force growth, merely maintaining the same increase in the capital–labor ratio as in the past would have taken less new capital formation. After rising from $26,100 per worker in 1948 to $44,900 in 1979 (where both are stated in 1989 dollars), the amount of plant and equipment in U.S. business was still just $49,200 per worker in 1989.

Some observers of these events have claimed that government deficits do not matter for business investment, usually attempting to demonstrate the lack of any connection by pointing to the example of Japan, where the deficit has historically been larger (compared with national income) than in the United States, yet investment has been ample, and productivity and living standards have risen rapidly. What this argument ignores is that the Japanese also save far more of their incomes than Americans do—between two and three times as much, depending on conventions of measurement.

TABLE 7-3
Productivity, Wages, and Capital Intensity, 1948–89
*(Percentage Average Growth Rates per Year)**

Years	Growth in Output per Hour Worked	Growth in Capital per Worker	Growth in Real Wages
1948–65	2.7	2.1	3.0
1965–73	2.0	1.7	2.3
1973–79	0.6	0.7	0.5
1979–89	1.2	0.7†	0.3

SOURCE: U.S. Department of Labor, U.S. Department of Commerce.

*Productivity and wage data are for the nonfarm business sector. Capital per worker includes the entire private economy. Wage and capital data are in real terms.
†Indicates average for 1979–88 only.

If the United States had a private saving rate like Japan's, it too could run a high deficit and still have plenty of saving left to finance investment both at home and overseas. International comparisons of net national saving rates (that is, net private saving rates plus the overall government surplus or minus the overall government deficit), net investment rates, and growth of productivity and living standards deliver a consistent story (see Table 7-4). Among the world's five major economies, Japan ranks first in all four of these categories, Germany and France are always second and third, and Britain is usually fourth. Except for growth in consumption, where ever greater borrowing has kept the party going despite the lack of production to support it, the United States is consistently last.

Similarly, some people have argued that the current U.S. policy of high deficits even at full employment has not been harmful—indeed, is positively healthy—because the government is "using" the deficit to finance investment in infrastructure like roads, bridges, port facilities, and research stations. If that were so, then the government would be doing no more than what any soundly run business does when it relies on debt to finance capital installations that will be productive over a long period of time. Indeed, there is evidence that such public investments might, if carefully made, enhance the nation's productivity just as much as, and perhaps even more than, private investment in new plant and machines. If so, there is surely nothing wrong with using scarce private saving in this way. The same argument applies to investment in "human capital" through education.

But it is simply not true that such investment activity accounts for the high deficit that the United States has maintained since 1980. Some economists point to the fixed assets that the U.S. government owns—ranging from military installations to office buildings to undeveloped public lands—as if their existence somehow nullified the economic impact of the

TABLE 7-4

International Comparisons of Saving and Investment, and Growth of Productivity and Living Standards*

	Net National Saving Rate	Net National Investment Rate	Growth of Output per Worker	Growth of Consumption per Capita
Japan	20.5%	18.4%	4.7%	4.9%
Germany	13.9	12.0	2.8	3.1
France	12.2	11.2	3.0	3.4
United Kingdom	8.2	8.0	2.2	2.3
United States	7.6	6.8	0.7	2.4

SOURCE: OECD.

*Saving and investment data are averages of annual percentages of GNP for 1960–88. Productivity and consumption data are average per annum growth rates, for 1967–87 in the case of productivity and 1961–88 in the case of consumption.

government's current borrowing. But such an inventory of assets accumulated in the past says nothing about the purposes for which the government is currently absorbing so much of the nation's private saving. In fact, just as the federal deficit rose to record magnitude after 1980, the share of federal spending devoted to investment that might plausibly improve productivity shrank to an all-time low. During 1981–89, investment in all civilian infrastructure activities accounted for just 1.2 percent of federal spending. Spending on education, by both federal and state and local government, has been either stagnant or declining.

In the end, the fact that the United States has not been investing adequately in any of the makings of a strong economy—not business plant and equipment, nor public infrastructure, nor a well-trained work force—has already resulted in the first business expansion since the 1930s in which the average wage paid to workers in U.S. business has not even kept pace with inflation. The 1980s may have been a success in terms of what Americans spent and consumed, but not in terms of what they produced and earned (see again Table 7-3). In 1983, the average U.S. worker earned $281 per week. By year-end 1989, the average weekly paycheck, stated in 1983 dollars, was just $271. To continue on with the current policy of high deficits at full employment probably means more of the same.

INTERNATIONAL IMPLICATIONS

Because the United States is not a closed economy, but rather one country operating in an increasingly integrated structure of world markets, there has been a second, and perhaps even more worrisome, cost of the high-deficit

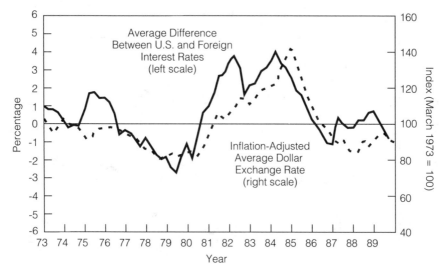

FIGURE 7-3 *Real Dollar Exchange Rates and Real Interest Rate Differentials, 1973–89*

fiscal policy of the 1980s. U.S. real interest rates in the 1980s were high not just by the standards of prior U.S. experience but also compared with what investors could get in other countries. Foreign investors therefore competed among themselves to acquire dollars with which to buy high-interest U.S. bonds and other dollar IOUs, and for half a decade the dollar became ever more expensive in relation to other countries' currencies (see Figure 7-3). As the dollar rose, the ability of U.S. industries to compete with foreign producers all but collapsed, not only overseas but in home markets too.

With the dollar so overvalued, the United States therefore increased what it consumed faster than what it produced, not only because the nation failed to invest adequately but also because it increasingly used overvalued dollars to import more than it exported. The $25 billion gap between U.S. merchandise imports and exports in 1980, considered a major problem at the time, grew to $160 billion in 1987 (see Figure 7-4). As the country paid for this growing excess, it sent more and more dollars abroad, and foreigners then invested these funds in U.S. financial markets. Indeed, because so little of what Americans saved was left over after the government financed its deficit, this re-investment of U.S. dollars by foreign lenders has accounted for most of the inadequate supply of capital that U.S. business has had available for investment in recent years. In 1989, total gross investment in new plant and equipment by U.S. business was $512 billion, or only $84 billion beyond the mere replacement of worn-out facilities. The net flow of investable funds into U.S. markets from abroad in 1989 came to $97 billion.

As the U.S. trade deficit continued to grow throughout the 1980s, the resulting accumulation of dollars in foreign hands gradually saturated the foreign appetite for dollar-denominated assets and therefore eventually

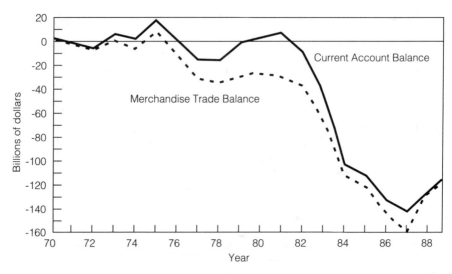

FIGURE 7-4   *U.S. International Position, 1970–89*

drove the dollar back down. By 1988, the dollar was about back to where it was in 1980. With the dollar cheaper, the U.S. trade deficit began to shrink. But since then the dollar has risen again, and the improvement in the trade balance has likewise stalled. Moreover, a projection to 1990 of the trends that had characterized long-run exchange rate relationships before 1980 suggests that even if the dollar were now at the 1980 level, it would still be overvalued by some 20–30 percent.

Further, even if the dollar were correctly valued in the financial markets, a return to balance in U.S. international trade would still take time, in large part because the country has underinvested in its economy as a whole and especially in industries like manufacturing in which U.S. firms compete against foreign producers. The United States is increasingly learning that a cheaper dollar by itself is not enough. Its industries must also have the capacity to produce enough of what people at home and abroad want to buy.

Even more important in terms of long-run implications, as a result of excessive borrowing the United States has, within less than a decade, dissipated its net international holdings and run up the world's largest net debt. Now, therefore, there is not one debt problem but two: the debt that the U.S. government owes as a result of borrowing to finance its string of record budget deficits, and the debt that the United States as a national economy owes as a result of borrowing from abroad to finance its string of record trade deficits. Even if U.S. imports and exports somehow regained the equilibrium they had displayed for so many years until the 1980s, the United States' new international burden would not disappear.

The excess of imports over exports that the United States ran throughout the 1980s meant that Americans spent far more, on all goods and services combined, than the nation produced. Between 1980 and 1989, total spending in the United States—including consumer spending, all business and residential investment, and all spending by government other than mere transfers and interest payments—rose by 34 percent after allowance for inflation. But total U.S. production rose by only 30 percent during these years. The widening gap between what Americans spent and what they produced required importing an ever greater volume of goods produced abroad, in excess of the U.S.-made goods exported for use elsewhere.

The problem is that Americans also had to pay for this excess, and they did so by borrowing from abroad. As they borrowed from foreigners, in even larger amounts, to finance the growing gap between the goods they bought and the goods they sold, the debt they owed to foreigners accumulated. It has already far eclipsed the debt that foreigners owe to Americans, and it will continue to accumulate as long as the country's international trade remains out of balance. Even on the most optimistic trajectory, the debt that the United States owes abroad (over and above what foreigners owe the United States) will continue to grow in relation to U.S. income for several more years. Indeed, it is not implausible that the country may, not long thereafter, reach a debt-to-income ratio comparable to that of many of today's hard-pressed developing countries.

Like any newly developing country, especially one that was a colony of a larger and older country, the United States too began its economic life as a net borrower from abroad. Foreign borrowing was especially important to U.S. economic development during four key periods, all during the nineteenth century. But by the early 1890s, much of the nation's rail and telegraph network was in place, and so were the makings of its new industrial base. Just as importantly, incomes were higher, and therefore so was the country's own available saving. The United States had grown past its period of need for foreign capital. Net inflows of foreign saving, in excess of outflows of U.S. saving, slowed sharply in the early 1890s. From 1897 on, Americans were investing more of their own saving abroad than the amounts of foreign saving that they took in. Apart from World War II and a few other scattered years, they continued to do so until 1982.

As the United States after 1896 continued to be a net supplier of saving to foreign countries, rather than a net user of other countries' saving, the accumulated U.S. net foreign debt shrank. Two decades proved sufficient to eliminate this net indebtedness altogether. The last year in which Americans owed more abroad than foreigners owed them was in 1914. U.S. foreign lending surged to new record volumes as World War I began, and early in 1915 the United States became a net creditor. For the next 6 1/2 decades, the United States continued to be a net lender to the rest of the world in almost every year. As it did so, the U.S. net foreign asset position steadily grew, eventually reaching a peak of $141 billion in 1981.

The reversal of the U.S. international financial position since then has been just as spectacular as the decline in the country's competitiveness that lay behind it. The United States officially became a net debtor country again in early 1985. By the end of that year, foreign assets in the United States exceeded Americans' foreign assets by $111 billion—almost as much as the difference going the other way had been, just a few years earlier. The United States' net foreign borrowing *in just one year* had exceeded the entire outstanding indebtedness of Mexico or Brazil. Since then the pace has quickened. By year-end 1988, the U.S. net foreign debt was $533 billion, twice as much as that of Mexico, Brazil, and Argentina combined. By year-end 1989, it was probably in the $650–700 billion range, even still counting all of U.S. banks' foreign loans at 100 cents on the dollar. Estimates of a net debt position surpassing $1 trillion by early in the 1990s, which once seemed absurd, now appear to be a virtual certainty.[1]

Net foreign debt on even the current scale has already placed the United States at the top of the roster of world-class debtors. Worse still, the United States is rapidly becoming more heavily indebted than any other major country, even in relation to its large size. The $650–700 billion that the nation probably owed on a net basis at the end of 1989 represented roughly 13 percent of the country's total income for that year—a large net debt ratio, to be sure, but still well below comparable net foreign debt ratios in the range of 20 percent for Argentina, 30 percent for Brazil, or 40 percent for Mexico. But if the U.S. net foreign debt continues to grow at the current rate of $150 billion per year, while national income grows at 7 percent per annum, the U.S. net debt position will reach 20 percent of U.S. income by 1995.

In 1980, the United States could easily afford its $25 billion excess of merchandise imports over merchandise exports, because it also earned $36 billion more on its foreign holdings than foreign investors earned on their U.S. holdings. That advantage, however, depended largely on owning more assets abroad than foreigners owned here. Now the high-deficit fiscal policy has dissipated the differential in ownership, changing what used to be a net foreign *asset* position into a net foreign *debt* position. As a result, the U.S. surplus of income earned from foreign assets is shrinking, and in time it too will disappear. After it does, the only way the United States will be able to avoid running up an ever larger net foreign debt position is for Americans to live on less than what they produce and earn. The fact that the incomes out of which they will have to pay debt service to foreigners will already be diminished, as a result of inadequate capital formation and sluggish productivity growth, will only make the resulting deterioration in the country's ability to raise its citizens' standard of living all the greater.

In short, the United States as a debtor nation will have to maintain a continual trade surplus. But the proceeds of that surplus will not accumulate into wealth held abroad by Americans, nor even go toward reducing U.S. international indebtedness. Net proceeds from international trade in the amount of 1–2 percent of the country's total income will merely be enough to pay the interest on the debt already owed as of the end of the 1980s. Actually paying down this debt, as the United States did between the mid-1890s and the beginning of World War I, would require an even larger trade surplus.

When and how the United States will make the major adjustment that moving from trade deficit to trade surplus involves is not entirely, or even largely, up to this country's discretion. As is the case for any kind of borrower, after some point a debtor country's ability to keep increasing what it owes depends mostly on choices made by others. In this case, the speed and extent of the adjustment that the U.S. economy must make will mostly depend on how much appetite foreign investors have for owning assets in this country. As long as foreign investors continue to want to increase their holdings in the United States rapidly enough, compared with the pace at which Americans are increasing their holdings of assets abroad, this country can continue to borrow what it needs to pay interest on its outstanding international debt and finance an ongoing excess of imports over exports. But the ability to do so will hinge crucially on foreigners' continuing demand to own ever more U.S. assets—importantly including not just debt instruments (issued by the U.S. Treasury, U.S. banks, or yet other private U.S. borrowers) but also equity securities and the entire available range of direct investments.

Once foreign investors have accumulated enough holdings in the United States that they are increasing their ownership of U.S. assets no more rapidly than Americans are increasing their ownership of assets abroad, the United States will not even be able to borrow the debt service it owes—much less finance a continuing trade deficit. It is at this point that the U.S. trade balance will have to move into surplus in order to enable the country to earn, not borrow, whatever it needs to pay the interest and dividends it must pay each year to foreigners. The dollar will then have to fall to whatever level is necessary to enable U.S. exports to exceed U.S. imports, by at least enough to earn each year's debt service. A continuing inability of U.S. industry to compete even at a lower exchange rate, or a continuing large appetite of Americans for foreign-made goods even at higher prices, means only that the dollar will have to fall so much further.

What will make servicing the U.S. foreign debt all the harder at this point is that in the 1980s the United States borrowed not to invest, but to consume. After all, issuing debt in order to finance new facilities is standard practice for most soundly run businesses. And most developing countries rely heavily on net inflows of foreign capital to finance their early industrialization—as the United States did in the nineteenth century. If a business is successful, it will earn enough revenue from its new facilities to service its debt, and add to its profits too. If a country's economic development is successful, as the United States' was, it will generate enough income to service the country's foreign debt and also raise its citizens' standard of living.

But the United States in the 1980s has been running up foreign debt without putting up domestic investment. Whether or not the returns from the country's additional capital formation might prove sufficient to finance the country's foreign debt service is not an issue, because there has been no additional capital formation in the first place. In large part because of the high-deficit fiscal policy, the share of U.S. income going into net business investment in the 1980s has not been greater than ever before, but smaller (see again Table 7-1).

Americans since 1980 have been borrowing from foreign lenders on a scale that exceeds even what their great-grandparents borrowed during the peak period of U.S. foreign borrowing, in the late 1860s and early 1870s. Even at this previous height of the country's reliance on foreign capital— to finance its expanding railroads, its new steel industry, and the beginnings of its manufacturing industries—the annual net inflow of saving from abroad averaged just 2.2 percent of annual U.S. income. Since 1985, when the U.S. economy regained approximately full employment but large government deficits continued on anyway, each year's net inflow of saving from abroad has averaged 2.7 percent of yearly U.S. income.

But unlike a century ago, the United States since 1980 has simply borrowed to maintain an artificially inflated level of consumer spending. In the United States in the 1980s, there was no equivalent to a transcontinental railroad link, or Carnegie's new steel works, or New England's manufacturing plants—only higher levels of consumer spending, compared with the country's total income, than ever before.

MISLEADING ASSUMPTIONS

How was all this allowed to happen? Understanding the impetus behind the adoption of a fiscal policy that broke so dramatically with nearly two centuries of prior U.S. experience is presumably more a matter of politics, or sociology, than economics. Even so, several major lines of economic thinking probably played some part at least in enabling advocates of the tax and spending measures that formed the basis of this policy to construct an internally coherent (albeit badly mistaken) case for them.

The first of these mistakes was to overestimate—not just at the usual margin of debate about economic uncertainties, but by a whole new order of magnitude—the effect of across-the-board tax rate reductions in stimulating individuals' work effort. In the 1980 presidential campaign, Ronald Reagan argued that these incentive effects would be sufficient to deliver higher tax *revenues* despite lower tax *rates*, and do so even within one year's time. Some well-known economists made the same argument, although with a two-year horizon. With lower tax rates, it would therefore be possible to balance the government's budget despite the sharp increases in military spending that Reagan was proposing, and without having to cut or eliminate nondefense programs that citizens genuinely valued. The potential consequences of government deficits were simply not an issue, because the government would run no deficits.

Lower tax rates do provide incentive effects of many kinds, but the effect on work effort is nowhere near what the architects of the new fiscal policy apparently expected. Nor was there any real basis for this expectation in the first place. The evidence on U.S. labor supply behavior that was available in 1980 pointed to only a modest positive effect of lower tax rates on individuals' overall work effort. The experience since the Economic Recovery Tax Act of 1981 cut tax rates across the board by 25 percent has been consistent with that evidence.

In retrospect, the idea that reducing tax rates in an across-the-board fashion would increase tax revenues, and thereby finance a major defense build-up without cuts in major spending programs like Social Security or Medicare, was a joke. Although President Reagan consistently blamed Congress for the deficits that averaged $180 billion per year during 1982–88 (the 1981 budget was still President Carter's), the difference between the spending that Congress voted and what he proposed—including defense and nondefense programs—averaged only $17 billion during these years. Even if Congress had adopted each of the Reagan budgets down to the last dollar item, the aggregate deficit for these years would have been not even 10 percent smaller. The real cause of the deficits the government ran during these years was that Congress approved the Kemp–Roth tax cut, which President Reagan strongly supported, without matching spending cuts that neither Congress nor the president was willing to propose. The same overall policy remains in place as of the time of writing.

The second major assumption lending support to a policy of high deficits even at full employment was that higher interest rates—after taxes, and after inflation—would spur people to save more out of what they earn. A higher saving rate would have been essential to boosting the country's investment rate even if the government budget had actually remained in balance. The emergence of a chronic deficit of large magnitude, which itself absorbed large flows of saving, only made the need for a higher saving rate all the greater. Supposedly, the way to deliver that additional saving was a higher rate of return for savers, to be realized through lower tax rates, slower inflation,[2] and a more profitable overall business climate.

By contrast, one of the strongest lessons of the 1980s is that higher after-tax real rates of return do not reliably stimulate saving. Even as of 1980, there was no solid evidence to support the belief that higher interest rates elicit greater saving. But now the experience of the 1980s has dramatically contradicted this idea. Interest rates have been at record levels compared with inflation throughout the decade, and marginal tax rates have fallen sharply. Inflation has slowed. Specifically targeted tax incentives, like the opportunity to contribute to Individual Retirement Accounts (IRAs), have been available for most families (fewer after the 1986 tax reform). Notwithstanding all that, the economy's net private saving, measuring the saving of both businesses and individuals, has not risen but fallen (see again Table 7-1). So has the more familiar personal saving rate out of disposable income (see Figure 7-5). Instead of more saving, to finance the government's swollen requirements and perhaps some additional investment too, there has been less.

The third potentially supporting assumption behind the new fiscal policy was that the mere fact of all that government borrowing, once it

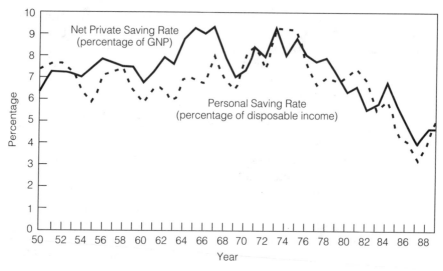

FIGURE 7-5   *Private-Sector Saving, 1950–1989*

became known, would by itself stimulate more saving. After all, why is taking money away from the private sector by selling Treasury bonds any different from taking the money by collecting taxes? If people know that the government is borrowing instead of collecting taxes—so the argument goes—they will cut back their spending anyway, in order to save for the day when the government finally will have to raise their taxes to pay the interest due on what it owes. Even huge government deficits therefore need not diminish what the country is able to invest, nor damage its international competitiveness by forcing it to rely on extra saving drawn in from abroad.

It is true, of course, that taxes and government borrowing are both ways of taking money from the private sector. But the two are not equivalent. Taxes, especially on individuals' incomes, force changes in spending that government borrowing does not. After all, that is why taxes are unpopular. The idea that people will maintain the same spending as before despite a rise in taxes, simply financing their higher tax payments by reducing what they save, is irrelevant for families who do no saving anyway. The idea that people will maintain their spending when taxes go up by borrowing more on their own, in order to finance the higher tax payments, is likewise irrelevant for families with no ability to borrow. Detailed studies of income and spending patterns suggest that as many as one-half of all U.S. families either do substantially no saving, or have no practical ability to borrow, or both.

Moreover, even families whose spending is not so tightly constrained by their after-tax incomes may still regard the government's borrowing as far from equivalent to their own. At the most practical level, few individuals can borrow money at anything like the interest rate that the government pays on Treasury securities. Why should they be indifferent to whether they borrow on their own or the government borrows for them? Having the government borrow at a lower interest rate than they can get reduces the cost of deferring their tax payments from today into the future. By doing so it enables them to spend more, either now or later, or perhaps both now and later.

Even if someone did regard government borrowing as just deferring payments from the present into the future on a fully equivalent basis, any individual's responsibility for meeting those payments could be greater or smaller than if they were due right away. Some people will retire, and therefore fall into lower tax brackets. Others will die and pay no taxes at all. In either case, they will increase their saving in response to the fact of government borrowing only if they are somehow trying to pre-fund future tax payments to be levied not on them but on their heirs (if they plan to leave estates at all). Moreover, as the country's population grows, as a result of ordinary demographics as well as immigration, the average taxpayer's share of whatever taxes are deferred will shrink over time anyway.

Finally, even the basic premise that taxes deferred by government borrowing necessarily lead to taxes levied in the future ignores the important possibility that inflation will serve as a substitute for those taxes by reducing the real value of the government's debt once it is outstanding. If investors who buy the government's securities fully anticipate whatever inflation will occur, then interest rates will have to be higher to compensate them for their loss, and so taxes will have to be higher too. But investors do not always know what the future will bring. If inflation takes them by surprise, once they already own government bonds bearing fixed interest payments, then the loss of value on these bonds takes the place of taxes that the government would otherwise have to collect.

Americans need look no further back than the experience of the past two decades to find ample demonstration that when the federal government borrows, it sometimes ultimately imposes the cost on bond investors rather than collecting ordinary taxes. The record of losses that bond investors suffered when both inflation and interest rates rose in the sixties and seventies suggests that investors are not always adept at spotting such trends before they start, or even while they are developing. Who can be confident today that the government will not eventually choose to deal in the same way with the enormous debt it has run up in the 1980s?

In the end, the experience of the 1980s dramatically contradicted this line of thinking too. Government *dis*saving compared with national income rose to peacetime record levels, and remained. Private saving, instead of increasing so as to leave the overall national saving rate unchanged, actually declined as well (see again Figure 7-5). The U.S. national saving rate therefore declined not just fully in pace with the increase in government saving, but even somewhat more (see Figure 7-6).

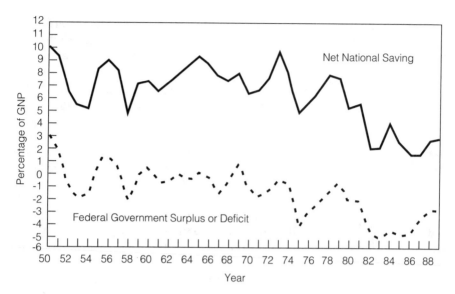

FIGURE 7-6   *National Saving and Government Dissaving, 1950–89*

WRONG CONCLUSIONS

As is probably inevitable in any discussion of complex matters of great public import, the debate over the U.S. high-deficit fiscal policy and what to do about it has not only embraced some misleading prior assumptions but also generated more than a few misperceptions after the fact. Perhaps the most straightforward of these is that the deficit is somehow going away on its own, and therefore that nothing need be done. During the 1988 presidential election campaign, for example, George Bush repeatedly called attention to the decline in the deficit from $221 billion in the 1985 fiscal year to $155 billion in fiscal 1988. But that pace of improvement has not continued. The deficit in fiscal 1989 was $152 billion. As of the time of writing, the most recent official deficit projection for fiscal 1990 is $218 billion—almost as large as in 1985—or $161 billion without counting the savings-and-loan bailout.

More importantly, virtually all of even the very limited improvement that has occurred since the mid-1980s has merely reflected the Social Security System's growing surplus—a surplus created by increases in the payroll tax for the explicit purpose of boosting national saving, not just to offset ever greater government dissaving. The 1988 overall deficit of $155 billion, to which Mr. Bush pointed as evidence of great progress, represented a $41 billion surplus for Social Security together with a $196 billion deficit for everything else the government does. The slight further improvement to a $152 billion overall deficit in 1989 was actually the combination of a $52 billion Social Security surplus and a $205 billion general account deficit. The latest "baseline" projection by the U.S. Congressional Budget Office, representing its judgment of the most likely outcome under a continuation of current tax and spending policies, shows a further widening of the general account deficit in every coming year to 1995. Whatever one may think of the deficit and its consequences, high deficits even at full employment remain the fiscal policy of the U.S. government.

A second major misperception that the debate over the deficit has spawned is that the resulting overconsumption, underinvestment, and foreign borrowing have all had no serious implications, and indeed will have none in the future. This argument is wrong even in retrospect, in that it ignores the stagnation of real wages in the current business expansion, as well as the episodic loss of influence that the new U.S. status as a debtor nation has already brought. It also ignores the devastation of the economy's agricultural sector and many of its key manufacturing industries—automobiles, steel, and electric machinery—in the years when the dollar was especially overvalued. It also ignores other U.S. industries' continuing loss of sales to firms from countries where production costs are lower, in part because U.S. firms have underinvested.

Even so, it is true that the most important costs of the current high-deficit fiscal policy are not dramatic and obvious, but subtle and gradually corrosive over time. Moreover, it is also true that the costs incurred to date are small compared with those that are likely in the future.

Power and influence in world affairs have historically accrued to creditor countries. People simply do not view their debtors in the same light as they do their creditors. It is no accident that the United States emerged as a major world power simultaneously with its transition from a debtor nation, dependent on foreign capital for its initial industrialization, to a creditor supplying investment capital to the rest of the world. The same situation occurred in Spain in the sixteenth century, in Holland in the seventeenth century, and in Britain in the nineteenth century.

But the United States is now a debtor country again, and its future role in world affairs is in question. If the country continues on its current trajectory, over time that role will gradually shift to Japan and Germany, or still other new creditor countries that are able to supply resources where the United States cannot, and U.S. influence over nations and events will ebb. Watching its economic power shift to these new creditors as they begin to finance the exciting evolution of Eastern European countries into market economies, for example, or cope with the developing world's debt, or step in to prevent a "dollar crisis"—in each case, presumably in ways that promote their own commercial or diplomatic advantage—is part of the price the United States will have to pay for its high-deficit fiscal policy.

Most Americans continue to think of themselves as creditors, and the United States readily offers unsolicited advice to other debtor countries, as if they had fallen into a trap that this country had successfully avoided. At the same time, the Japanese and Germans often still appear to think of themselves as debtors. But attitudes toward world leadership will change soon enough, as the United States' own financial problems increasingly circumscribe its scope for maneuver in world affairs while the new creditors' financial strength does the opposite. The contrast between the U.S. role in supporting the post-war development of Western Europe via the Marshall Plan, and its virtual absence from current post-Communism development efforts in Eastern Europe, is just one striking example. Just how large a departure from recent history the resulting new international arrangements will represent is impossible to say. But especially in light of the astonishing events now taking place not only throughout Eastern Europe but even in the Soviet Union, continuing to rely on U.S. military prowess to guarantee the nation's international clout, when its underlying economic basis is being dissipated, is a highly risky strategy at best.

And at home, to persist in a policy of high deficits at full employment—and simply sustain the resulting underinvestment, slow productivity growth, and stagnant wages that stem from it—is, in the long run, to risk the material basis for what has been unique about the "American experiment" since its beginnings. The continued dedication to the ideal of forward progress, which has shaped U.S. thinking in so many different spheres of the nation's activity, would surely have been difficult if not impossible to maintain without the fact of a standard of living that roughly doubled once per generation. Over time, therefore, the fact of continual economic progress affected the character of U.S. society in the broadest possible terms.

A rising standard of living is worth having not only on its own account but, even more so, because it provides the material basis for a free and democratic society. The nature of the choices any society has to make is bound to be different when its citizens' incomes are regularly doubling every generation than when incomes stagnate. The openness, the social mobility, the commitment to individual opportunity, and the tolerance of diversity that have given U.S. society its unique flavor are all inseparable from a continually rising overall living standard. So is the ability to make crucial choices, affecting the shares of competing groups in the nation's output, without destructive social conflict.

But all this depends on progress and continuity—and hence on achieving adequate rates of saving and of investment in productive business assets as well as in the nation's stocks of housing and social capital. How will the attitudes of the first generation of Americans to live no better than their parents differ from the attitudes of Americans in the past? How long will it take before the social rigidity, the political divisiveness, and the acceptance of mediocrity characteristic of economically stagnant societies elsewhere set in here too? Which of the United States' open and democratic institutions can survive the more fractious disputes over a national income that is not growing? Questions like these are what the long-run consequences of a fiscal policy based on high deficits at full employment are all about. The fact that there are no straightforward, simple answers cannot make the issue go away.

HARD CHOICES

Finally, it is also wrong to conclude that all this is some kind of historical inevitability, about which nothing can now be done. To be sure, no change of policy, economic or other, can now neatly restore the damage done by the high-deficit policy of the 1980s. The assets that this policy has dissipated are gone. The debts that both the federal government and the nation as a whole have incurred under it are real. The full impact of these new economic facts has not yet reduced U.S. living standards, because the excess of consumption over income that the deficit fosters is still under way. But the overconsumption cannot go on forever, because the burden of both the domestic debt and the foreign debt will continue to mount until, as many developing countries have found, no one is willing to hold either.

To limit the damage means, in the first place, not committing so much of U.S. private saving, and foreign borrowing, to finance the federal deficit. Even so, there is nothing magic about balancing the budget. There are times when either a deficit or a surplus is more appropriate to the nation's economic needs. Moreover, simply matching government income and expenditure makes even less sense when accounts are as crudely and arbitrarily measured as the U.S. government's. There is no reason to think that the many mismeasurements and outright omissions that are by now so familiar simply offset one another.

The best measure of a government's fiscal position, over long periods, is whether its debt is rising or falling compared with the country's national income. Throughout two centuries of U.S. peacetime experience—until the 1980s—the federal government's debt was almost always declining in relation to U.S. national income. The ratio of federal debt to income rose, sometimes sharply, in each of the wars the United States fought. But once each war ended, the government returned to repaying that debt, if not through outright budget surpluses then at least in the economic sense that, if the debt rose at all, it rose less rapidly than the nation's income. The only exception—again, until the 1980s—was in the early 1930s, at the bottom of the Great Depression.

By contrast, under the policy of high deficits even at full employment, the outstanding federal debt rose from 26 cents for each dollar of national income in 1980 to 43 cents in 1987. Since then, under the pressure of restraint in federal spending (including a reversal in the build-up of defense spending relative to income, which characterized most of the Reagan years), as well as the accumulation in the Social Security Trust Fund, the debt ratio has held about steady at that level.

The chief aim of U.S. fiscal policy in the aftermath of the 1980s should now be to restore the federal debt to a solidly declining trajectory compared with the nation's income (and to do so without rekindling inflation). A declining ratio of debt to income will mark a return to the traditional U.S. fiscal posture. The 1980s will then have been a highly costly, one-time aberration. The nation will no longer be following a policy that is obviously unstable in the long run.

Moreover, in calculating the ratio of federal debt to national income, this fiscal policy strategy should not take into account the accumulating Social Security surpluses (to recall, already $52 billion in 1989, and growing much larger in the 1990s). To do so would defeat the purpose for which Social Security contribution rates were raised in 1983, namely to increase national saving so as to enable the Social Security system to cope with the burdens it will face early in the next century, when the aging of the postwar baby boom generation will sharply raise the number of retirees receiving benefits compared with the number of workers making contributions. Without these surpluses now, there will be no choice but to raise payroll taxes for that era's workers to unacceptably high levels, or reduce benefits sharply—just the outcomes that the 1983 legislation was intended to avoid. The target of a declining ratio of federal debt outstanding to national income should therefore include whatever amount of federal debt the Social Security Trust Fund may accumulate, and the budget deficit for purposes of this target should likewise include whatever part of each year's deficit the Social Security surplus may appear on paper to offset.

One way to meet this target is to implement substantial cuts in government spending. Smoke-and-mirrors accounting gimmicks are beside the point, as are sales of government-owned assets (which absorb private saving, just like sales of Treasury bills). Making genuine progress in narrowing the deficit means making genuine cuts in federal programs.

The notion that there are no possible areas in which to make these cuts is simply wrong. The U.S. Congressional Budget Office's annual publication titled "Reducing the Deficit: Spending and Revenue Options" typically lists about 100 possibilities, ranging from the tiny to the huge. What is presumably impossible, however, is finding spending cuts that are politically painless. Rhetoric about needless government programs notwithstanding, more than three-fourths of all federal spending now goes for defense, Social Security, Medicare and Medicaid, and interest on the national debt. And the remaining one-fourth includes such items as federal law enforcement, the courts, drug enforcement, U.S. embassies abroad, the immigration authority, tax collection, highway construction, the space program, the national parks, disaster relief, public health, public housing, veterans' benefits, federal civilian and military retirement pensions, and child nutrition.

The relevant question is not whether it is possible to identify further potential reductions in government spending. There is no lack of possibilities. The real issue is whether citizens actually want to implement these potential cuts, in sufficient magnitude to bring total government spending into line with total government revenues. The standard political rhetoric of the 1980s has repeatedly asserted that a consensus for such cuts exists. But the experience of the 1980s, including the fact that President Reagan's total spending requests came so close to the total spending actually voted by Congress, suggests that it does not. Even in the wake of the remarkable turnaround in U.S.–Soviet relations and in the political posture of Eastern Europe, there has been little consensus on the need for *specific* cuts in defense spending. With so much of the nation's military budget now, in effect, part of the welfare state—including not just low-income jobs on military bases, but also high-income jobs in defense industries—it is not hard to see why.

The other possibility, of course, is a tax increase. With enough spending cuts, it may be possible to do the rest of the job with such standard "revenue enhancements" as higher taxes on gasoline, tobacco, and alcohol, and higher user fees for services that the government provides. (Many of these devices are attractive, in that they serve other objectives beyond merely raising revenues.) Otherwise, solving the problem will require either an increase in income tax rates or the introduction of some new kind of tax. A consumption tax would probably be preferable, for reasons of economic efficiency and incentives.[3] So would a value-added tax.[4] But if nobody has the will to reopen the debate about what form of tax structure the United States should have, it is worth remembering that merely raising the two benchmark rates in the current income tax schedule from 15 percent and 28 percent today to 17 percent and 30 percent, respectively, would generate more than $50 billion per year of additional revenue.

From an economic perspective, it makes little difference which of these routes to correcting its chronic fiscal imbalance—spending cuts or tax increases—the United States takes. A combination of the two would also suffice, of course, and in the end that solution is probably the more likely on political grounds. But in contrast to any of these actions, the fiscal policy that the United States pursued in the 1980s was based on tax cuts not matched by spending cuts, and therefore on continuing large deficits even with the economy at full employment. That is the contrast that matters.

NOTES

This paper draws on my recent research and writings, including especially *Day of Reckoning: The Consequences of American Economic Policy Under Reagan and After*, New York: Random House, 1988.

1. Although public discussion of this issue has at times focused on well-known shortcomings in the official international accounts, on balance there is no reason to believe that a more accurate set of accounts would be more favorable from the U.S. perspective. The main adjustments in the United States' favor—evaluating at current market prices both U.S. gold holdings and U.S. foreign direct investment—would probably about offset the effect of allowing for unrecorded capital inflows and evaluating at current market prices U.S. bank loans to less developed countries. More importantly, what matters in this discussion is not the current position but the trajectory on which the United States is now traveling, and about that there is little dispute.

2. Slower inflation matters in this context because taxable investors pay tax on nominal interest earnings. For example, if the nominal interest rate earned is 12 percent and inflation is 8 percent, the *after-tax real* rate of return earned by an investor in the 25 percent bracket is just 1 percent ($1\% = 12\%(1 - 0.25) - 8\%$). If the nominal interest rate and the inflation rate both fall by 4 percent (so that the before-tax real interest rate remains unchanged), the investor's after-tax real rate of return becomes 2 percent ($2\% = 8\%(1 - 0.25) - 4\%$).

3. By taking what people spend, not what they earn, a consumption tax would not discourage saving or work effort. Although many critics regard a consumption tax as regressive, a well-designed combination of tax rate structure and family exemptions can easily make a consumption tax as progressive as the current U.S. income tax (or more so).

4. The value-added tax (VAT) is a close relative of the consumption tax, which shares most of its virtues and is, perhaps, more acceptable politically. The VAT is essentially a sales tax paid on all purchases made by domestic final users of goods and services. Hence investment goods, and goods sold for export, are excluded. Like the consumption tax, the VAT is often regarded as a regressive tax, but in fact a well-designed system of exemptions and credits—for example, excluding from the tax all purchases of food, clothing, shelter, and medical care—can eliminate much or all of this problem.

8 U.S. Budget Deficits: Views, Burdens, and New Developments

EDWARD M. GRAMLICH

Economists have argued about the burden of the public debt for as long as there has been a public debt. Not surprisingly, these arguments took on new force in the 1980s, when the outstanding U.S. federal debt held by the private sector more than tripled. Opinion was basically divided into what Charles Schultze identified as three schools of thought regarding debts and deficits—the wolf at the door theory, where deficits were an immediate problem; the pussycat theory, where deficits were no problem at all; and the termite theory, where deficits were a long-term problem but not a short-term problem. As the decade progressed, the debt mounted, and immediate difficulties were not encountered; those who cried wolf gradually stopped crying, and almost no respectable economist believes in the wolf theory any longer. But there is still a vigorous argument between the pussycats who think the debt is no problem at all and the termites who think it presages a long-run problem. In this essay, I try to distinguish the pussycat from the termite view, illustrating the main points with real world data. I then describe some important recent developments and how they bear on the argument.

The termite, or neoclassical, view of the burden of the public debt is the most conventional, and is held by the most economists. It can be stated either in stock or flow form. In stock form, the argument is that government debt is treated as net worth by the private sector, which then substitutes for holdings of real capital in its asset portfolio. Since real capital determines future real living standards, the public debt in effect reduces future living standards. In flow form, the government deficits that lead to this debt reduce national saving, which in turn reduces the amount added to the nation's capital stock and future living standards. There is no ultimate difference between these two statements of the termite view, though most students these days find the flow statement more familiar. Either way, the essential tradeoff is between present consumption and future consumption. Debt or deficits now mean that the nation is not taxing itself (reducing present consumption) enough to pay for its public goods, thereby increasing present living standards to the detriment of its real capital stock and future consumption.

One can be a pussycat by believing that any of the links in the termite chain of reasoning do not hold up. To clarify, I use the flow version and reduce the termite, or neoclassical, view to the following four controversial propositions:

1. The first controversial proposition is that budget deficits reduce national saving. This is true by definition as long as budget deficits are not offset by increases in private saving, which implies that the proposition can be evaluated directly from the behavior of national saving rates. The only problem is that it is not always easy to define and predict national saving, and the late 1980s turn out to be one such time.

2. The second controversial proposition is that reductions in national saving reduce some combination of investment in new capital and net exports. This is again true by definition when there are not large capital gains on the existing capital stock. But there were such gains in the late 1980s, making for another empirical quandary.

3. The third proposition is that reductions in this combination of investment and net exports reduce future living standards. This proposition is not as controversial as the first two, but it is also not true by definition. It will be true under the reasonable supposition that a lower stock of domestic or foreign assets lowers some combination of future worker productivity and future income from assets.

4. The fourth controversial proposition is that reductions in national saving are undesirable in the sense that they move the nation away from its preferred saving rate. Unlike the first three propositions, this one is normative rather than descriptive—that is, it is about policy goals. That makes it more subjective than the others, but it is still possible to develop some rules of thumb for what national saving and government deficits should be, and to assess fiscal policy from this standpoint.

Given the difficulty of measuring variables and relating them to each other, nothing is ever perfectly clear in macroeconomics. But in the middle of the 1980s, evidence on all four propositions pointed strongly in the direction of a sizable debt burden from the path of fiscal policy. There was little doubt that national saving rates were down, that the combination of domestic capital stock and foreign assets was down, that future living standards would eventually be down, and that budget deficits were too high from any standpoint. But by the late 1980s, new developments raised doubts on all but the third proposition:

• The abrupt collapse of the Warsaw Pact in 1989 made it less clear that properly defined national saving rates were down throughout the 1980s, and also led to the prospect that national saving could increase sharply in the 1990s.

- The large capital gains on new and existing capital opened up the question of whether in market value terms this capital stock was really down.
- The small reduction in real deficits that did take place satisfied at least a minimum standard for deficit reduction, and lowered the priority of further deficit reduction.

This chapter goes into each of the propositions and new developments in more depth. The bottom line is that I continue to believe, as I have believed all along (Gramlich, 1984), in the termite theory: There was a substantial burden of the debt created in the 1980s and more deficit reduction is desirable. But I do admit that both the severity and the certainty of these arguments is lessened by the new developments.

BUDGET DEFICITS AND NATIONAL SAVING

The national income accounts (NIA) define net national saving (NS) as:

$$(1)\ NS \equiv PS + GS \equiv NI + NX$$

Here PS refers to private saving of households, business, and for reasons to be explained, state and local governments. GS refers to saving by the federal government, the difference between federal taxes and spending. It follows, of course, that GS also refers to the federal budget surplus, and the negative of GS to the federal budget deficit. NI refers to net investment, the difference between gross investment and depreciation. NX refers to net exports, the difference between exports and imports. The equation represents nothing more than the old truism that saving equals investment, with the definitions expanded to include the government and foreign sectors. The equation is also an accounting identity —true by definition. It is true by definition either in real or nominal terms, but throughout the chapter I will define variables in real terms unless otherwise stated.

The first proposition focuses on just the left side of the equation—the definition that national saving is the sum of private and federal government saving. Pussycats point to two reasons why an increased federal deficit, or a drop in federal saving (GS), may *not* reduce national saving (NS).

The first reason is the famous paradox of thrift. Keynesian economists argue that a drop in GS—basically, deficit spending—will for a time increase gross national product (GNP). In this case, it can be shown that NS will be higher or lower depending on whether NI is stimulated by the higher income more than it is deterred, or "crowded out," by interest rates that would also be higher. But it is important to remember that this reaction is mainly for the short term: if deficits persist over time, the economy is likely to run into capacity constraints and not have GNP remain persistently above its long-run path. Then no investment would be stimulated, and there would be no doubt that NI and NS would be reduced.

This crowding-out effect is magnified if the foreign sector is important in shaping macroeconomic behavior, in which case the economy is said to be "open" to trade and capital flows. In this open economy case, the drop in GS raises interest rates, attracts foreign capital, and raises the value of the dollar relative to other currencies. This in turn means that U.S. exports cost more and are reduced, while foreign imports cost less and are increased. The resultant drop in net exports (NX) limits the rise in GNP and any rise in investment that might be stimulated. So the Keynesian paradox of thrift argument becomes much less important in an open economy world. Since the U.S. economy, like most other current economies, now operates very much like an open economy, and since the U.S. budget deficits under consideration have lasted a long time, this Keynesian paradox of thrift argument seems increasingly unimportant.

The second reason why a government budget deficit may not reduce NS involves another famous argument, this one termed Ricardian equivalence.[1] Under this argument, rational and far-sighted households realize that taxes now are equivalent to taxes later, and since taxes postponed do have to be paid eventually, these households save now to build up an account to pay their future taxes. Or to will to their children so the children can pay their future taxes. In effect, households are so far-sighted and altruistic toward their heirs that they do not let the deficits affect their own consumption. A drop in GS is then followed by a corresponding rise in PS, with no change in NS.

There has been a great deal written, pro and con, about Ricardian equivalence. Without dredging up all the arguments, the proof of the pudding is in the behavior of NS. If NS does not drop when government saving drops, this first link is broken and there is no obvious burden of the debt. If it does drop, at least the first link in the termite view is holding.

With these points in mind, I now turn to some real world data for the United States. Figure 8-1 uses official NIA data to compute the path of net national saving (NS) and federal saving (GS). In this and the other figures, all variables are shown as a percentage of net national product (NNP) to eliminate any time trends due to the growth of the economy. Also in this and the other figures, depreciation is subtracted from both gross national saving (to give net national saving) and GNP (to give NNP) so that all numerators and denominators will be on the same basis.

When GS is below the zero line, the federal budget is in deficit. As can be seen, since 1970 the federal budget has been in deficit, and since 1982, very much in deficit. Over this latter time period, national saving has dropped sharply too, indicating that neither the Keynesian nor the Ricardian objection to this first proposition has proven very important.[2]

But Figure 8-1 is in terms of officially defined NIA variables, and there have been a number of measurement questions raised about the proper interpretation of both NS and GS in Figure 8-1. The main measurement questions that have been raised, and how they affect both NS and GS, are given below:

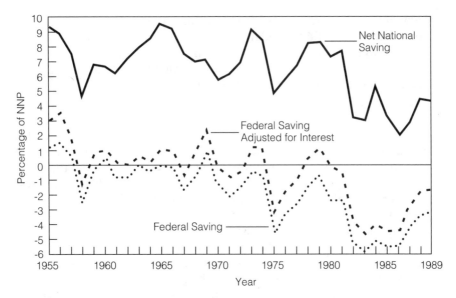

FIGURE 8-1   *Budget Deficits and National Saving (Percentage of NNP, 1955–89)*

1. **Consumer durables.** The NIA records such consumer durables as autos and furniture as if they were all consumed within one period. In fact, the service flow from these durables is consumed over many periods. Adjusting the accounts to put them on a service flow basis will shift the NS series up slightly (Hendershott and Peek, 1989) but not affect the GS series. The observed 1980s relationship between GS and NS is also not much affected by this change.

2. **Federal government physical investment.** The NIA records all federal spending as consumption, when in fact some of it is for long-lived physical investments that yield a flow of services over a period of time. Adjusting the accounts so that federal net investment is treated like private net investment, with both federal and national saving similarly redefined, raises both the GS and the NS series by the same slight amount (U.S. Congressional Budget Office, 1987). The reason the changes are slight is that the federal government simply has not invested much more than the depreciation on its own capital over this period. Moreover, the observed 1980s relationship between NS and GS is unchanged by definition.

3. **State and local surpluses.** State and local governments typically run fairly large surpluses in their employee pension funds, and no surpluses aside from that. One might think that state and local pension sur–pluses should be lumped with the federal budget variable and treated as a reduction in government deficits, but in fact if these pension surpluses were treated in the same way that the NIA treats pension surpluses for other employers, the state and local pension surpluses

would be considered part of private saving. So it is proper treatment to omit them from the GS line in Figure 8-1, as was done. Moreover, any change in the location of these pension surpluses would involve just a reshuffling of saving—no change in overall NS by definition. So this point does not change either the GS or the NS line.

4. Interest correction. It is well known that the nominal interest rate (i) equals the sum of the real interest rate (r) and the expected rate of inflation (g). Robert Eisner and Paul Pieper (1984) have used this proposition to argue that federal interest payments are overstated because they include a premium for the inflationary losses on the value of the debt expected by private households. Adjusting federal interest payments to take out the inflation premium will clearly cut deficits, or raise GS, as shown by the adjusted government saving line, in Figure 8-1. But since the nation as a whole has net interest payments that are close to zero, there would be little change in the NS line because of this adjustment. Hence this point also only involves a reshuffling of saving between the federal government and the private sector. There is no change in overall national saving and, as can be seen, no noticeable change in the 1980s relationship between GS and NS.

5. Government subsidies. It has also been argued that the NIA government budget deficit is understated because subsidized federal loans to such groups as students and farmers are considered asset transfers and simply excluded. Under the NIA, this subsidy only shows up later as a reduction in interest receipts. Were the timing of these loans altered to count the subsidy up front, the path of GS would be affected. But this adjustment would again just involve a reshuffling of saving between the federal government and the private sector, with no change in overall national saving. The U.S. Congressional Budget Office (1990) has also shown that there would be no change in the apparent relationship between GS and NS.

Hence these measurement issues do not change the basic story any. Most of them involve simple reclassifications of saving between the private and the federal sector, with no impact on the overall total saving by definition. Those that do involve a redefinition of the total do not count for much. There still seems to have been a sharp decline in federal saving and a parallel sharp decline in national saving in the 1980s.

Or at least that was the picture until late 1989. But then there was an important new development that seems likely to have fundamental bearing on the national saving story—the collapse of the Warsaw Pact. Surprisingly, this important development could change both the interpretation of past numbers and the outlook for the future.

The backward-looking point is that the 1980s boom in defense spending could have represented a form of investment. This boom may have put a strain on the Communist bloc, led to the breakdown of these economies and the collapse of the Warsaw Pact, made possible lower future levels of defense spending and taxes, and released resources for higher levels of future consumption.[3] The simple budget numbers show that if the 1980s boom in defense spending were treated as investment, there would not have been much decline in federal saving. Until 1989, one would not have taken very seriously the argument that the boom in defense spending lowered future defense spending and taxes: Indeed, one would probably have argued that U.S. defense spending only induced the Soviets to spend more and caused an arms race that led to *higher* future defense spending and taxes. But the abrupt collapse of the Warsaw Pact may cast the 1980s boom in defense spending in a different light. It is obviously difficult to make judgments on this matter, but it is at least now not so clear that the defense-spending induced deficits of the 1980s were bad for the future living standards.

The forward-looking point is that national saving rates are now much more likely to increase. One reason is the straightforward point that lower defense spending should make it possible to reduce federal deficits, or to increase GS, through what is known as the "peace dividend." But there is also a second type of peace dividend that is more speculative, but for which the supporting empirical evidence is very strong. Joel Slemrod (1986) has shown that private saving is very highly correlated with measures of perceived freedom from nuclear war. The reason is obvious: Saving represents provision for the future, and households have no incentive to provide for the future if they do not think there will be a future. Because of the Warsaw Pact collapse, there was a very sharp rise in perceived freedom from nuclear war in late 1989 and early 1990. If Slemrod is right, this freedom will show up as a sharp increase in private saving rates, enough to restore NS to its pre-1980s average in Figure 8-1.

Hence the bottom line in this section is one of irony. Throughout the 1980s, economists argued endlessly about the paradox of thrift, Ricardian equivalence, and a whole string of measurement issues, none of which now seems to have changed the basic story of a sharp drop in net national saving in an important respect. But late in the decade there was an unforeseen event—the collapse of the Warsaw Pact—that not only could change the way we read the past evidence but also the future prognosis. It was this unforeseen event, and not any of the decade-long haggles, that leads to the lessened certainty about how much national saving really did, and will, drop.

NATIONAL SAVING AND NATIONAL WEALTH

The next proposition refers to the right side of the accounting identity in equation (1). Any drop in NS, whether from a federal deficit or any other source, must by definition reduce the sum of NI and NX. In the old days of a closed economy, the mechanism by which this drop took place is that the budget deficit raised interest rates and crowded out some capital investment directly. Then over time the parallel rise in GNP would push up prices,

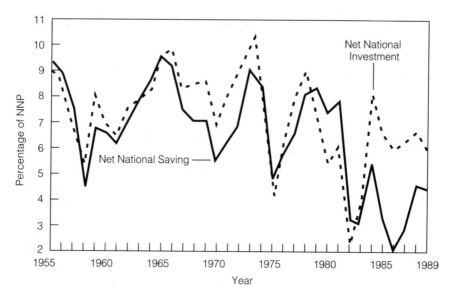

FIGURE 8-2 *National Saving and Investment (Percentage of NNP, 1955–89)*

reduce the real money stock, and crowd out more investment. In the end, there would be a new equilibrium, with GNP on its original time path but with both NS and NI lower.

In today's open economy world, these adjustments take place more quickly. As was explained earlier, the deficit would push up interest rates, attract foreign capital, drive up the dollar relative to other currencies, reduce exports, and raise imports. Hence, NX drops along with NI and the induced short-run rise in GNP is less. There is still a movement back to the original path of GNP, with the sum of NI and NX down by exactly the drop in NS. How much NI and NX drop depends on how much the economy behaves like a closed economy and how much like an open economy. But either way U.S. national wealth is down—in the first case, real capital is down; in the second, net claims on foreigners are down.

There is another way to put the open economy point. The balance of payments accounting identity shows that NX also equals the amount of net lending done by the United States to foreign countries. When NX falls, the United States either borrows more from abroad, or foreigners buy U.S. assets. This is what is meant by the oft-heard phrase "the selling of America." Either way, U.S. national wealth is down—either the real capital stock is down (when NI drops), or the real capital owned by U.S. citizens is down (when NX drops).

Figure 8-2 shows time series data for NS and NI, again as a percentage of NNP. The NS line is that already shown in Figure 8-1, with the sharp 1980s drop already noted. The drop in NI is seen to be less, about one-half of the drop in NS. From equation (1) we can then infer that the drop in NX also covered about one-half of the saving shortfall. Putting it in our

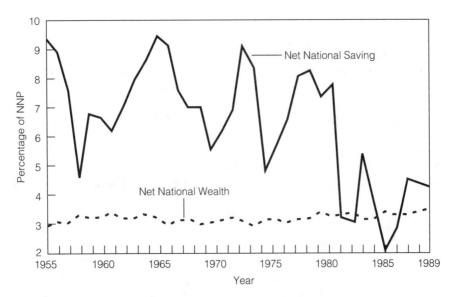

FIGURE 8-3   *National Saving and Wealth (Percentage of or Ratio to NNP, 1955–89)*

alternative formulation, about one-half of the decline in national saving showed up as a decline in real capital located in this country and one-half as a decline in the capital owned by citizens of this country.

But there is also a potentially serious measurement problem in the comparison of national saving and national investment. Suppose that for some reason the existing capital stock becomes more valuable. The relative price of this capital stock would rise, leading to what are known as capital gains. U.S. national wealth would then rise because of the revaluation of the existing capital even if the nation did not save any more. It turns out that this has happened in the United States, as is shown in Figure 8-3. The top line in the figure is the NS line we have already been examining, with the sharp 1980s drop. The bottom line is the ratio of net national wealth to NNP. For these purposes, national wealth is defined as household net worth less the outstanding federal debt, with the latter subtracted because this debt clearly does not make the nation as a whole wealthier. But even with the subtraction of federal debt, there has been such a sharp increase in the stock market valuation of the U.S. capital stock in the 1980s that the wealth ratio does not drop. Indeed it rises very slightly since the late 1970s.

What can we make of this discrepancy? The national saving rate declined in the 1980s, but the national wealth ratio has not declined because of very high capital gains. The thinking of economists is that it depends on the duration and source of the capital gains. Regarding duration, suppose these gains seem clearly to represent one-shot price adjustments that will not recur. Then the new national wealth is welcome, but the lower national saving rates will ultimately assert themselves and lower the value of the capital stock and future living standards.

Regarding source, the argument is more complicated. Suppose the capital gains reflect a shift in tax policy that benefits holders of capital without truly increasing the productive capacity of the economy. Again there is no likely recurrence of the gains, and this time the gains do not even reflect an improvement in living standards for the whole country. In this case, the lower national saving rate would be more meaningful than the unchanged wealth rate. Suppose the gains reflect a flight of international capital to this country because of a crisis of investor confidence in other countries. These gains may recur, and they may represent long-run improvements in national living standards, if the country is able to buy foreign goods more cheaply. In this case, some combination of saving and wealth rates might be appropriate. Suppose the gains arise from a wave of innovation that is likely to make new and old capital truly more productive at a continuing rate. Then the wealth figures are probably more meaningful— in effect, the country does not have to save as much to protect future consumption, and the present generation can raise consumption. So the question of whether to look at saving flows or wealth stocks is ultimately pretty unclear, but it should perhaps be reemphasized that low national saving rates are likely to recur until fiscal policies are changed, while capital gains can be, and have often been, nonrecurrent.

NATIONAL WEALTH AND FUTURE LIVING STANDARDS

The connection between the decline in national saving and future living standards is clearest in the closed economy case. In this closed economy case, all national wealth is in the form of tangible capital—there are no claims by or against foreigners. Assuming for simplicity that there are no capital gains either, the drop in national saving means that every year the country is devoting less of its productive capacity to building up its capital stock and more of its productive capacity to current consumption. Over time, the capital stock will drop, as will the output produced from this smaller capital stock. Hence, the drop in capital accumulation can also be reflected in a rise in present consumption and a drop in future consumption.

Now suppose the economy is open to trade and capital flows. In the short run, the drop in national saving drives up interest rates and the dollar, and through processes already described, leads to a decline in NX and a rise in net borrowing. The reduced ownership of capital leads to a decline in the returns on capital, and again to a decline in future living standards. To be sure, the decline is less abrupt in the open economy, because to the extent that the drop in saving does not reduce the capital located domestically, the country's income is still higher because of the earnings of workers employed at factories now owned by foreigners. From the standpoint of future living standards, a country that is undersaving should find it better to borrow than not borrow, but it is better still not to undersave.

TABLE 8-1
National Saving Rates and Trend Output Growth Rates (Percentage, 1955–89)

YEARS	NS	N
1955–59	7.44	2.88
1960–64	7.30	3.60
1965–69	8.06	3.60
1970–74	7.24	3.22
1975–79	6.72	3.04
1980–84	5.40	2.41
1985–89	3.29	2.68

The main problem in evaluating either the closed or the open economy version of this proposition is that the drop in investment and net exports is immediate, while the decline in living standards occurs gradually over time. It has proven very difficult to measure these links, and generally to explain worker productivity. There has, for example, been a well-known decline in worker productivity in the United States, but still a great deal of controversy about what has caused this productivity decline.

The numbers, such as they are, are given in Table 8-1. For each five-year period, the table shows the NS value described and shown earlier, and the percentage rate of growth in real potential output (n). For these purposes, potential output is used to measure growth in order to smooth out cyclical fluctuations. As seen already, the national saving rate drops over time, gradually at first and sharply in the 1980s. This drop implies that the capital stock will be dropping too, though as discussed above, with a lag. Eventually the trend output growth rate will also decline. It can be seen that the trend growth in output generally does follow such a pattern, dropping somewhat after the drop in national saving. Not all the wiggles match up, but the basic pattern does match up. Hence, it seems both theoretically and empirically reasonable to attribute some of the growth slowdown to the reduced national saving, though exactly how much remains in doubt.

HOW MUCH DEFICIT REDUCTION?

The final proposition has less to do with a positive discussion of the historical evidence than with a normative judgment about optimal policy. For the first three propositions, the concepts were clear and the numbers murky; now the concepts are not very clear either.

Perhaps the best way to discuss the question of how much deficit reduction is desirable is to contrast two standards, the minimum amount of deficit reduction desired and the maximum amount desired. After having done this, and having found a wide gap between the two, I will also introduce what might be a reasonable compromise goal for deficit reduction.

The minimum standard for deficit reduction is that federal deficits should be low enough that an unchanging fiscal policy should *not* result in steadily rising debt and interest burdens. To see what this means, the change in the outstanding federal debt (dD) in nominal terms can be expressed as:

$$(2) \ dD = F - T + iD$$

where F is federal spending apart from interest payments, T is federal taxes, iD is nominal interest payments, D is the stock of outstanding debt, and i is the nominal interest rate (equal to $r + g$ where r is the real interest rate and g is the expected rate of inflation). Now letting Y refer to nominal GNP and n to the growth rate of real GNP, as above, differentiation yields:

$$(3) \ d(D/Y) = (F - T)/Y + (r - n)D/Y$$

The dependent variable here is the change in what might be called the debt burden ratio, the change in the stock of the outstanding debt to GNP.[4] It is proportional to the debt service ratio (interest payments over GNP) often used in analyzing the debt problems of less developed countries. The variable (F – T) is known as the primary budget deficit, the deficit apart from interest payments, and (F – T)/Y is the primary deficit ratio. The expression $(r - n)$ is the difference between the real interest rate and the real GNP growth rate, an expression that can be shown to be positive for the United States, and also in general when a country saves as little as does the United States. Since $(r - n)$ and D/Y are positive numbers, the equation says that the debt burden ratio will typically rise *unless* the primary budget is in surplus. And the minimum standard is just that primary budget surplus that holds the change in the debt burden ratio, $d(D/Y)$, equal to zero.

Table 8-2 gives these numbers, both historically and under the latest Congressional Budget Office projections of the implications of current policies. The first column is the primary deficit ratio, (F – T)/Y, averaged over the relevant fiscal years to smooth out wiggles. The second column is the overall deficit ratio, dD/Y (very close to the negative of the GS variable used earlier), averaged over the same years. The third column is the change in the debt burden, $d(D/Y)$, from the start to the end of the period.

The story of the table is as follows. In the 1960s, the federal government ran primary budget surpluses and saw its debt burden ratio drop sharply. The primary deficit ratio rose in the 1970s, and the debt burden ratio stopped dropping sharply. In the bad years of 1983–86, the primary deficit ratio shot up and the debt burden ratio did likewise. Then there was a sharp improvement in the primary deficit ratio beginning in 1987, and the country is now following a trend where the debt burden ratio is once again declining. It will have to decline greatly to restore this debt burden ratio to its 1980 low point, but the debt burden ratio has stopped rising and is now declining.

What does all this say about the minimum standard for deficit reduction? Simply that the reduction in primary deficits that has already occurred

TABLE 8-2
Primary and Total Deficits (Percentage, 1962–94)

Years	(F − T)/Y	dD/Y	$d(D/Y)$
1962–70	−0.5	0.9	−15.8
1971–80	0.8	2.3	−2.4
1981–82	0.9	3.4	7.7
1983–86	2.4	5.5	8.6
1987	0.3	3.4	0.3
1988	0.1	3.2	−0.2
1989	−0.4	2.9	−0.5
1990–94	−1.0	2.0	−2.8

is enough to start the debt burden ratio on a downward trend. In the mid–1980s, a continuation of the then prevailing fiscal policies would have generated steadily rising interest and debt burdens. Now the same continuation generates slowly falling interest and debt burdens. In a word, the minimum standard for deficit reduction *has already been satisfied.*[5]

But a look back at Figure 8-1 suggests that while prevailing fiscal policies already satisfy the minimum standard for deficit reduction, that standard is not very ambitious. The federal deficit is still quite large by historical standards; national saving rates are still quite low. We can bound deficit reduction policy on the other side by finding the maximum deficit reduction that might be desirable.

This maximum deficit reduction that might be desirable is taken from the neoclassical growth models of Robert Solow (1956) and Edmund Phelps (1961). Were national saving rates very low, living standards would be also, because there would be very little investment in new capital. Were national saving rates very high, the capital stock and output would be high, but consumption and living standards would be low because little of this high output would be consumed. It stands to reason then that there is some national saving rate that maximizes the level of consumption across all generations—high enough so there is reasonable capital accumulation, but not so high that society runs into the law of diminishing returns on its capital investment. This standard is called the "golden rule" saving rate, because each generation is doing unto others (saving) as it would have had its elders do unto it. Without going into the details, the golden rule NIA saving rate is on the order of 20 percent, about the normal national saving rate in Japan but, according to Figure 8-1, well above the level that has ever been realized in the United States. The country would need to run enormous budget surpluses and have enormous rises in national saving, and drops in consumption, even to come close to this maximum standard.

Is there anything between the very unambitious minimum deficit reduction standard and the very ambitious maximum deficit reduction standard? A reasonable compromise might be to restore national saving rates to their level when the economy was growing at a healthy rate, roughly 7.5 percent of NNP as seen from Table 8-1. Compared with today's levels, federal budget deficits would have to be reduced at least by another 3 percent of NNP to bring this standard about. Comparing this with the progress that has already been made since the mid-1980s in Table 8-2, the job is roughly half done.[6]

IMPLICATIONS

The termite view of the burden of the debt, and the implications that flow from it, can be simply stated. The rise in federal deficits has lowered national saving, lowered some combination of capital investment and net exports, this will lower future living standards, and as soon as is practicable the U.S. should reduce its federal budget deficits another 3–4 percent of NNP to get back on a healthy growth track. This statement is much as would have been made throughout the 1980s, though the required deficit reduction then would have been larger.

But some recent developments may have altered the picture. The collapse of the Warsaw Pact raises the possibility that both federal and national saving did not fall so much in the past and will rise of their own accord in the future. The rise in comon stock values at least raises the possibility that the U.S. capital stock evaluated at market prices has not dropped relative to output. The little deficit reduction that has already taken place is enough to satisfy a minimum standard, though still a long way from other more ambitious standards.

All of these recent developments are welcome, and they all lessen both the severity and the certainty of the termite line of argument. But when all is said and done, there is still a great deal of evidence that present U.S. fiscal policy is placing a burden on future generations and that further deficit reduction is desirable, at least until there have been sustained increases in national saving.

NOTES

Robert Barsky and Paul Courant have made helpful comments.

1. Students of doctrine say that David Ricardo invented the point in the l9th century but did not think it would be very important. The main modern proponent of the point has been Robert Barro (1974). For some less approving theoretical discussion, see B. Douglas Bernheim (1989).

2. To be perfectly correct about it, the Keynesian claim should be evaluated in terms of levels of national saving, not ratios to NNP. I show that test in Gramlich (1989), finding no real change in the results.

3. This point was discussed in the abstract in Courant and Gramlich (1986). We had no idea how significant it would come to be.

4. The switch from NNP used earlier to GNP used here is benign. NNP is the proper deflator, and for the earlier numbers that was easy to get. These budget numbers are typically shown as a percent of GNP for fiscal years, with no record of NNP. So I have switched over to GNP for this section.

5. These numbers are based on the U.S. Congressional Budget Office estimates of January 1990. As the chapter went to press, the 1990–94 average deficit ratio went from 2.0 percent (in Table 2) to 2.7 percent without the full cost of the savings and loan bailout, and to 3.3 percent with the full cost. First off, for examining long-term trends the added savings and loan bailout costs should probably be ignored—these costs really were incurred earlier when the institutions failed, and they are one-time costs. Very large and maddening one-time costs, but still one-time costs. Secondly, even if deficits average 2.7 percent of GNP, the minimum standard for deficit reduction has been satisfied.

6. It might be felt that the aging of the American population, and the coming slower growth of the labor force, would require greater than normal saving. In fact Cutler et al. (1990) show just the reverse—other things equal a more slowly growing labor force requires less national investment and saving to equip. In this sense, the job may be slightly more than half done.

9 Random Thoughts on the Debt

GORDON TULLOCK

PARADOX, A PARADOX, A MOST INGENIOUS PARADOX

One of the first pieces of work I did on the debt—in fact, it came out of informal discussion of Ricardo long before Robert Barro (1974, 1989) wrote—was what I call "Tullock's fallacy." This fallacy has occasionally been mentioned in the literature and is part of the older oral tradition at the University of Virginia, but I have never formally put it in print before. Thus, the first thing that I will do in this chapter is to give you a correct version of a fallacious line of reasoning.

In general, we have to pay our taxes to the government in the year that they come due. Clearly, however, we would be better off if that were loosened up. For example, suppose that I can pay this year's taxes and next year's taxes in the corresponding years, or I can pay them both this year having a discount on next year's taxes equivalent to the rate of interest, or I can pay them next year with an interest payment added on this year's taxes. Clearly, I have added flexibility and would be better off.

As a matter of fact, that is the present situation for those members of the population with good credit. I can pay next year's taxes this year by the simple expedient of buying an adequate quantity of government bonds, and I can borrow money to pay this year's taxes and then pay it back with interest next year. Clearly, these additional opportunities benefit me: I have greater freedom in making my tax payments.

But let us suppose that the government decides to benefit me even further. Suppose they notice that the interest rate that they have to pay is lower than the interest rate that I have to pay[1] and, in addition, their credit is good so they can always borrow money.[2] They, thus, borrow money for all of their expenditures this year and permit individuals to purchase an adequate quantity of bonds to cover this year's tax liability or wait until next year. The interest that the individual pays if he or she waits until next year will be lower although the interest received if he or she pays this year will be the same. Clearly, this is a "super-Pareto" move. Not only is nobody injured, a great many people would be benefitted.

From this line of reasoning, we reach the conclusion that the government should collect no taxes this year, they should borrow money and then should collect this year's taxes plus interest next year. But note that the same line of reasoning would apply next year, and the next, and the next. . . . This is Tullock's fallacy, and I should warn the reader that although it is obviously a fallacy, it is very hard to put your finger on exactly what is wrong with it.

INFLATIONARY ACCOUNTING

Since about mid-1960, I have been trying, unsuccessfully until now, to get into print my view that good bookkeeping requires that the lowering of the real value of the national debt by inflation should be counted as a source of government revenue. This is not because I like inflation, but because it is simply true that at the inflation rate of 4 percent the bonds that were available at the beginning of the year are worth 4 percent less at the end of the year. If we are paying a higher rate of interest to compensate the bond holders for this effect, then either that additional interest rate should not be counted as an expenditure or we should offset it by entering the shrinkage of the debt in our budget.

I never succeeded in getting this into print, but Robert Eisner, of course, has—in fact, repeatedly (Eisner, 1989a, 1989c).[3] He has a much broader program than I. I simply want to get our bookkeeping accurate. With this form of bookkeeping, however, it will be noted that we ran practically nothing in the way of government deficits, for the federal government in any event, until the 1970s. The real value of the national debt was shrinking during most of this period even though it did not shrink very markedly. The nominal value, of course, sometimes went up.

The phenomenon continues. Last year, we ran a nominal deficit of $152 billion, and if we offset this with the shrinkage of the national debt due to the inflation, the net effect is $53 billion. The real effect of this kind of thing in years in which the holders of the debt are fooled is quite large-scale repudiation of the debt. For example, we entered the 1970s with $408 billion of debt. In each of the years from 1970 to 1980, we borrowed in nominal terms the amount shown in column 1 of Table 9-1, and in terms of 1971 value dollars, the amount in column 2. The total debt in nominal terms and in 1971 dollars is shown at the bottom, and it will be observed that a very considerable part of the national debt was repudiated.

But much of the debt in 1970 was long term and had interest rates which did not compensate for potential inflation. The market discounted this long-term debt down to a value which took into account the probability of a long-term inflation and, of course, we have, indeed, had a long-term inflation of about 4–5 percent. As a result, the market value of the total federal bonded indebtedness in 1980 was about $420 billion 1971 dollars, or only slightly higher than in 1970. Altogether, we are not really in a good

TABLE 9-1
Nominal and constant value of deficit

Year	Nominal Value, Billions of Dollars	Billions of 1971 Dollars
	Deficit	
1971	23.0	23.0
1972	23.4	22.3
1973	14.9	13.4
1974	6.1	5.0
1975	53.2	39.8
1976	73.7	51.9
1977	53.6	35.4
1978	59.2	36.4
1979	40.2	22.7
1980	73.8	38.2
1971–80	421.1	288.1
Debt of 1980	908.5	470.7

SOURCE: *Economic Report of the President,* Washington, D.C.: Government Printing Office, January 1989.

position to criticize the partial or complete repudiation of the debt of so many poor countries.

If we continue with the policy of this sort, the interest rate will rise to take care of the debt so that individuals will not be injured. They can be injured, however, by a faster rate of inflation and, in fact, they can make very substantial profits if the rate of inflation is slowed down. Of course, indexing the debt would be a far better way of dealing with this problem than counting the shrinkage of the national debt as income. In the early days of the Reagan administration, it seems likely that the simple indexing of all debt[4] would have restored the budget to surplus.

Note that all of this deals only with the debt instruments. The government owns many assets and, of course, those that are denominated in dollars, like import–export bank loans, are subject to exactly the same shrinkage that I have mentioned above. Most of them, however, are real assets such as, for example, 40 percent of the land area and all of the offshore waters of the United States. These will increase in nominal value but not real value as a result of inflation. It is sensible to make the bookkeeping adjustments, but the change should not be counted as income.

In this connection, it is particularly important to avoid what I call the English, or Thatcher, error. Margaret Thatcher has been selling consider-able amounts of British government property and counting the receipts as simple income;[5] hence, Britain has a budget which appears to be pretty much in balance. Actually, selling assets is roughly equivalent to borrowing money in its effect on your wealth. Personally, I feel that disposing of these assets has increased the efficiency of England, but that does not mean their sale has generated real income.

But although selling assets is roughly equivalent to borrowing money, if you have the gigantic collection of assets that the United States has, there may well be strong arguments for selling them and repaying a good part of the national debt that way. If it is thought that the national domain, for example, should in the long run be in the hands of the government, then selling it now and then buying it back later would be roughly equivalent to borrowing money and repaying it later. Thatcher, of course, has been selling things which are better placed in the private sector.

REPUDIATION

Of course, this assumes that the money will be repaid. I have just pointed out that, by inflation, we have gotten rid of a good deal of our long-term debt and this is simply a particular form of repudiation. A great many other countries in the world have been more direct in repudiating their debt. North Korea and Vietnam seem to have been the pioneers and, interestingly enough, the banks that they refused to pay responded by trying to keep that fact a secret.[6]

But this start has been followed by a very large volume of partial or complete debt repudiation by other countries. Actually, they do not announce that they are not going to pay. Indeed, North Korea and Vietnam did not so announce; they simply stopped. The more recent procedure, in general, is to either put a limit on repayment which is much below the amount owed, or stop payments and announce that this is temporary. In general, from the standpoint of the country repudiating its debt, this is a sensible policy granted the debt is held by foreigners. This is particularly so since the repudiations are partially concealed by U.S. and European banks who do not want to simply list these bonds that they hold as worthless. In general, however, the underdeveloped countries that have debt problems have made only very modest payments. They are willing to accept a rescheduling, particularly if the rescheduling involves loaning them a new sum of money greater than the amount that they themselves owe, but, in general, they are not willing to pay the entire amount.

There is usually some political squabbling in the country, with the left-wing parties being in favor of outright repudiation and the right-wing parties wishing to disguise it and perhaps even make some payments. Many of the leftist parties are arguing that they are positively morally virtuous in refusing to pay. Much the same attitude would have been found in France during the early 1930s when they were refusing to pay their debts to the United States. Apparently, a good many people do not like to admit even to themselves that they are doing something immoral; hence, they invent new moral rules which legitimize their repudiation.

The United States has chosen, as have so many other countries, repudiation by inflation rather than direct repudiation, but it should not be forgotten that, in the 1840s, almost all of the local governments in the United States directly repudiated their debts to English bond holders.

I have said that repudiating your debt is generally sensible—although, of course, you should try to disguise it a little bit—and this is not in accord with the current conventional wisdom. It is pointed out that normally this will prevent you from borrowing more money in the future. It is not obvious that it will, because the new money borrowed in the future can be borrowed by, say, private companies in your country, or you can have a drastic change in government with the announcement that you will from now on pay your bonded indebtedness. The latter is more reasonable in terms of attracting credit if it is alleged, probably truthfully, that the previous loans were accompanied by a good deal of corruption; hence, the banks who made them should be punished.

In any event, short-term commercial credit covered by the cargo should normally be easily obtained at all times. The basic problem, and it is not a very large one, would be efforts on the part of the banks to seize property that is not within, say, Peru. If the Peruvian government takes the simple precaution of never owning anything outside Peru—and that is a fairly easy thing to do in the present-day market—they should be immune to that response.[7]

The cutting off of new loans is, of course, an inconvenience but, in general, much less of an inconvenience than paying off the existing loans. Assume that you, like most governments, have, in fact, sovereign immunity and cannot be forced by the sheriff to repay your loans. Say you bought a $125,000 house, paying $25,000 down and having a $100,000 indebtedness. The indebtedness is to be paid off at $4,000 per year and the rate of interest is 5 percent, so you must pay $9,000 per year this year, gradually reducing the amounts over the next 25 years.

If you repudiate, you are immediately better off by $100,000. The only problem is that it would probably be difficult for you to get a mortgage on a new house in the event that you decide to move up. It is best to delay repudiation until you have borrowed the maximum amount you think you can get. Still, in most cases, the saving on repayments will more than compensate for the inability to borrow.

This is, of course, the reason that we have a complicated legal procedure to enforce the payment of loans. If nonpayment had a negative present value, there would be little or no need for sheriffs, officers, courts, and so on to enforce payment. People, in fact, would pay.

There is a myth that floated around the banking community not many years ago that governments do not go bankrupt. I cannot imagine who dreamed that one up. A better explanation for the international banks' activity is the one which I have seen in a number of places in the economic literature: "International bankers behave like a herd of sheep." It should, of course, be remembered that there was strong government pressure to offer development loans to what were in those days referred to as undeveloped countries.

FUTURE GENERATIONS

Let us now, however, assume at least temporarily that the government will, in fact, in one way or another be forced to repay its obligations. Further, let us consider not short-term obligations of the sort which traditionally were entered into by the U.S. government to finance wars,[8] but assume that we borrow money now and that it will be repaid by the next generation and, once again for now, we will assume that the entire debt and repayment is domestic.

At this point, the effects of the debt depend to some extent on how the money is spent. If it is simply consumed paying for current expenses of the government—like the New York payment of its police force—then we have one effect, and we have another if it is productively invested. Let us start by assuming a pure consumption use of the loan.[9]

In this case, we find ourselves dealing with a subject which for some obscure reason has attracted a great deal of attention. Presumably, the government being in the market for loans would move the interest rate up, and this would mean that somewhat more money was saved and invested. Given normal assumptions about elasticity, however, the net effect of this would be that the money available for private investments would be lower. Since we are currently assuming that the government spends and does not invest its borrowings, the net effect of this is that the total volume of productive investments in society goes down.[10] Since the mechanism that lowers it is a rise in interest rates, presumably the investments that continue to be made are the most productive ones.

To repeat what I said above, for some obscure reason this rather simple economic proposition has been controversial, and there have been a number of statistical tests as to whether or not the government debt does, indeed, crowd out private investments. Efforts to empirically determine the outcome have been difficult, not least because our tax system is so designed that a great many productive investments do not appear that way in the national accounts.[11] Granted we accept the view that when you increase the demand for some product by a new purchaser—in this case, the product is investable funds—the total amount available for others goes down and the price goes up. Retaining our assumption that the government borrowing is for consumption, it is obvious that there will be less investment; hence, the next generation will have a lower total income.

Note that there would be some transfer effect here, too. Those members of the next generation who are able to live on interest income would be better off to some extent, and those who are compelled to live by their labor—which, after all, is most of us—would be worse off. It is not even certain that the people who are living on invested income would be better off. The reduction in total GNP might be enough so that their larger share of GNP is still worth less than it would be had this situation not developed.

But this is a second order effect. The primary effect would be that those in the next generation who are working for a living would find themselves transferring fairly large sums of money to those who are not. If we temporarily assume that the people who receive the bonds are not foreigners, that all of this is within the country, then one can say, as was so popular in the 1930s: "We only owe it to ourselves."

Clearly, then, consumption today can be increased by this method, and consumption for the next generation will be lower. Further, there will be a switch in the next generation between laborers and capital owners as to who does the consuming. In the current generation, the level of consumption should go up, but at least while the debt is still small the consumption by the laborers should go up while the consumption by investors is not very firmly specified. The investors would certainly increase the total amount that they are investing and would be able to spend the income. In the early days, the former of those two effects would be greater than the latter. After the system has been going awhile, it might well be that the owners of government bonds would find that the increase in their interest income more than counterbalances the additional amount of money that they were saving because of those higher interest rates.

This naturally raises something which is very misleadingly called the Ricardo effect. Since Ricardo, although he mentioned it in his book, specifically said that it was not true, it is not at all clear as to why his name is attached. For quite some time, I thought that only Robert Barro believed in the Ricardo effect, but apparently there are some other people who do, too. This is the view that since individuals are concerned about their descendants,[12] they would regard government borrowing of money as roughly equivalent to a tax because they would immediately set aside enough money so that their descendants could cover that part of the future tax liability represented by the loan.

Note that this requires that the individual regard his or her descendants as more or less the same as himself or herself. The individual regards transferring debt to them as much the same as transferring debt to a later period in his or her own life. I doubt that this is true, but there is a stronger reason for objecting to this scheme.[13]

Let us divide the population of the world into those who will leave to their descendants very little in the way of an estate and expect that their descendants, like they themselves, will make their living by working, as category A. Category B is those people who have enough money so that they will leave a significant estate to their descendants. Let us further assume, which I think is true, that almost everyone assumes that living standards will rise and the returns for labor will increase over the predictable future. Under these circumstances, if Mr. Jones puts the same weight on the well-being of his daughter as of himself, and if both are people who make their way by work, he would assume that his daughter will have a higher income than he; hence, he would be interested in transferring funds from his daughter to himself.

There is, however, no direct way in which he can borrow money to be repaid by his daughter.[14] If the government borrows money and spends it on consumption goods now with the intention that it be repaid with taxes drawn from his children, however, it would be such a transfer. From his standpoint, such a government deficit is sensible. Note, by the way, that if the child also values the consumption of her father as high as her own consumption, she would have no objection to such a transfer.

A person who is going to leave a positive estate, however, has no motive of this sort. He can increase his current consumption by simply reducing the size of that positive estate which he would leave. Since he can, if he wishes, have a living standard twice as high as that which he proposes to leave to his daughter without worrying about the need to directly borrow money, he simply spends money he has on hand.

Thus, there is here a conflict of interest between the laboring class, which makes up well over 80 percent of the population—probably 95 percent, if you count all kinds of labor—and that rather small part of the population which will leave sizeable positive estates. It is, of course, true here that a rise in interest now makes that particular conflict somewhat greater.

There is, here, another effect. If I can in one way or another reduce the amount of capital that I am leaving to my daughter without, however, having other people join me in this reduction, the net effect on GNP in return for labor through reducing investment is substantially nil. On the other hand, if all of us do that—and, of course, government debt is an example of that—then the reduction in current investment, and hence, the reduction in the return for labor in the next generation, would be significant. Thus, once again there is a conflict of interest with the upper-income people being opposed to government debt and the lower-income people having something to gain from it.

So far we have been assuming that the government borrows the money for the purpose of consumption expenditures. Let us now consider the cases in which the government borrows money for investment purposes, and let us assume that we can tell what is an investment as opposed to consumption and that the government is reasonably efficient in choosing among potential investment projects. It is, of course, clear that there are many things in which the government puts money which are investments by ordinary standards, even if there is no direct return. The highway system would be an obvious example.

In this case, in the first place there is no reduction in the total amount invested in society although there will be, of course, a readjustment in the particular subjects of investment. We would have more highways and fewer factories, but, clearly, there is no law of nature which says that this is undesirable. Indeed, the highways are necessary for the factories to function.

Thus, private investment would be crowded out but it would be replaced by public investment, and if we assume that both investments are run out to the point where their margins are equal, the total economy would be more efficient.

However, it would, of course, be possible to pay for these investments out of current revenue. The problem here is rather like that of a corporation which contemplates building a new factory and can finance it by direct payment out of its profits or can pay the profits out to the stockholders and borrow the money to build the factory. Many economists would say that the corporation should choose that alternative which maximized the present discounted value of the corporation to the stockholders, but it is not obvious that that particular bit of advice would be much practical help. The absence of anything directly similar to the stockholders in government makes the problem considerably more difficult.

If we could regard the present voters as the people whose well-being would be maximized and ignore future generations, then clearly, borrowing the money rather than paying for the, say, new bridge out of tax funds is reasonable. Local governments, of course, with their strong tendency for the voters to turn over by migration and the normal life cycle, would be particularly strongly motivated to do this and a great many of them do.

It is clear, however, that for the next generation things would be better if the government decides to make the investment out of its current revenue rather than borrowing money. This has the opposite effect of crowding out. Since the government will not be borrowing the money, the interest rate will be somewhat lower than it otherwise would be—there will be, in fact, somewhat smaller savings as a result—but the total resource available for private investment would be greater.[15] In this case, note that the transfer goes the opposite way. On the whole, people with investable capital will be injured right now by the decision to make the investment out of tax money rather than borrowing, and since they presumably will pay a proportionate amount of the tax, their injury is relatively greater than that to the workers. All the workers in the next generation, on the other hand, will have the benefit of the additional government expenditure, but there will be no repayment of the debt or payment of interest on the debt, and taxes, in general, will be somewhat lower.

In general, if one believes that the government should be encouraging investment in capital, then one simple way of doing so is to never borrow money and to buy all capital goods out of current revenue. Further, except for emergency situations, this is normally a fairly easy thing to do because governments are such large organizations that the amount of new investment coming up each year tends to be more or less stable. Nevertheless, this is a quite different level of argument than what we have dealt with before. Obviously, if you are trying to encourage investment in productive assets, you do not borrow money and consume it. Indeed, there would, I presume, be strong arguments for the government not only covering all of its own investments out of its own tax revenue, but buying common stock and bonds in the market for the same purpose.

All of this assumes that people should be compelled one way or another to save more than they would voluntarily, and it is not at all obvious that this is a good thing. Growth, after all, is not the only goal of our society.

I would like to be able to argue that people's behavior reflects these considerations, but, as a matter of fact, I do not see any evidence that it does. I presume that the computations are too difficult for either the average voter or the upper-income voter. Popular attitudes on whether the government should run large deficits seem to be more a matter of fads and "ideology" than these rather material motives.

In this connection, I should perhaps say that dictatorships and democracies seem to behave much the same with respect to this issue. I happened to be visiting Venezuela and noticed that in many ways, including debt, the Venezuelan government was much better run than the Mexican government, although the two in natural conditions have much in common. I thought it might be a reflection of Venezuela's functioning democracy as contrasted with Mexico's semidictatorship.

On returning to the United States, I got one of my colleagues, Gary Anderson (1988), to look into the issue, and he found that the dictatorships tended to have somewhat larger deficits than the democracies. This inspired Erol Balkan and Kenneth V. Greene to respond in an article (which has been accepted for *Public Choice* but not yet published) in which they, using better data than were available to Anderson, argued that there really is not much difference. Surely if there is a difference, it is not very large.

MORE ACCOUNTING ERRORS

One of the intriguing features of the U.S. government is that in its official statistics, money that it owes to itself is considered as part of its debt. As far as I know, there is no other entity that does this. Corporations, when they own their own bonds, simply remove the bonds from their bonded indebtedness and, of course, do not carry them as assets. When the Federal Reserve Board or the Federal Deposit Insurance Corporation buys government bonds, however, this is not true. In my data in this chapter, I have adjusted for this bizarre nature of the government statistics.

There is one rather astonishing exception to this which has to do with the social security old-age pension scheme. The old-age pension scheme is difficult to discuss in terms of debt because, as a matter of fact, if you assume that the government is under an obligation to pay the pensions that it has now promised to pay, the total obligation is monstrous. Further, it is quite impossible to tell exactly how big it is because it depends upon how long people live, which in turn depends upon medical research. In recent years, the life expectancy of older members of the population[16] has been increasing quite rapidly, and I have heard people saying that 150 as normal death age does not seem to be beyond the range of possibility. Clearly, if medicine does make that kind of progress, we will have to radically change our old-age pension system.[17]

The issue here has been complicated by recent acts of Congress. Having discovered that actuarial predictions implied that the pensions could not be paid for by the total receipts in the twenty-first century, Congress passed a law which raised the receipts of the program now with the idea of saving money to pay out later. Money which is being saved, however, is being "invested" in special government bonds. This means that the effect on the taxpayer when these bonds come due will be exactly the same as if no such "saving" had been made.

This, indeed, is beginning to bother Senator Patrick Moynihan and various other people. There are congressional hearings going on as this chapter is written looking into the problem. Notably, these hearings concern only that half of the payroll tax which is officially collected from the laborer. As economists, we know that both halves are really paid by the laborer, but the Social Security Administration puts much effort into denying that fact.

The political importance of the matter is that the bonds purchased for the social security "trust fund" are not counted as part of the deficit under the Gramm–Rudman Act. Offhand, this seems to be a simple, straightforward example of fraud on the part of the federal government.

This is not the only place where bookkeeping turns out to be odd. There are very large numbers of entities, like the Farm Credit Administration, that have the right to borrow money on the credit of the federal government. Indeed, the list of bonds issued by such entities in *The New York Times* financial pages is twice as long as the list of direct government securities. It is not, of course, true that these expenditures are in and of themselves as large as the regularly calculated government debt, but they are very large. On the other hand, in most cases, there are at least some assets to offset them.

In many cases, the assets are very much less than the debt, but there are undeniable cases in which the U.S. government has guaranteed a loan in which the chances of the loan being repaid—hence, the guarantee not being implemented—are very good. There are other cases in which the U.S. government through one of its agencies has built something and borrowed money on the credit of the federal government but in the name of the agency and whatever is built is, in fact, valuable enough so that the guarantee is not particularly dangerous.

The problem here, then, is not simple debt; it is the fact that we do not know how big the debt is. I have been talking about accounting difficulties here, and it seems to me that these issues are, indeed, very severe accounting difficulties. The savings and loan crisis is, of course, a current example. Here again, we do not know how much it will cost, because the amount to be realized on the foreclosed assets is still uncertain.

There is, then, another large collection of areas where the federal government has guaranteed something or another, but we do not have any positive account for it. For a long time, for example, the federal government was offering insurance to nuclear facilities at prices which were thought at the time to be a bargain. Since, as a matter of fact, the federal government has made money on it, I do not suppose we can argue that they were. Both Lockheed and Chrysler were bailed out by a use of federal government credit and, in both cases, the federal government actually did very well on the transaction. Unfortunately, this is likely to lead to similar efforts in the future, and I do not think the luck will hold.

In all of these areas, except possibly the old-age pensions, which are currently indexed, the government has a great deal to gain from inflation. Its debts will go down, its obligations will shrink, and, on the whole, there will be no counterbalancing reduction in its assets or its income. You may recall that not long ago New York City was on the verge of bankruptcy, and although they did a good deal about pretending to save money and so on, they were actually rescued by the inflation which cut the value of their obligations about in half while making it possible for them to raise their tax revenue without much difficulty. The federal government may well benefit from the same set of circumstances in the future. Certainly many other countries have at one time or another.

HISTORY

At the time of the French Revolution, two-thirds of the revenue of the king of France was going to pay the interest on his debt—unfortunately, denominated in gold. At the same time, the king of England was spending one-half of his revenue on the same not very pleasant account. The French republic got rid of the national debt by a simple inflationary procedure, but the British never did. They let their debt grow throughout the Napoleonic wars and then simply did not repay it. The growth of the British economy during the nineteenth century was so great that by the time they got around to another major war, their debt was more or less insignificant.

Historically, in the nineteenth century, one of the standard arguments for democracy as opposed to royal governments was that democracies were more fiscally responsible. I think it is hard to look at the nineteenth century, or for that matter, the eighteenth century record without agreeing that this was, indeed, so. But it should be remembered that in those days democracies were quite rare, and secondly, in most democracies—the United States was an exception—only people in the upper-income brackets were permitted to vote.

In the twentieth century, many people have argued that the deficit is a product of democracy.[18] Since dictatorships do at least as badly as democracies, this seems to be unlikely. In any event, what is a really remarkable characteristic of all of this tale is that a good many governments—including a good many communist governments—actually pay off their debts. The temptation to repudiate, or in the twentieth century to inflate it out, would seem to be overwhelming, and yet many governments do not succumb to it. Indeed, as we have mentioned, a good many governments, like the United States and England in the nineteenth century or Switzerland now, have maintained a balanced budget, even governments with excellent credit.

All of this makes prediction difficult. My own personal feeling is that the United States is on the edge of getting rid of this debt by inflation. It should be pointed out, however, that this is not quite as easy as one might hope. We now have to pay quite significant interest because people assume we will inflate. If we count the inflation as revenue, however, the debt is shrinking as a share of GNP, and, in fact, its real value is shrinking as a share of GNP no matter how we account for it.

Assume we just balance our budget in conventional terms, which means that we will continue paying an interest rate high enough to counterbalance inflation but will not count the shrinkage of the debt as part of our revenue. Then, at our present rate of inflation, the real debt will be cut about in half in 14 years. Since we could anticipate at least a 50 percent increase in GNP during that period, this would mean that the burden on the economy would be about one-third of what it is now without any nominal repayment.

If we stabilized our currency, the short-term debt would, I imagine, rapidly adjust with a much lower level of interest with the result that our apparent budget balance would improve. On the other hand, the longer-term debt with its, generally speaking, higher interest rates, would simply rise in present-day capital value and, from the standpoint of the bondholder, this would be marvelous. However, taxpayers would now not only face paying these high interest rates but not be compensated for it by the shrinkage of the capital.

So far, I have been assuming that we will not actually take steps to repay the debt, but it should be kept in mind that at various times in the past, we have. Anyone looking at our farm program or the Central Arizona Project immediately realizes very large savings are possible in government expenditures. There are, of course, numerous other expenditures which could be cut to pay off our debt.

CONTAGION?

The question of why we began sometime after 1960 running large peace-time deficits is one for which I have no positive answer. It should be noted first that we were not the pioneers in this development and, in fact, we never became one of the leading countries in debt production. Such staid conservative places as Belgium were borrowing far larger shares of GNP than we were for many years. Indeed, so was Japan, although Japan has now stopped. Since we are a very large country, our total debt does loom large, but the tendency to talk only about U.S. debt is simply another example of how our alleged allies like to blame everything on us.

But why did the debt begin to grow when it did and stay as large as it did in a considerable number of countries? There are a number of theories, none of which is very good. The first of these is that it is somehow a consequence of democracy—which is obviously absurd because dictatorships are doing it too, and because democracies, until quite recently, did not run large debts. Of course, neither did dictatorships until recently.

Something must have happened somewhere between 1960 and 1970 which made a good many countries—regardless of their political system—change their policies. It should, of course, also be said that it may be that they always wanted to borrow the money but the bankers had more brains earlier. Since I see no positive evidence that bankers' intelligence has declined, I do not agree that that is a very strong contender for the explanation.

Another explanation is that it is the very much delayed effect of Keynesianism. Since I have dealt with this elsewhere (1987), I will only say that it seems to me that it is odd that the effect of a book published in 1936 should only have been felt in 1960. It is also odd that it should have affected a lot of countries that do not seem to have very much Keynesianism in their blood. Again, Belgium is a good example and so is Japan. It is, however, hard to really definitively disprove this proposition.

There is another possibility which I should call the Colin Clarke explanation, although it is not exactly what he hypothesized. He argued that when any country's expenditures on government get above 25 percent of GNP, then inflation automatically follows, which will bring it back down to 25 percent. There has been a good deal of inflation recently, but it certainly has not brought government expenditures down to 25 percent.

We could, however, modify Clarke to something different. Roughly, we suppose that there is some threshold value above which the taxpayers are no longer willing to pay for government expenditures but where political pressures bear on the government to continue making the expenditures anyway. When this threshold is reached—and the modern welfare states would be particularly good candidates for this kind of reasoning—deficits follow.

As one illustration, the Japanese went in for a welfare state, ran up very large deficits, and are now attempting to get the whole thing back under control by way of a sales tax. The sales tax is very unpopular and almost cost the party that has dominated Japanese politics since World War II an election. This would fit the modified Clarke theory which I have just given, although, of course, a single observation of that sort is not much evidence.

In order for this theory to be true, it would be necessary that the threshold in which the government reaches this problem be different in numerical value in different countries. Since the rise in deficit financing occurred in most countries sometime in the 1960s or 1970s, they would have passed any given number, Clarke's magic 25 percent, for example, at quite different points in time. Still, again, I cannot think of any firm way of disproving or proving this hypothesis.

The last example which I will turn to is one that I myself have invented and, I may as well inform the reader, that I do not think is very good. It fits better than anything else, but, unfortunately, that is not very strong praise. I call this the contagion theory.

According to this theory, politicians thought that it was literally impossible to run large deficits during peacetime. Whether they thought that some law of nature made it impossible or whether they thought that the voters would throw them out if they did so,[19] is not necessary to specify here. In any event, this would mean that they would keep expenditures and taxes in balance.

Then, one country—probably by accident, possibly because the politicians did not believe the proposition about debt—in fact, ran a large deficit in one peacetime year. It was observed by the politicians in that country that there was certainly no immediate disaster, so they ran one the following year, and with no disaster from that year, they continued. Meanwhile, other countries noticing what was going on began experimenting with the same technique. The deficit then spread, in essence, like a contagious disease with all of the politicians deploring it but doing nothing about it.

But note that for this to be feasible, it would be necessary that the voters, given their choice among continuing to run a deficit, raising taxes, or cutting expenditures, prefer running the deficit. As far as I can see, that is a correct statement about U.S. voters and I suspect it is about other voters, too.

A deficit of this sort clearly means that future generations will not be as well off as they would be if the government paid for its expenditures, possibly including its capital expenditures, out of current taxes. Indeed, the present voters in a few years will not be as well off because there will be less capital to mix with their labor. Still, they are better off this year, whether we take them as taxpayers who pay less taxes or as investors who face a slightly higher interest rate.

Can this kind of policy continue forever? I think the answer is: "Yes, provided it is done modestly." In the United States today, inflation is rapid enough so that it comes close to canceling the deficit. We end most years with a debt which is in real terms about what it was at the beginning of the year, in spite of the fact that nominally it is bigger.

We are also increasing our GNP fairly rapidly with the result that the debt as a share of GNP is declining. I mentioned before that the English war debt from the Napoleonic wars was never paid off, but by 1914 it was insignificant. If we keep borrowing money and inflating, so it does not increase the real value of the debt by much, the same would be true. Even if we borrow enough money so that the real value of the debt increases substantially, as long as it increases less rapidly than GNP, the effective burden of the debt will fall.

But all of this is not to recommend our present policy which, on the whole, I dislike, but to point out that it does not have the negative effects that are usually criticized. It does mean that we will be poorer in the future than we would be if we followed other policies, but, heaven knows, there are many government policies of which that can be said.

ENVOI

I titled this Chapter "Random Thoughts on the Debt." I take it that no one will quarrel with that title. I do not think I have offered any solutions, or even any basic explanations. What I have done is clear away some of the underbrush so that it will be easier for other people to see both the woods and the trees.

NOTES

1. So long as the debt is denominated in dollars, this will always be so, even in inflationary periods. If the debt is denominated in something else—gold bars for example—then the government interest rate can be, and frequently has been, higher than that of private persons.

2. Once again, in paper money.

3. I feel rather jealous since I apparently made my first efforts to get it into print before he started his crusade. I cannot avoid the impression that his success and my lack thereof are due to our different political positions.

4. Which would have raised legal problems, but we can ignore them here.

5. Of course, when the property was acquired, the cost was counted as simple expenditure.

6. Many of the bankers had loaned this money inspired by vaguely anti-American motives. They obviously had particularly strong reasons for keeping it secret.

7. It would be theoretically possible for foreign creditors to seize the value of the Peruvian contribution but not the value added. Thus, Peruvian copper arriving in France after having been purchased by a Japanese company could be seized, with the Japanese company being reimbursed for its contribution to the value. Practically, however, this does not seem very useful.

8. The War of 1812 and the Civil War were paid for by borrowing money which was then reasonably quickly repaid. Significant repayments were made on the debt for World War I also, but the Great Depression intervened. Minor wars, like the war with Mexico or the one with Spain, were also financed to some extent by borrowing, but the amount was so small it was repaid very quickly. The Revolutionary War, a more serious difficulty, was only partially paid for. In this particular case, the matter is very remarkable because the officers and men in the army were, in general, paid in part by promises of payment at the end of the war which were simply repudiated. The federal government was not established until six years after the end of the war, but under Hamilton's influence, the formal debt of the Confederation and also that of the states was repaid.

9. Note that a number of cases are a little hard to classify. For example, it could easily be argued that the borrowing of money to finance the Revolutionary War was actually an investment that paid off very well and would have paid off even if the Americans had met their obligations and paid off the officers and men of the Continental Army. It is not the ordinary kind of investment, however, and I will skip this problem for the rest of the chapter. As mentioned above (note 8), the actual bonded indebtedness was paid off eventually.

10. The higher interest rates should attract foreign funds; hence, part of the reduction in productive investment will occur abroad.

11. I am on the board of directors and a substantial shareholder of a small company. We make use of the tax law when we can and, as a result of this, I myself, let alone government statisticians, do not know exactly how much we are investing.

12. I do not have any.

13. The actual history of this particular idea is amusing. As I suppose is obvious from what I have said above, I have never taken the Barro proposition very seriously; hence, I have not read up much on it. The *Journal of Economic Perspectives* (Spring 1989, 3, 17–93) ran a whole symposium on the budget deficit, which I read as a way of refreshing my memory. This led me to quickly write up about four pages giving the objection to the line of reasoning which will be found in the next few paragraphs of the main text. I sent them into the journal and they were rejected with the very polite note that did not tell me why. I met Joseph Stiglitz, the editor, in Chile and he told me the reason they were rejected was because Allan Drazen (1978) had already said this. This seems to be odd for a journal that does not claim to be a research journal, but since I had become accustomed to editorial arbitrariness through my long association with *Public Choice*, I did not protest.

Shortly thereafter, I saw an article by Alex Cukierman and Allan H. Meltzer (1989) which with much greater complication made the points I had made in my submission, and I am sure it was submitted to the *American Economic Review* before my article was submitted to *Journal of Economic Perspectives*. It also contained a footnote to Drazen. Nevertheless, I regard this as evidence of something I have always been aware of—the inherent arbitrariness of the refereeing process.

14. There are ways that this can be done legally if his daughter is an adult, but, in general, they are not only rather impractical but they would no doubt immediately raise suspicion on the part of any bank he would approach.

15. Once again, part of the effect will be felt abroad.

16. Like me, unfortunately.

17. The easiest way to do this is simply raise retirement age, but this is politically difficult.

18. The Nobel Committee in awarding its Prize to Buchanan cited this as one of his accomplishments.

19. Or some other dictator would replace them if it was a dictatorship.

Part Three

Opinion of the Various Opinions

10 Is the National Debt Really— I Mean, *Really*— a Burden?

ALAN S. BLINDER

INTRODUCTION

The budget deficit of the U.S. government must be both the most overrated and understated problem in contemporary American life. There are those who paint cataclysmic pictures of the adverse effects of deficits—and, indeed, who painted these same pictures almost a decade ago. There are others who view deficits as an accounting fiction of no real economic importance, or even as a blessing. It seems doubtful that both groups can be right for this particular time in this particular place.

My role in this volume is that of a wise man. Readers who have come this far have encountered a variety of economists advocating their own particular views—some of them highly idiosyncratic; some of them, perhaps, rather extreme. Most of the arguments and counterarguments in earlier chapters contain more than a germ of truth. But many fail to do justice to the other side. My assignment—as befits a middle-of-the-road, middle-class, middle-aged economist—is not to promote any particular view, but to help you wade through the claims and counterclaims and separate wheat from chaff. That is what I will try to do.

I can think of no better summary of the reasonable, middle-of-the-road position that I am supposed to represent than the following quotation:

> More and more talk is being heard these days that the federal-budget deficit is not such a problem after all. Should Americans learn to stop worrying and love the deficit? I think not. But neither should we view it as a sword of Damocles. A bloated deficit is more like having a few termites in the house: It's better to clean them out right away, but a little procrastination will do only a little damage, and an excessively toxic pesticide might do more harm than good.[1]

Notice that two points are being made here. First, that the budget deficit, while hardly a good thing, is certainly not a cataclysm. Second, that dealing with it is not an emergency—the sooner the better, but hasty actions are not called for. I wrote those words in *Business Week* in February 1989 and see no reason to change them now.

In this essay, I want to explain the reasoning behind them. But before we can discuss the burden of the debt logically and dispassionately, there are three *logically prior issues* that must be dealt with. Each has come up prominently in earlier chapters of this book, and, unless you dozed off frequently, has probably left you somewhat confused. An analogy may help you think through each of them.

LOGICALLY PRIOR ISSUES

Is Debt Any Different from Taxes?

When we talk about a "burden" of the debt, we mean possible adverse consequences of a decision to finance government expenditures by debt rather than by taxes. We want to know what "burden," if any, might arise from substituting debt for taxes.

Why pose the question this way? Because, as Robert Barro never ceases to remind us, *using debt is like deferring the tax payments to the future*—when the interest and principal come due.[2] It is a fact of financial life that the present discounted value of these *future* interest and principal payments must equal the market value of the bond that is issued. So, if we cut taxes by $1,000 and issue a bond that sells for $1,000, the present discounted value of the future tax liabilities must be exactly $1,000—for that is what determines the market value of the bond. In this sense, a substitution of debt for taxes is just a swap of tax liabilities through time. The citizens agree to pay the tax collector later rather than now.

The key question here is: Does such a swap affect people's economic behavior? If it does not, then the whole question of burden from the debt—and thus this whole book—makes little sense. We should just be asking about the costs and benefits of government expenditures on different items at different times. The timing of taxes would be of second-order importance, if that. This is precisely Barro's position.

Typically, Barro's argument is phrased intergenerationally. The government borrows today, postponing taxes to our children and grandchildren. But people (who have infinite horizons!) do not want their children's positions worsened by government financial operations. So they save just enough more to undo the government's attempted intergenerational transfer, and leave the funds as a bequest. In this way, private saving exactly compensates for government dissaving, leaving no net effects on anything.

Notice that I rank this question first among my three "logically prior issues" because, if Barro's position is correct, the rest of the debate is pointless. If government financial operations of this sort are undone by the private sector, they certainly cannot have any real economic effects.

Barro's view is often parodied for incorrect reasons. Of course, few people have infinite planning horizons. And most practical people find his implicit model of bequest behavior fanciful, if not actually humorous. But, in fact, neither an infinite horizon nor bequests are critical to Barro's argument, because government borrowing is overwhelmingly short term.

Rhetoric aside, the real question is this: If you raise people's *current* after-tax incomes, but do not affect the present discounted values of their *lifetime* after-tax incomes, will they alter their economic behavior in any significant way? In particular, will they spend more and save less today (as the mainstream view claims)?

That brings me to my first analogy. Ask yourself the following question: If a friend gives you money on Monday, to be repaid on Friday, will that affect your economic behavior? Probably not. Now suppose the loan lasts a month instead of a week. Or a year. Or ten years. As the horizon lengthens, it becomes more and more believable that, for example, your spending might rise as a result of the loan.

It is from such reactions that a burden of the debt can arise. How? A rise in current consumption expenditures means that less is being saved out of any given flow of income.[3] With a smaller pool of saving, interest rates will probably rise, thereby crowding out some investment. (An alternative, to be discussed later, is that the exchange rate might rise instead of the interest rate.) And that means that a smaller capital stock will be willed to the future. Note that "the future" does not mean future generations. Since the average useful life of the U.S. capital stock is in the neighborhood of 10–12 years, most of the burden will fall on the people alive when the financing decision was made.

Now let's move from personal loans to the real issue: government borrowing versus current taxation. When the U.S. government issues debt instruments, it borrows for periods ranging from three months to 30 years. The mean maturity of the public debt is now six years, but the *median* is under three years. So the practical question is: Will cutting people's taxes now and raising them in three years lead to more spending today?

Unfortunately, econometric evidence on this point is sufficiently ambiguous that people can cling tenaciously to their pet theories without fear of being *decisively* contradicted by the data. Why is the evidence so inconclusive?

One main reason is that—until the 1980s—we had precious few episodes in which the *cyclically adjusted* deficit moved a great deal. Note the adjective. The deficit is the difference between tax receipts and expenditures, both of which vary with national income. So it can change *either* because policy changes *or* because national income changes. If you study U.S. fiscal history, as James Rock does in Chapter 1, you are led to the conclusion that—until the early 1980s—most large changes in the federal deficit were due to the business cycle. When the deficit jumped upward, it was generally because a recession slowed the growth of revenue. For example, the federal deficit rose about $50 billion from fiscal 1981 to fiscal 1982, but the cyclically adjusted deficit hardly moved. The only major exceptions to this rule were wars, when surges in government spending precipitated large deficits despite growing revenues.

Juxtaposed against this historical backdrop, the Reagan fiscal policy represented a somewhat unique, and very nearly controlled, experiment—a deliberate attempt to substitute debt for taxes without changing the path of government expenditures much.[4] And the effects—as Benjamin Friedman, Edward Gramlich, and others in this volume (but not Barro) have said—were more or less in line with what mainstream theory predicted.

To see this, look at Table 10-1. So as not to be unduly swayed by starting and ending points, and also to hold cyclical conditions roughly constant, the table compares the decade of the 1970s with the decade of the 1980s. Starting with the top panel, we see that the overall government deficit—government expenditures minus taxes, or G – T—including state and local as well as federal budgets, rose from 0.9 percent to 2.6 percent of gross national product (GNP), an increase of 1.7 percentage points. Barro's theory would seem to imply that the ratio of private savings to GNP (S in the table) should have *increased* by 1.7 percentage points. In fact, it *decreased* by 1.4 percentage points. That's quite a discrepancy.[5]

According to the mainstream view, the large deficits of the 1980s (relative to the 1970s) should have pushed up long-term real interest rates. The third panel shows an estimate I have constructed of the real interest rate on 10-year government bonds in the 1970s and 1980s.[6] My estimate might easily be off in any particular year, but it ought to be fairly accurate over a decade. It shows that real long-term interest rates were drastically higher in the 1980s than in the 1970s. Again, this is just as conventional theory predicted.[7]

The theory goes on to predict that private investment as a share of GNP (I in the table) should have fallen. The first panel suggests that this did indeed happen, though the fall in investment is less than the rise in the government deficit. However, most of the apparent decline is an illusion. During the 1980s, official government data show that the prices of investment goods rose only about one-half as rapidly as the prices of consumer goods.[8] That means that the same share of *nominal* GNP bought relatively more *real* capital goods in 1989 than in 1979. In fact, the second panel shows that the ratio of investment to GNP actually *rose* slightly in real terms. And many economic scholars believe the Commerce Department's indexes overstate the inflation of capital goods prices, and hence understate real investment.[9] Thus, on this score, the mainstream theory seems to fail.

Why? Table 10-1 (either the first or second panel) shows that net exports (X – IM) absorbed the blow, falling by roughly 2 percent of GNP. Thus net exports were crowded out instead of domestic investment. (More on the mechanism below.)[10]

So my tentative conclusion is that the substitution of debt for taxes in the United States in the early 1980s probably was *not* neutral. It *does* seem to have raised real interest rates and crowded out net exports. Is that bad?

TABLE 10-1

	1970s	1980s	Change
A. Shares of Nominal GNP			
G – T	0.9%	2.6%	+1.7
S	17.8	16.4	–1.4
I	16.7	15.6	–1.1
S – I	+1.1	+0.8	–0.3
X – IM	+0.2	–1.8	–2.0

Memo: G – T = (S – I) – (X – IM)

B. Shares of Real GNP			
C	62.8	64.5	+1.7
I	16.3	16.9	+0.6
G	20.2	19.8	–0.4
X – IM	0.8	–1.3	–2.1

C. Ex Post "Real" 10-Year Government Bond Rate			
	0.86%	6.47%	+5.61%

I will return to that question later, where I will give an affirmative answer. But the answer to the first of my three logically prior questions is: Yes, in our imperfect world, debt does seem to be something different from taxes.

Do We Really Have a Big Deficit?

Robert Eisner and, to a lesser extent Peter Bernstein and Robert Heilbroner, argue that we really do not have a big deficit. Eisner in particular makes several valid and important points. I answer them by posing a seemingly unrelated question: Is 40 degrees cold?

The answer, as everyone knows, depends on where you are and on the time of year—and also on whether you are measuring in centigrade or Fahrenheit! The analogy to deficits is this: In judging whether the deficit is too large, we must consider the time period and the country we are dealing with; and we must understand the units of measurement.

First, an elementary point with which all the authors in this volume agree: Certainly we should express the deficit *as a percentage of GNP*. A $100 billion deficit sounds like a huge sum. But, relative to today's GNP, it is the same as a $50 billion deficit in 1980 or a $19 billion deficit in 1970. People often forget how big the U.S. economy is. Table 10-2 shows that by 1989 the deficit was down to 2.9 percent of GNP—down from 4.9 percent in 1986 (row 1).

Beyond this obvious and noncontroversial adjustment, Eisner makes three valid points about measuring the budget deficit, each of which trims its size.

First, we should certainly reckon the *state and local government surplus*—which is now running around $45 billion, or 0.9 percent of GNP—into the calculation. After all, macroeconomic (and probably also microeconomic) effects do not depend on which level of government makes an expenditure or levies a tax. This adjustment alone reduces the measured deficit by almost one-third (see line 2 of Table 10-2). However, making the same correction to the 1981 figures reduces the deficit by about $30 billion, or 1.1 percent of GNP. So including the state/local surplus makes the growth of the deficit in the 1980s look even longer. (Compare lines 1 and 2 in Table 10-2.) In other words, Eisner is right; but the adjustment does not help his case.

Next, we certainly should do *inflation accounting*, as Eisner and Tullock say—and for precisely the reasons they give. There are two equivalent ways of thinking about this issue. One is to say that receipts from the *inflation tax* on holders of government debt should be counted like any other tax receipt. The other is to argue that part of what we now count as interest expense is actually return of principal, and hence should not be treated as an expenditure. Either approach leads to the same conclusion: We should subtract from the deficit an amount equal to the product of the inflation rate times the outstanding debt. Nowadays, this reduces the measured deficit by about $75 billion, or 1.4 percent of GNP. However, in 1981 this same correction would have been about $50 billion—or about 1.6 percent of GNP. Thus, once again, making the correction that Eisner wants makes the rise in the deficit since 1981 look even larger. (Compare the third and fourth lines of data in Table 10-2.)

Third, there is the matter of separating capital expenditures from current operating expenses. Eisner explicitly and Bernstein and Heilbroner implicitly argue that it would be better to have a separate capital budget. There are arguments on both sides of this issue, but I basically agree with Eisner. However, it is often hard to separate current from capital expenditures in the budget in practice. (For example, how do you treat education expenditures?) More important, if separate budgetary accounts are maintained, allowance must be made in the current operating budget for depreciation. Doing so would probably leave the current operating deficit more or less where it is now—if we restrict ourselves to *physical* investment—because *net* physical investment is around zero. However, Eisner would like to define investment more broadly—to include *human* investments—and subtracting this larger sum would produce a lower deficit number.[11]

Thus, when you cut through all the rhetoric—which is literally correct, but somewhat misleading—you are left with the conclusion that the government budget deficit *rose more* from 1981 to 1986 and *fell less* from 1986 to 1989 than naive accounting suggests. (Compare the first and fourth lines of data in Table 10-2.)

TABLE 10-2
Deficit as Share of GNP

	1981	1986	1989	Change 1981–86	Change 1981–89
1. Conventional accounting	–2.1%	–4.9%	–2.9%	–2.8%	–0.8%
2. Include state/local	–1.0%	–3.4%	–2.0%	–2.4%	–1.0%
3. Cyclically adjusted	+0.1%	–2.5%	–2.0%	–2.6%	–2.1%
4. Inflation accounted	+1.7%	–1.7%	–0.6%	–3.4%	–2.3%
5. Addendum: Private Saving	18.0%	15.8%	15.4%	–2.2%	–2.6%
6. Line 5 *plus* line 1	15.9%	10.9%	12.5%	–5.0%	–3.4%

Does that mean that recent deficits are "too big"? That's a much tougher call. As a share of GNP, they are smaller than those run in recent years by Japan, West Germany, and many other European countries, as Bernstein and Heilbroner point out. But, as Friedman notes, those people save much more than Americans do. Remember now the accounting identity that says:

✘   National saving ≡ Private saving – Government deficit

This subtraction is displayed in the last line of data in Table 10-2.

Many other countries, especially Japan and West Germany, do much more private saving (relative to their smaller GNPs) than we do.[12] So they can easily afford to run larger budget deficits. Because the United States is a spendthrift nation, *we have a smaller capacity to run budget deficits.*

Thus, I conclude that our recent deficits have been large (a) by U.S. historical standards and (b) compared with foreign countries, once you take account of our private saving behavior. This resolves my second logically prior question in the affirmative. But it does not yet establish that our deficit is *too large.* How can we tell? What does this phrase even mean?

Surely the most obvious and critical sense in which a public sector deficit could be excessive is if it were so large that the debt was growing faster than GNP. That would simply be an unsustainable position. Earlier in the decade, the U.S. government budget deficit was in fact this large, and the debt/GNP ratio rose rapidly. Today, we are just about at the dividing line: The debt/GNP ratio has been roughly constant and will remain so with a $140–$150 billion deficit—which is about what we have, if social security is included.[13] This is one major reason why Eisner and some others dispute the notion that the deficit should be reduced.

Those, like me, who argue for smaller deficits must be implicitly arguing that the debt/GNP ratio should be *lower* than it is now. That invites a rhetorical (but legitimate) question from deficit optimists: How do you know? The usual answer is that it would be better for the country if interest rates were lower, investment were higher, the trade deficit smaller, and so on. I will return to that theme shortly.

A second way to appraise the size of the deficit is to look at how it has changed since about 1980 or to compare it with postwar historical norms.[14] As the first line of Table 10-2 shows, the officially measured deficit as a share of GNP rose by 2.8 points from 1981 to 1986 and then fell by 2.0 points from 1986 to 1989. By this metric, then, we have already corrected more than two-thirds of the fiscal aberration of the early 1980s. But the fourth line paints a less optimistic picture: When measured more appropriately, the deficit as a share of GNP rose 3.4 points from 1981 to 1986, but fell only 1.1 points from 1986 to 1989. That is one reason why I think we still have a way to go to restore fiscal normalcy.

I hasten to agree with Eisner and Bernstein and Heilbroner, however, that a deficit can be *too small* as well as *too large*—especially if fiscal stimulus is needed to spur a sluggish economy. That was an important point in, say, 1982 or 1983. But I do not think the United States, with its 5.3 percent unemployment rate, is in this position today.[15] I, like Friedman, ask: Why should the U.S. government be running deficits (appropriately measured) of 2.3 percent of GNP in a full-employment, peacetime economy? I find it hard to think of answers.[16]

⌈So I think there are reasons, though certainly not ironclad ones, to believe that the current U.S. government budget deficit is too big. However, its size is certainly not overwhelming, and there is no reason to shoot for a balanced budget by current accounting standards.⌉

The Business Cycle and Other Influences

Bernstein and Heilbroner, and to some extent Eisner and Barro as well, criticize the mainstream view that Friedman and Gramlich represent on the grounds that the observed correlations among economic variables are often not what the theory calls for. Let me deal with this, and some related issues, with yet another analogy. Think about the following question: In a free market, do we expect quantity to rise or fall when price rises?

Even beginning students of economics will recognize this as a trick question. There is no correct answer. If price rises because of surging demand, we expect quantity to rise. But, if price rises because of shrinking supply, we naturally expect quantity to fall. Thus the correlation between price and quantity can be positive or negative, depending on why price changes.

Here is the analogy to deficits. *Question*: Do we expect higher interest rates when the deficit is higher? *Answer*: It depends why the deficit rose. If a larger deficit was precipitated by fiscal policy changes that increased government spending or reduced taxes, then mainstream theory does predict higher interest rates. If that does not happen, then the theory is in trouble. (Unless world capital markets are highly integrated. Then the exchange rate may rise instead of the interest rate. More on this below.) But if a larger deficit is due, say, to a recession, we expect it to be accompanied by *lower* interest rates, not higher ones, because the demands for money and credit decline in a business downturn. Hence the correlation between deficits and interest rates could be positive or negative. By itself, this raw correlation tells us nothing.

This problem of interpretation, by the way, is one reason why it is important to look at the *cyclically adjusted* deficit, which is unaffected by changes in national income. But this is hardly a full solution, for even the cyclically adjusted deficit can fall sway to two-way causation if, for example, fiscal policy actions respond to the state of the economy. More generally, as Bernstein and Heilbroner emphasize, numerous factors influence both interest rates and the budget deficit, causing potentially disparate comovements in different periods.

The point I have just made is very general; it applies to other correlations, such as the one between budget and trade deficits. The mainstream theory predicts that a deliberate, policy-induced increase in the budget deficit will lead to a trade deficit. (I will explain how shortly.) But, if a recession comes, the budget deficit should *rise* (because tax receipts fall) while the trade deficit should *fall* (because imports decline).

Nor is the business cycle the only factor we must worry about. As Bernstein and Heilbroner note, if some exogenous force reduces our net exports, our national income (and hence tax receipts) will fall, producing a larger budget deficit. In general, a variety of changes in the economy— or in other economies—can affect the budget deficit, the trade deficit, interest rates, exchange rates, saving and investment, and so on. Thus simple correlations tell us little. We must look through the data to the economic mechanism and try to solve the chicken-egg problem as best we can.[17] In this respect, the Reagan tax cuts form a particularly clean example because an ideologically motivated president cut taxes drastically for no good reason!

The mention of recession brings up another point emphasized by Eisner. In opposing policies that reduce the deficit, he notes that there are worse things than a deficit—such as a recession. I agree completely and enthusiastically. But I do not see that as a choice we now face. In this time and place, I believe, the Federal Reserve will use monetary stimulus to replace whatever fiscal stimulus is taken away by deficit reduction. Thus when people like Friedman, Gramlich, and myself talk about cutting the deficit, we do not advocate a contractionary policy. We advocate, instead, *a shift in the policy mix toward easier money and tighter budgets*. That should lower interest rates, raise the investment share of GNP, and boost the capital stock that we transmit to the future. Even Eisner agrees that that is a desirable outcome.

BURDEN-OF-THE-DEBT ARGUMENTS

With this as background, let me now run over the main burden-of-the-debt arguments as I see them.

I begin with two very old-fashioned arguments that were based mostly on myths and misunderstandings. These arguments accounted for most of the traditional Republican abhorrence of deficits for decades. And I believe they are still an important part of the popular folk wisdom. But they have not played a prominent role in the current scholarly debate, and so I treat them briefly.

Argument #1: The interest and principal that will have to be paid later is a burden on future generations.

Wrong! Future generations will indeed have to pay higher taxes. But they will also receive the principal and interest payments. Thus, the debt service payments, when they come, will just amount to shuffling dollars from one group of Americans to others living at the same time. Timothy Smeeding argues that this reshuffling may not be distributionally neutral and, for that reason, may be undesirable. I agree. But it does not mean that the debt burdens *the nation as a whole.*

However, this argument *does* have validity to the extent that we borrow from foreigners, for then the debt service payments leave the country. I will come back to this in another context.

Argument #2: If we borrow too much, the nation will go bankrupt.

This may be true for Brazil, Mexico, or Poland; but not for the United States. Why? As long as our borrowing is denominated in dollars, we never need fear defaulting for we can always print as many dollars as we need. It may be wise or foolish to incur more debt. But fear of default is simply a red herring in the U.S. case.[18]

Argument #3: Running excessive deficits can be inflationary.

This danger was much discussed when Reaganomics was first being debated; but it sounds silly now. As you probably know, inflation fell rapidly just as the large budget deficits were opening up.

But concern about the inflationary consequences of deficits is not at all silly in Latin America and in several Eastern European countries, where large deficits are at the root of hyperinflation. Why? In those countries, but not in the United States, deficits are typically financed by expanding the money supply because the government is unable to float bonds on the world market at reasonable interest rates. In such an environment, a large deficit quickly leads to excessive money growth and to a classic inflation with "too much money chasing too few goods."

In our country, things are quite different. The cumulative rise in the net national debt since 1980 has been about $1,400 billion.[19] But the rise in bank reserves and currency during that same period has been only about $135 billion, or roughly 10 percent as much. Thus less than 10 percent of our deficits have been turned into money. If the U.S. national debt is a burden, it is not because it has left us a legacy of high inflation.

Argument #4: Budget deficits crowd out private investment.

This is the classic burden-of-the-debt argument, represented in this volume most clearly by Friedman, but discussed by almost every author. It runs, briefly, as follows. Higher deficits raise the ratio of debt to GNP (relative to what it otherwise would have been). This, in turn, raises real interest rates. Higher interest rates deter some investment spending, so the capital stock—and hence potential GNP and standards of living—grow more slowly than they would have with smaller deficits.

As we have already noted, this did not happen in the United States in the 1980s. (See, especially, the second panel of Table 10-1.) Why? What went wrong?

Clearly, the problem was not with the link from debt to interest rates. Real interest rates soared. But investment spending did not fall. One reason may have been that tax incentives for business investment cancelled out the deleterious effects of higher interest rates. But the main reason, as I have already suggested, is that net exports were crowded out instead. We saved investment by savaging our international trade position. This brings us naturally to the next argument.

Argument #5: Deficits crowd out net exports and turn the nation into an international debtor.

There are two ways to tell the story. The first version begins (as in Argument #4) with deficits raising interest rates. In a world economy with open and fluid financial markets, this prompts inflows of financial capital from international investors seeking higher returns on their money. These inflows make the currency appreciate (if exchange rates are floating), and discourages exports and promotes imports. So net exports fall.

The second version starts with the accounting identity implicit in the first panel of Table 10-1:

$$G - T \equiv S - I - (X - IM)$$

Now suppose that a change in fiscal policy raises the deficit (G - T). If this policy action does not drive saving (S) up or investment (I) down, then X − IM must fall. This much follows by the laws of arithmetic. The only question is whether S − I will rise to match the increase in G − T, thereby shielding X − IM.

Suppose personal income taxes are cut, as happened in the United States between 1981 and 1984. Will savings rise? The Barro theory of debt neutrality says yes: People will save their tax cuts so as to have the funds to pay future tax bills. Reaganomics also said yes, though for a different reason. The tax cuts, we were told, provided powerful incentives that would induce households to raise their personal savings substantially. The mainstream theory, of course, denies the empirical validity of both of these scenarios. And, as we have seen, the data do not look favorable to the Barro/Reagan view.

The other possibility is that investment might fall—the old crowding out story. It will happen to the extent that interest rates rise a lot and investment is sensitive to interest rates. But international capital mobility blunts the rise in any one country's interest rates by tying together interest rates all over the world. Now one country's deficit must raise *world* interest rates in order to cause (domestic) crowding out. And, even if this happens, investment will be crowded out in many countries, not just in one country that ran the deficit.

What we learned from the U.S. experience in the 1980s is:

1. that the United States is big enough to push world interest rates around (which was no surprise);
2. that international capital markets limit the impact of U.S. deficits on U.S. interest rates (also not much of a surprise);
3. and that net exports appear to be far more sensitive to exchange rates than domestic investment is to interest rates (which *did* catch us by surprise).

Thus the conclusion seems to be that, for the contemporary United States, a larger budget deficit causes a larger trade deficit. But remember the warning issued before: This applies to a budget deficit *deliberately caused by a policy change*. If a budget deficit rises *because of a recession*, the trade deficit should fall.

This seems an appropriate place to stop and ask an important question that has been postponed until now: Why should this be considered a burden? Why is it a bad idea to run a trade deficit and borrow from abroad? After all, it means that foreigners send us goods and services in return for paper IOUs.

In fact, there are two clear circumstances in which it is a very good thing to do. One is if we never have to pay back what we borrow. This might be called the "junk bond solution"; but it is not very plausible for the United States. I believe, as do the world capital markets, that the United States will in fact meet its debt service obligations. Once again, the story may be quite different for Latin America, as Kenneth Jameson discusses in Chapter 3.

The second scenario is if we invest the borrowed money wisely, yielding enough future income to repay interest and principal and leave something over for ourselves. This might be called the Washington/Jefferson solution, because it is exactly what the United States did in its early days (and for most of the century that followed). Barro wants us to believe that this is what happened in the 1980s. Suppose the Reagan tax cuts and/or the general resurgence of pro-capitalist attitudes made the United States a particularly attractive place to invest—not just for Americans, but for capitalists all over the world. Then funds would have flocked to our shores, the dollar would have appreciated, and a large trade deficit would have opened up.

This scenario is logically clean but empirically flawed. If this is what happened in the 1980s, we should have seen the investment share of GNP rising right away, which we did not. (See Table 10-1.) A few years later, we should have started seeing the productivity fruits of all these marvelous investment opportunities, which we still have not.

What really happened, as Friedman indicates, is that the United States went on a consumption binge. We threw a party, to which—as Rock and Smeeding remind us—the wealthy were especially invited. In consequence, when we must pay back the foreign loans, we will not have enough income-producing properties to service the debt. We will, instead, have to reduce our standard of living by consuming less than we produce—just as we raised our standard of living in the 1980s by consuming more than we produced.

There is another sense in which financing our national debt by borrowing from foreigners has burdened not only the United States but the world. It's our new status as the world's largest debtor. I think it is realistic to say that America's new and unaccustomed debtor status undermines our geopolitical clout and moral authority on a variety of issues. Although it is not strictly an *economic* burden, Friedman emphasized it in his chapter, and I agree. Furthermore, I am enough of an American chauvinist to think that the whole world will lose when and if leadership of the free world passes out of our hands and into others.

These last two arguments constitute the mainstream view, as amended in the light of recent experience. (The amendment is to emphasize crowding out of net exports rather than crowding out of domestic investment.) But I would like to add one further respect in which the budget deficit is now putting a burden on America's future.

Argument #6: The unending deficit "crisis" makes for myopic budget policy that shortchanges the future.

Washington's perpetual preoccupation with the budget deficit is making a mockery of federal budgeting. And the foolish, myopic incentives created by the Gramm-Rudman-Hollings Act make matters even worse. Congressmen and women these days seem to care more about how some program affects the Gramm-Rudman calculation than they do about the program's merits.

Here I agree with Barro, Eisner, Bernstein and Heilbroner, Smeeding, and others, who argue that a fixation on today's deficit can be harmful to the economy's long-term future. Specifically, *government investments*, just like private investments, entail expenditures today in order to reap returns tomorrow. Two of my favorite examples are:

1. Public infrastructure capital like roads, bridges, airports, and waste treatment facilities, which were mentioned by Eisner and Bernstein and Heilbroner. There is evidence that the United States has underinvested in these items, that they have high rates of return, and that they would raise private-sector productivity and capital

formation.[20] But all of them cost money to build *now* and yield benefits only *later*. In today's budget climate, that intertemporal tradeoff is a loser.

2.   Early intervention on behalf of children at risk, which was mentioned by Smeeding. There is strong evidence that prenatal care, postnatal care, and preschool education have very high financial rates of return.[21] Providing these services to those who are incapable of providing them for their own children is probably the most effective antipoverty program we know. It would, in addition, be a profound humanitarian gesture. But, once again, the expenditures come now and the benefits come *much* later, perhaps as much as a generation later.

In our current fiscal environment, it is hard to get members of Congress to take proposals like these seriously—they all "raise the deficit." At a hearing on infrastructure in the summer of 1989, Congressman Lee Hamilton asked me and three others whether we would vote for $15 billion in additional spending on public infrastructure, if that spending would add $15 billion to the budget deficit. I think he was surprised when three of the four of us said we would.[22] Three-quarters of the Congress, I am certain, would not.

Instead, Congress continuously looks for gimmicks that can cut the present deficit even if that comes at the expense of future deficits. The current debate over the capital gains tax is a fine example. In 1989, a proposed *temporary* decrease in the tax rate on capital gains drew a great deal of political support because it would have provided a "window of opportunity" for holders of appreciated assets to realize their gains—and thus would have raised revenue for the fiscal 1990 budget at the expense of future budgets. Even today, the transitory increase (but long-run decrease) in tax revenue that a capital gains tax cut is likely to yield remains a strong selling point.

THE SOCIAL SECURITY SURPLUS

Finally, I should not conclude without saying something about the much-ballyhooed social security surplus and its relation to the burden-of-the-debt issue.

Under plans laid out by the Greenspan Commission in 1983, the government will take in more in payroll taxes than it spends on social security benefits until, roughly, the year 2010. These annual excesses of receipts over disbursements constitute the social security surplus and are the major reason for both past and projected progress in reducing the overall federal deficit.

Some numbers will illustrate. (See Table 10-3.) Looking backward, the social security surplus grew from zero to about $52 billion between fiscal years 1984 and 1989, while the overall deficit declined just $33 billion.

TABLE 10-3
Changes in the Budget
(in billions of dollars)

	1984–1989	1990–1995
Social security	+$52	+$62
Rest of budget	–$19	–$42
Total	+$33	+$20

Thus the non-social-security deficit *rose* by about $19 billion. Looking forward, current CBO projections see the social security surplus growing about $62 billion between fiscal 1990 and fiscal 1995. During this time, the overall deficit is projected to decline just $20 billion. So the non-social-security deficit is expected to rise about $42 billion. Under current projections, the social security trust fund may just about buy up the *current* national debt. What will happen to the *actual* national debt outstanding by the year 2010 depends, of course, on what happens to the non-social-security portion of the budget between then and now.

Most people are confused about the nature of the social security trust fund. Many people think of it as a kind of bank account into which they make "deposits" while they work so as to be able to make "withdrawals" when they retire. Nothing could be further from the truth. In fact, the fund is an accounting fiction. Most payroll taxes are used immediately to pay benefits to retirees. The rest is invested by law in U.S. government securities—which is where the accounting fiction comes in.

The U.S. government is now running about a $150 billion overall deficit comprised of a $50 billion surplus in social security and a $200 billion deficit in the rest of the budget. So the Treasury issues $200 billion in new bonds each year. But the social security trust fund buys $50 billion of them, which amounts to one branch of the government lending to another. Only $150 billion is left to be sold to private investors. That is the true sense in which social security is being used to finance part of the non-social-security deficit.

Both Budget Director Richard Darman and Senator Daniel P. Moynihan object to this practice. But there is a good reason for it. If we insist on matching taxes to benefits year by year, as Senator Moynihan now wants, the graying of the U.S. population will require much higher payroll tax rates in the next century. Rather than let that happen, Congress decided to run surpluses in social security for about 25 years and then to "spend" the accumulation by running social security deficits. Legally, that decision meant that the accounting fiction we call the social security trust fund would first rise enormously and then fall even more. Economically, it meant that social security would swallow up much of the national debt—but only temporarily.

The effects of this massive fiscal operation depend sensitively on which view of the burden-of-the-debt debate is correct.

Under the mainstream view, the large accumulation of funds in social security—that is, the large reduction of the national debt—will ease the burden of paying future social security benefits. How? Either it will:

1. lower interest rates and thereby raise investment, so there will be more capital and hence higher output per worker in the future.

2. limit our need for foreign borrowing, so that when the future rolls around, more U.S. assets will be owned by Americans.

In either case, the same payroll tax *rates* should generate more revenue.

On the other hand, the Barro debt neutrality view implies that none of this matters. Adopting the Moynihan proposal to cut payroll taxes would have no effects whatever! And, under the Eisner view, the government budget surpluses that social security is producing might be a drag on the economy. So the Moynihan plan probably has merit. So, you see, it really does matter who is right. I hope by now to have convinced you that I am.

NOTES

1. Alan S. Blinder, "Is the deficit too high? Yes. Should it be higher? Maybe." *Business Week,* February 20, 1989, page 17.

2. Except where otherwise noted, all references are to earlier chapters in this volume.

3. As Bernstein and Heilbroner, Eisner, and others remind us, the size of the flow of income may depend on saving decisions for Keynesian reasons. I return to this important point later.

4. Here I separate Reaganite rhetoric from Reaganite actions. *In word,* Reaganomics cut government spending. *In deed,* it mainly replaced social spending by defense spending.

5. I am being unfair to Barro here. Other influences than government financial policy move the private saving rate and could have been pushing it downward.

6. Since there are no market data on real interest rates, this calculation needs some explanation. For the 1970s, I subtracted from the 10-year government bond rate the *actual* inflation rate over the following 10 years to get the *ex post* real rate. For the 1980s, I followed the same practice as far as I could and then extrapolated a 4.5 percent inflation rate into the future. Thus, for example, expected 10-year inflation in 1985 was assumed to be actual inflation in 1985–89 and 4.5 percent per annum thereafter.

7. Barro, and to a lesser extent Bernstein and Heilbroner, make much of the fact that *short-run* variations in investment do not match up well with *short-run* variations in interest rates or the deficit. That is not inconsistent with the claim made here. After all, many factors other than the deficit affect interest rates; and many factors other than interest rates affect investment. More on this later.

8. The price increases are mainly for structures. Prices of equipment (which includes computing equipment) have been roughly constant since 1982.

9. See Robert J. Gordon, *Measurement of Durable Goods Prices,* National Bureau of Economic Reasearch, University of Chicago Press, 1990.

10. Bernstein and Heilbroner, in particular, would have us believe that some other factor (such as lagging U.S. industrial productivity) caused both the decline in U.S. net exports and the rise in the budget deficit. That is, as I will note shortly, a logical possibility. However, it is hard (for me at least) to see how adverse productivity trends could have created the two deficits so quickly. No one maintains that the level of U.S. industrial productivity dropped.

11. It would also open a Pandora's box of measurement problems. As with physical capital, we must reckon depreciation into the operating budget. But how are we to measure the depreciation of human capital?

12. I do not find it useful, in this context, to count what we spend on Sony televisions and Hondas as saving, as Barro and Eisner want to do. If we do so, international savings gaps shrink.

13. It can be argued—fairly cogently—that we should omit the social security surplus, which is meant to bolster savings for other reasons. More on this at the end of the chapter.

14. In practice, the two concepts of "normalcy" differ only slightly.

15. These words were written in March 1990. The unemployment rate began to rise in July. Higher unemployment rates call for higher deficits.

16. Eisner and Bernstein and Heilbroner, of course, dispute the premise that a 5.3% unemployment rate is about full employment.

17. This is what economists try to do with their models.

18. It is *not*, of course, in the Latin American case, as Kenneth Jameson reminds us.

19. The adjective "net" means that I exclude the portion of the public debt that is owned by government agencies like the social security trust fund.

20. David A. Aschauer, "Is Public Expenditure Productive?" *Journal of Monetary Economics,* March 1989, pp. 177–200.

21. Committee for Economic Development, *Children in Need,* New York, 1987.

22. *Public Investment in Human and Physical Infrastructure,* Hearing before the Joint Economic Committee, U.S. Congress, July 19, 1990.

Glossary

Ability-to-pay principle: A taxing principle, based on the belief that the last (marginal) dollar earned by the rich is worth relatively less to them than the last dollar earned by the poor. Consequently, it advocates that tax liability should be a larger fraction of income and wealth for high-income/high-wealth receivers than for low-income/low-wealth receivers. Such a taxing scheme is called "progressive." See *Taxes*.

Absolute advantage: The ability of one country to produce a specific good or service with fewer resources (more cheaply) than other countries. See *Comparative advantage*.

Actual budget: See *Budget, public*.

Adjustable peg system: See *Bretton Woods system; Exchange rate*.

AFDC: See *Aid to Families with Dependent Children*.

Aggregate demand: The total quantity of goods and services consumers are willing and able to demand (that is, effective demand) at various economy-wide price levels. Also known as aggregate expenditure. See *Gross national product; Keynesian economics; Macroeconomics*.

Aggregate supply: The total quantity of goods and services producers are willing and able to supply at various economy-wide price levels; also known as aggregate output. See *Macroeconomics*.

Aggregation: Summing individual units or data into one unit or number. For example, national income accounts is an aggregation of all individual transactions. Price indexes are a sum of the value of all prices divided by the number of prices.

Aid to Families with Dependent Children (AFDC): A state-administered and partly federal-funded program that provides aid if dependent children do not have the support of a parent because of his or her death, disability, or desertion. See *Public assistance programs; Transfer payments*.

Appreciation (depreciation) of a currency: See *Exchange rate appreciation (depreciation)*.

Asset: Anything having exchange value in the marketplace; wealth; listed on the left-hand side of a balance sheet or income statement. See *Balance sheet; Income statement; Liability.*

Automatic stabilizer: Federal revenue or expenditure items that automatically respond countercyclically to changes in national income; for example, unemployment benefits, progressive income taxes. See *Budget, public.*

Balanced budget: A situation in which current revenue is exactly equal to current expenditures. Some Keynesian economists advocate a cyclically balanced budget: Government expenditures for goods and services and net tax collections are equalized over the course of a business cycle, and deficits incurred during periods of recession are offset by surpluses obtained during periods of prosperity. Some New Classical economists advocate annually balanced budgets. See *Budget, public; Keynesian economics; New Classical economics.*

Balanced budget amendment: Proposed constitutional amendment that would require Congress to balance the federal budget annually by assuring that federal revenues would cover expenditures.

Balance of international payments: A tabulation of a nation's transactions with other countries for a given period, typically a year, using a double-entry system of accounting. Each transaction creates a flow of exports or imports and a flow of capital (capital account) to pay for it. A surplus means that the home country has added to its wealth or reduced its debt to foreigners; a deficit indicates the opposite. The flow of exports and imports is published in three basic balances: balance of trade or merchandise trade (exports and imports of goods), goods and services (includes net investment income, as well as goods and services), and current account (includes all the others plus unilateral transfers). Historically, the current-account balance falls between the other two. See *Balance of trade; Capital account; Current account.*

Balance of trade: The difference between the value of a nation's exports and imports of merchandise or goods ("visibles"); one component of the balance of payments. If exports exceed imports, the balance is positive, otherwise it is negative. See *Current account.*

Balance on capital account: See *Capital account.*

Balance on current account: See *Current account.*

Balance sheet: An accounting statement of the wealth position of an enterprise as of a particular date. Net worth is positive if assets exceed liabilities. A balance sheet tallies stocks (time reference, at a specific date); an income statement tallies flows (time reference and time dimension, for example, per year). See *Income statement.*

Barter: The direct exchange of one good for another, without the use of money: Goods buy goods. See *Monetary economy.*

Base year: A year chosen as a comparison or reference point with regard to other years.

Bond: A contractual agreement, generally long-term, acknowledging a debt, carrying a specified amount and schedule of interest payments, and (usually) a date for redemption of its face value; an IOU. Government bonds and shorter-term securities (bills and notes) are used to fund the federal-budget deficit.

Bretton Woods system: The rules and institutions established in 1944 at Bretton Woods, New Hampshire in 1944 to regulate the international economic system. Its system of "adjustable pegs" remained in effect until August 1971. The principal Bretton Woods institutions are the World Bank and the International Monetary Fund. See *Exchange rate; International Monetary Fund; World Bank.*

Budget, public: A statement of a government's anticipated expenditures and revenues for a fiscal year. For the federal government it is called the federal budget.

> *Federal-budget deficit:* The shortfall of federal revenues (taxes) relative to expenditures (government purchases and transfer payments), measured at an annual rate.

> *Federal-budget surplus:* The excess of federal revenues relative to expenditures, measured at an annual rate. See *Deficit; Government purchases; NAIRU; Taxes; Transfer payments.*

> *Full-employment budget:* Derived assuming the lowest sustainable unemployment rate compatible with reasonable price stability; what government expenditures and revenues (and the surplus or deficit) would be in such an economy.

Built-in stabilizer: See *Automatic stabilizer.*

Business cycle: A wavelike fluctuation of national income around its trend value, after seasonal fluctuations have been removed; alternating periods of economic growth and contraction.

Business saving: Net business saving is the after-tax profits of corporations not distributed as dividends to stockholders; gross business saving includes a capital consumption allowance. See *Saving.*

Capital (or capital resources): A factor of production or resource, which is composed of physical capital, financial capital, and human capital; all three are used as inputs for production. Capital—unlike labor, land, and entrepreneurship—must first be produced itself before it is available for use in further production. Capital stock is the term commonly used for the aggregate quantity of capital goods, which is increased and decreased by investment and disinvestment.

Capital account: The section in a country's balance of international payments that records securities transactions, long- and short-term loans, deposits in financial institutions, and the net reserve position. A surplus or deficit in this account is matched by an offsetting one in the current account. See *Balance of international payments; Current account.*

Capital consumption allowance: The national income accounting estimate of the depreciation (and obsolescence) of the value of capital goods; the value of the nation's production equipment used up in producing other goods. It indicates how much investment is needed to keep the nation's capital stock intact and is subtracted from gross national product to obtain net national product.

Capital flight: The movement of financial and human ("brain drain") capital from less desirable countries to more desirable countries to avoid government expropriation, taxation, and high rates of inflation or to realize better investment opportunities.

Capital formation: Investment in physical, financial, and human capital.

Capital gain (loss): The monetary gain (loss) realized when securities or properties are sold for a price greater (less) than the price paid for them.

Capitalization of assets: The value of an asset measured by calculating the present value of its expected future income. See *Present value.*

Categorical grants: Federal grants to state and local governments for specific expenditures.

CEA: See *Council of Economic Advisers.*

Central bank: A government-established agency that controls the supply of money and supervises the country's commercial banks. The central bank of the United States is the Federal Reserve System. See *Federal Reserve System.*

Central economic planning: Government determination of the objectives of the economy and the direction of its resources to the attainment of these objectives, in contrast to laissez faire. See *Laissez faire.*

Ceteris paribus: Literally, "other things being equal"; a simplifying assumption used by economists in which only the specific variables under consideration change and all other variables remain constant.

Classical theory of employment: The macroeconomic generalizations accepted by most economists prior to Keynes' *General Theory* (1936), which led to the conclusion that a capitalistic economy would tend to employ its resources fully. See *Keynesian economics; New Classical economics.*

Coincidence of wants: A situation in which the item (good or service) one trader wishes to obtain is the same item another trader desires to give up and in which the item the second trader wishes to acquire is the same item the first trader desires to surrender. This is a necessary condition for barter trade. See *Barter.*

COLA: See *Cost-of-living adjustment.*

Comparative advantage: A principle of international trade stating that a nation should produce and export goods where its efficiency relative to other nations is highest. Specialization and, consequently, opportunities to benefit through trade depend on comparative, not absolute, advantage. See *Absolute advantage.*

Conspicuous consumption: The use of certain goods and services to display the owner's wealth and to gain prestige and the envy of others. See *Consumption.*

Constant dollars: Amounts measured in base-year dollars (that is, according to the purchasing power of the dollar in some earlier year) to express value in a way that corrects for changes in the price level. See *Consumer Price Index; Current dollars; Index number; Nominal; Price index; Real.*

Consumer Price Index (CPI): An index number representing a weighted average of the prices of basic, uniform-through-time goods and services purchased by representative families in an economy; a measure of the cost of living. See *Constant dollars; Index number.*

Consumption: The market value of purchases of goods and services by individuals and nonprofit institutions and the value of food, clothing, housing, and financial services received by them as income in kind.

Cost-benefit analysis: A technique for evaluating government policies. The sum of the opportunity cost to all parties is compared with the value of the benefits to all parties.

Cost-of-living adjustment (COLA): Automatic adjustment of nominal income at the same percentage as the rate of inflation.

Cost-push inflation: See *Inflation, cost-push.*

Council of Economic Advisers (CEA): Three persons appointed by the President under the authority of the Employment Act of 1946, whose job it is to conduct research and to advise the President on economic matters (including the preparation of the *Economic Report of the President* to Congress). See *Employment Act of 1946.*

Creditworthiness: The ability to secure a loan. The least-cost loan terms are given to those thought to be the most creditworthy.

Crowding in (crowding out): A favorable (or adverse) effect on private-sector investment spending, owing to the positive effect on aggregate demand, output, and the utilization rate of capital equipment on (or owing to the negative effect of higher interest rates associated with) federal deficits. See *Investment.*

Currency appreciation (depreciation): See *Exchange rate appreciation (depreciation).*

Current account: The section in a country's international balance of payments that records transactions arising from trade in goods ("visibles," or balance of trade), in services, and from interest and dividends that are earned by capital owned in one country and invested in another ("invisibles"). A surplus or deficit in this account is matched by an offsetting one in the capital account.

Current-account deficit indicates either borrowing, gifts from abroad, or increasing the reserves held by the foreign central authorities.

Current-account surplus indicates either loans and gifts to foreigners or the reduction of reserves of dollars held by the foreign central authorities. See *Balance of international payments; Balance of trade; Capital account; Deficit.*

Current dollars: The value of present-year dollars; also called nominal or money dollars. See *Constant dollars; Money illusion.*

Cyclical: Referring to economic impacts—for example, deficits and unemployment—caused by the business or trade cycle. See *Secular.*

Debt: Generally, amounts owed to one's creditors. The national debt is a summation of the annual budget deficits and surpluses. The net foreign debt, likewise, is a summation of the annual current account deficits and surpluses. The present value of future debt is diminished by inflation and increased by deflation. See *National debt.*

Debt servicing: The interest required on an outstanding debt by contractual agreement.

Deficit: The excess of expenditures over revenues.

> *Twin deficits* are the federal budget deficit and the international current account deficit. The federal budget deficit (or simply budget deficit) is a state of domestic budget imbalance in which expenditures exceed receipts. The international current account deficit (or simply current account deficit), in balance of payments accounting, is a condition in which negative or debit entries exceed positive or credit entries.

> *Real deficit* is the actual deficit adjusted for the net balance sheet gain experienced by government because of inflation (actual deficit minus the inflation rate times the net federal debt outstanding).

> *Structural deficit* is the total federal budget deficit minus that portion arising because the economy is operating below (what is defined as) full employment. See *Current account; Federal-budget deficit.*

Deficit financing, national: Funding those expenditures that are in excess of current receipts through borrowing or monetizing. See *Monetization.*

Deficit Reduction Act (1984): Delayed elimination of the telephone excise tax, canceled the $100 per person net interest exclusion from individual income taxes, and changed other small items in an attempt to reduce the federal budget deficit.

Deflation: A decrease in the average level of prices of goods and services. See *Inflation.*

Demand: The desire to buy at certain prices. Effective demand is the desire and ability to buy at certain prices; aggregate demand is national effective demand. See *Aggregate demand; Effective demand.*

Demand for money: The quantity of money people wish to hold at alternative interest rates and income levels. The demand for foreign currency is called the demand for foreign exchange.

Demand-side (Keynesian) economics: An approach to macroeconomic stabilization policy that emphasizes stimulating aggregate demand to encourage full employment. See *Keynesian economics; Supply-side economics.*

Depository Institutions Act of 1982: Extended the 1980 Depository Institutions and Monetary Control Act and dealt specifically with the problem of failing thrift institutions; also known as the Garn–St. Germain Act.

Depository Institutions Deregulation and Monetary Control Act of 1980: Allowed, among other things, savings banks, credit unions, and savings and loan associations (depository institutions) to accept checkable deposits, to use the check-clearing facilities of the Federal Reserve, and to borrow from the Federal Reserve; subjected them to the reserve requirements of the Fed; and provided for the gradual elimination of ceilings on the interest rates that could be paid by depository institutions on savings and time deposits.

Depreciation (of capital): See *Capital consumption allowance.*

Depreciation (of currency): A fall in the free-market value of domestic currency in terms of foreign currency—that is, a rise in the price of foreign exchange.

Depression: A persistent period when national output is well below its potential, with very high unemployment and high excess capacity; a severe recession; a very severe panic or crisis.

Derived demand: Demand for labor and other inputs not as ends in themselves but as means to produce other things; demand for a resource that depends on demand for the products it can be used to produce.

Devaluation of currency: A decrease in the defined value of a currency; under the gold standard, a decrease in the value of a currency as a consequence of an increase in the price of gold.

DIDMCA: See *Depository Institutions Deregulation and Monetary Control Act of 1980.*

Discount: The practice of paying or receiving the present value of bills of exchange, securities, or promissory notes before their maturity date minus a deduction to cover interest for the purchaser.

   Discount rate: The interest rate the Federal Reserve charges depository intermediaries for loans; more generally, the rate of interest used to discount a stream of future payments to arrive at their present value. See *Present value.*

Disinflation: A reduction in the rate of inflation.

Disposable personal income: The amount of personal income that people can keep after paying personal taxes and certain nontax items; the amount available to households for either saving or consumption spending.

Dissaving: Spending for consumer goods and services in excess of disposable income; a negative saving flow that leads to a reduction in wealth.

Distributions of income and wealth: See *Gini coefficient; Lorenz curve.*

Dividends: Profits paid out to shareholders of a corporation.

Dollar bloc (dollar standard): See *Exchange rate.*

Double coincidence of wants: See *Coincidence of wants.*

Durable good: A consumer good with an expected life (use) of one year or more.

Easy (tight) monetary policy: Monetary policy that expands (contracts) the money supply and is supposed to lower (increase) interest rates, although inflationary expectations could reverse the effect. See *Federal Reserve System.*

Economic cost: The cost of obtaining and retaining the services of a resource. See *Opportunity cost.*

Economic efficiency: The least-cost method of producing a good or service. It depends on prices of resources and on technology; technological efficiency depends only on the amount of resources used.

Economic growth: An increase in output resulting from an increase in resource supplies or an improvement in technology.

Economic integration: The complete or partial unification of the economies of different nations; the elimination of the barriers to trade among these nations; the bringing together of separate national markets into one large international and intranational common market.

Economic perspective: A viewpoint that individuals, firms, and institutions make rational or purposeful decisions based on a consideration of the benefits and costs associated with their actions.

Economic Recovery Tax Act (1981): Also known as the Kemp-Roth tax cut. It reduced personal income tax rates, lowered capital gains tax rates, allowed a more rapid write-off against taxes of business expenditures for new plants and equipment, lowered the rates at which corporate incomes are taxed, and provided for the adjustment of tax brackets for inflation. It was also supposed to increase tax revenue according to the Laffer curve. See *Laffer curve.*

Economics: The study of how scarce resources are allocated among alternative uses to satisfy human wants.

Effective demand: Demand backed up by purchasing power. See *Keynes' Law; Purchasing power of the dollar.*

Efficiency vs. equality tradeoff: See *Tradeoff, equality vs. efficiency.*

Employment Act of 1946: Committed the federal government to the maintenance of economic stability (full employment, stable prices, and economic growth); established the Council of Economic Advisers and the Joint Economic Committee; provided for the annual economic report of the President to Congress. See *Council of Economic Advisers; Joint Economic Committee.*

Employment rate: The percentage of the labor force employed at any time. See *Labor force.*

Engels' Law: The tendency for the percentage of a family's budget spent for food to decline as its income rises.

Equality vs. efficiency tradeoff: See *Tradeoff, equality vs. efficiency.*

Equilibrium: A situation in which there is no tendency for change.

European Monetary System: An agreement among the countries of the European Community to fix exchange rates among their own currencies and then let their joint rate float against the dollar. See *Exchange rate.*

Exchange rate: The relative or real price of a foreign currency in terms of another; the number of units of one currency that one unit of another currency can purchase.

Adjustable peg system is another name for the Bretton Woods system of exchange rate adjustment which was in effect from 1945 until August, 1971. Exchange rates were fixed in the short term but were occasionally changed in response to imbalances in the balance of international payments. Each nation defined, or "pegged" its currency in terms of gold or the dollar.

Dollar bloc (dollar standard) is an international monetary system under which countries hold reserves, write contracts, and settle debts with U.S. dollars, even though the dollar is not backed by gold or any other physical source of monetary value. Some Latin American countries use the dollar as their standard.

Fixed exchange rates, maintain (manage) the exchange value of a nation's money within a small range around its publicly stated par value. To do this, a country's central bank or an international monetary agency buys and/or sells official reserves in the foreign-exchange market; a metallic (usually gold or silver) standard also allows a fixed exchange rate. This system of monetary control uses aggressive intervention to keep exchange rates at certain levels rather than permitting them to fall in response to market forces.

Flexible exchange rates (also called floating or free exchange rates) can move up or down in response to shifts in demand and supply that arise from international trading and finance and that are not purposefully influenced by government action.

Gold standard is a method of determining exchange rates, which prevailed off and on until the 1930s; specified that currencies were convertible into a certain amount of gold.

Managed floating exchange rates use central bank intervention in the foreign-exchange market in pursuit of an official exchange rate target; they are also called "dirty floats."

Purchasing power parity (PPP) exchange rate between any two national currencies adjusts to reflect changes in the relative price levels in the two nations. See *European Monetary System.*

Exchange rate appreciation (depreciation): An increase (decrease) in the value of one currency relative to another; an increase (decrease) in the relative price—the exchange rate—of two currencies.

Expectations: What consumers, business firms, and others believe will happen or what conditions will be in the future.

Adaptive expectations: The proposition that people determine their expectations about future events (for example, rates of inflation) on the basis of past and present events.

Keynes' theory of expectations: ". . . a large proportion of our positive activities depend on spontaneous optimism rather than on a mathematical expectation. . . . Only a little more than an expedition to the South Pole, is it based on an exact calculation of benefits to come. Thus if animal spirits are dimmed and the spontaneous optimism falters, leaving us to depend on nothing but a mathematical expectation, enterprise will fade and die . . ." (Keynes, 1936, pp. 161–62).

Rational expectations: The theory that people's spending decisions are based on all available information. Consequently, consumers understand how the economy works and learn quickly from their mistakes; although they may make random errors, they do not make systematic and persistent errors. Their price-level expectations adjust quickly when contractionary or expansionary monetary or fiscal actions are taken, so that government stabilization policies have little effect on real output in the economy. See *Keynesian economics; New Classical economics; NAIRU; Policy ineffectiveness theorem.*

Expectations-augmented Phillips curve: See *Phillips curve.*

Exports: Goods and services sold to foreign buyers, which increase the amount of foreign money held by the citizens, firms, and governments of a nation. See *Imports.*

External value of the dollar: The value of the dollar expressed in terms of foreign currencies. Changes in the dollar's external value are measured by changes in the exchange rate. See *Exchange rate.*

Externalities: Costs (or benefits) of a market activity that are borne by a third party; the difference between the social and private costs (benefits) of a market activity.

Factors of production: Economic resources—namely land, capital, labor, and entrepreneurial ability; also called resources.

Fallacy of composition: Incorrect reasoning that what is true for the individual (or part) is therefore necessarily true for the group (or whole).

"Farming out" of taxes: See *Taxes.*

Federal Deposit Insurance Corporation (FDIC): A federal government agency that insures deposits in certain financial institutions.

Federal Reserve System: A system of twelve district Federal Reserve Banks and a Board of Governors, established in 1913. The Board of Governors is composed of seven members appointed by the President for 14-year terms; their function is to promote the nation's economic welfare by supervising the operations of the U.S. money and banking system.

Federal Open Market Committee (FOMC) is the Federal Reserve System's most important policy-making committee. It has twelve members: the seven members of the Federal Reserve Board plus a specific rotation of five of the twelve presidents of the Federal Reserve Banks (always the president of the New York bank). The FOMC is responsible for controlling bank reserves and the money supply by buying and selling securities for the system. See *Monetary policy.*

Fiat money: Money that attains its value by government decree and has little value as a commodity. All U.S. currency and coins today are fiat money.

Fiscal federalism: The system of transfers (grants) by which the federal government shares its revenues with state and local governments.

Fiscal instruments: Taxing and spending devices used to influence the performance of the economy. See *Government purchases; Taxes; Transfer payments.*

Fiscal policy: The use of government taxes and spending to alter macroeconomic outcomes.

Fiscal year: The twelve-month period used for government accounting purposes; begins October 1 and ends September 30.

Fixed exchange rates: See *Exchange rate.*

Flexible exchange rates: See *Exchange rate.*

Floating exchange rates: See *Exchange rate.*

Foreign exchange control: The control a government may exercise over the quantity of foreign money demanded by its citizens and business firms and over the rates of exchange, in order to limit its outpayments to its inpayments (to eliminate a current account deficit).

Foreign exchange market: The market where national monies, or claims to these monies, are traded against one another.

Foreign exchange rate: See *Exchange rate.*

Foreign exchange reserves: Holdings of foreign exchange by an official government agency, usually the central bank or treasury.

Foreign trade crisis: The large and expanding current account deficits of the United States during the 1980s.

Free exchange rate: See *Exchange rate.*

Free trade: The absence of government barriers to trade among individuals and firms in different nations. The absence of government intervention in international trade implies that imports and exports must not be subject to special taxes or restrictions levied merely because of their status as "imports" or "exports."

Frictional unemployment: See *Unemployment.*

Full employment: The use of all available resources to produce goods and services; a condition in which the real output of the economy is equal to its potential real output. Keynes allowed for frictional and structural unemployment but no cyclical unemployment. The "natural" rate of unemployment—the lowest rate of unemployment compatible with price stability—has been variously estimated at between 4 and 6 percent. See *NAIRU; Phillips curve.*

Full Employment and Balanced Growth Act of 1978: A supplement to the Employment Act of 1946, also called the Humphrey-Hawkins Act; requires the federal government to establish five-year goals for the economy and to make plans to achieve these goals.

Full-employment budget: See *Budget, public.*

Full-employment GNP: See *Gross national product.*

Functional finance: A federal government policy to promote the socially optimal combination of unemployment and inflation, even at the risk of unbalancing the budget over considerable periods.

Garn–St. Germain Act: See *Depository Institutions Act of 1982.*

GATT: See *General Agreement on Tariffs and Trade.*

General Agreement on Tariffs and Trade (GATT): An international agreement reached in 1947 by 23 nations, including the United States, in which each nation agreed to give equal and nondiscriminatory treatment to the other nations, to reduce tariff rates through multinational negotiations, and to eliminate import quotas.

General price level: An average of all prices in the economy.

Gini coefficient: A measure of income (wealth) inequality; the area between the Lorenz curve and the diagonal of a rectangle (horizontal axis is percentage of the people, and vertical axis is percentage of total income or wealth), expressed as a percentage of the area of one-half the rectangle. See *Lorenz curve.*

GNP: See *Gross national product.*

GNP deflator: The price index for all final goods and services used to adjust the money (or nominal) GNP to measure the real GNP; also called the GNP implicit price deflator. See *Index number; Price index.*

GNP gap: The difference between full-employment (potential) GNP and actual GNP.

GNP per capita: Total GNP divided by total population; average GNP.

Golden (market) rule: "Them that's got the gold makes the rules."

Gold standard: See *Exchange rate.*

Government purchases: Government spending on final goods and services, excluding transfer payments. State and local governments are often separated from federal government and included with the private sector, because they have run a surplus.

Government transfer payments: See *Transfer payments.*

Gramm-Rudman Act: See *Gramm-Rudman-Hollings Act.*

Gramm-Rudman-Hollings Act (1985): Requires annual reductions in federal budget deficits and, as amended, a balanced budget by 1993; mandates an automatic decrease in expenditures when Congress and the President cannot agree on how to meet the targeted reductions in the budget deficit.

Great Depression: The period of severe unemployment, falling price levels, and economic stagnation extending through the decade following the stock market crash of 1929. See *Depression.*

Gross domestic product (GDP): National income as measured by the output approach; equal to the sum of all values added in the economy or, what is the same thing, the values of all final goods produced in the economy.

Gross national product (GNP): The value of total output produced and incomes earned by domestically based producers and factors of production. Measured from the expenditure side of the national accounts, it is the sum of consumption, investment, government expenditures on final output, and net exports; measured from the income side, it is the sum of factor incomes plus capital consumption allowance plus indirect taxes net of subsidies. See *National income accounting.*

Potential gross national product—also called potential national income, high- or full-employment GNP, or high-employment national income—is the level of GNP that can be attained when the economy is operating at full capacity or full employment. See *NAIRU.*

Human capital: See *Capital.*

Humphrey-Hawkins Act: See *Full Employment and Balanced Growth Act of 1978.*

Hyperdeflation: A situation in which unemployment and falling prices induce pessimistic expectations of such magnitude that the recession feeds on itself, becomes worse, and is not alleviated by further falling prices.

Hyperinflation: A situation in which the price level rises rapidly, causing an increase in the velocity of circulation of money and usually culminating in the breakdown of the monetary system.

Identity: A statement whose two sides are equal by definition.

IMF: See *International Monetary Fund.*

Imports: Goods and services purchased from foreign sources.

Income equality (inequality): The equal (unequal) distribution of an economy's total income among persons or families in the economy. See *Gini coefficient; Lorenz curve.*

Incomes policy: Any direct intervention by the government to influence wage and price formation.

Income statement: A financial report showing the revenues and costs that arise from the firm's use of inputs to produce outputs over a specified period. See *Balance sheet.*

Inconvertible currency: The money of a country that does not allow it to be freely exchanged for money of other countries.

Indexing: A system that automatically builds an inflation or deflation adjustment into agreements for wage rates, savings accounts, taxes, interest rates, bond values, and other contracts. It has a pro-cyclical effect. See *Automatic stabilizer.*

Index number: The average changes over time of such variables as the price level and industrial production, expressed as a percentage relative to a base period given the value 100. See *Price index.*

Induced expenditure: In macroeconomics, an element of expenditure that is explained by variables within the theory; also called endogenous expenditure, in contrast to exogenous (autonomous) expenditure. In the aggregate desired expenditure function, it is any component of expenditure related to national income.

Industrially advanced countries (IACs): Countries such as the United States, Canada, Japan, and the nations of Western Europe, which have developed market economies based on large stocks of technologically advanced capital goods and skilled labor forces; the First World. See *Worlds of development.*

Infant industry argument for tariff production: The position that new domestic industries with potential for economies of scale or for learning by doing need to be protected from the competition of established, low-cost foreign producers, so domestic producers can grow large enough to achieve costs as low as those of foreign producers.

Inflation: A significant and sustained increase in the general level of prices, usually measured by the rate of change in some price index number. If inflation is anticipated (that is, if the rate of increase in the price level is equal to the expected rate), recent theory says it is not a burden to anyone; however, the information costs of inflation are high.

Deflating is the process of converting values expressed in current dollars into values expressed in constant dollars, to correct for changes in the price level during inflationary times. See *Deflation; Disinflation.*

Expectational inflation develops from anticipation that the price level will rise in the near future. It is inflation that occurs because decision makers raise prices (so as to keep their relative prices constant), in

the expectation that the price level is going to rise. See *Expectations*.
Pure inflation is a rise in money prices but not relative prices.

Inflation, bottleneck: Inflation that results from converting a war economy to a peacetime economy.

Inflation, cost-push: An increase in the price level initiated by an increase in the cost of production, usually from higher wage rates and raw-material prices.

Inflation, demand-pull: Increases in prices caused by "too much money chasing too few goods"; an excessive aggregate demand.

Inflation, profit-push: An increase in the price level initiated by producers' attempts to raise profit margins; a variant of cost-push inflation.

Information cost: The cost of obtaining information.

Infrastructure: The basic physical capital installations and facilities usually provided by the public sector, such as transportation and communications systems, waste treatment facilities, and municipal water systems. Some would include the basic financial and human capital systems as well.

In-kind transfer: The distribution by government of goods and services to individuals, for which the government receives no currently produced good or service in return; a government transfer payment made in goods or services rather than in money. See *Transfer payment*.

Interest rate: The annual amount that a borrower must pay for the use of a creditor's asset. See *Real interest rate*.

Interest rate parity: A condition in international capital account transactions in which the domestic-money rate of return is the same as the foreign-money rate of return after conversion to domestic money.

Intergenerational burden: The costs imposed by the current generation on future generations by bequeathing an inadequate physical, financial, or human capital stock. Intergenerational equity is a very subjective goal.

International balance of payments: See *Balance of international payments*.

International Bank for Reconstruction and Development: See *World Bank*.

International Monetary Fund (IMF): An organization established in 1944 for the purpose of stabilizing exchange rates in international trade; a pool of gold and foreign exchange from which loans can be made to help countries stabilize foreign exchange rates. See *Bretton Woods system*.

Inventories: Stocks of raw materials, goods in process, and finished products, resulting from short-term fluctuations in production or sales.

Investment: Financial, human, and physical capital investment. Gross domestic private investment plus net foreign investment equals national investment.

Gross domestic investment is all additions to the nation's stock of private investment goods—that is, all investment spending (including purchases of tools, equipment, and machinery), all construction expenditures, and the change in total inventories.

Net domestic investment equals gross investment less capital consumption allowances. Net investment is the expenditure flow that augments capital stock. See *Capital*.

Net foreign investment: Net exports, or exports minus imports. When it is negative, it is the current account deficit. See *Deficit.*

Invisibles: Services and payments for the use of capital. See *Current account.*

Involuntary unemployment: See *Unemployment.*

Joint Economic Committee (JEC): A committee of the Congress established by the Employment Act of 1946 to conduct research and advise Congress on economic policy. See *Employment Act of 1946.*

Keynesian economics: Schools of economic thought based on the work of John Maynard Keynes (1883–1946), particularly *The General Theory of Employment, Interest and Money* (1936); the belief that a capitalistic economy does not tend automatically toward a full-employment equilibrium. Hence, Keynesians advocate activist monetary and fiscal policies. See *Classical theory of employment; Expectations; Monetarism; New Classical economics.*

Keynes' Law: The reverse of Say's Law; it applies to monetary economics, whereas Say's Law does not. Effective demand creates its own supply. See *Effective demand; Say's Law.*

Labor force: All persons over age 16 who are employed plus the number of those unemployed who are actively looking for work and are willing to take a job if one is offered. These people are called labor-force participants.

Labor productivity: The average amount of output that can be obtained for every unit of labor.

Laffer curve: A curve, in the shape of a hill, that shows the relationship between tax rates (horizontal axis) and government tax revenues (vertical axis). As tax rates increase from 0 to 100 percent, tax revenues rise but then begin to fall. In other words, after the crest of the hill, higher tax rates result in lower tax revenues. See *Reaganomics.*

Laissez faire: Literally, "let do"; a policy position favoring the market economy and opposing interference in the economy by the government; a belief that the efficiency of the market will more than offset the inequalities or inequities that may result.

Lender of last resort: A responsibility of Federal Reserve banks to make loans to member banks facing a liquidity crisis.

Less-developed countries (LDCs): The countries with the lowest per-capita incomes, most of which are in Asia, Africa, and Latin America; also called underdeveloped countries, developing countries, or the Third World. Living standards are lower for many reasons: because modern technology has not been applied to production processes, because natural resources are few, because population density is too great. See *Worlds of development.*

Liability: An obligation to make future payments; an IOU.

Life-cycle theory: A hypothesis of Richard Brumberg and Franco Modigliani that the level of a household's planned consumption expenditure is based on what it believes to be its expected lifetime income rather than, as in Keynes' theory, its current income. See *Consumption.*

Liquidity crisis: Lack of sufficient money and creditworthiness to make a market economy work. Keynes believed that classical economic theory (that is, the theory that supply creates its own demand, also known as Say's law) did not take account of the fact that an industrial society is a money economy and not a barter economy. Effective demand, demand backed up with ample liquidity as purchasing power, is needed to create supply. Crises ensue because of too great a demand to hold money broadly defined, which is a "riskless" asset as long as there is no inflation. See *Keynes' Law.*

Liquidity preference: The strength of the demand to hold liquid rather than illiquid assets at different rates of interest. The level at which interest rates are so low that people have an unlimited demand for liquidity is called a "liquidity trap." See *Demand for money.*

Lorenz curve: A graphic illustration that measures income (wealth) inequality by showing what percentage of the people (horizontal axis) receive what percentage of total income or wealth (vertical axis). The size of the area between the Lorenz curve and the diagonal is a measure of the inequality of the distributions of income and wealth. See *Gini coefficient.*

Macroeconomic equilibrium: A hypothetical situation in which all the goals of government policy are met, such as full employment, price stability, economic growth, and balance of international payments.

Macroeconomics: The study of the economy as a whole; the determination of national economic policy. See *Fallacy of composition; Microeconomics.*

Managed exchange rate: See *Exchange rate.*

Marginal propensity to consume: The fraction of each additional dollar of disposable income spent on consumption; the change in consumption divided by the change in disposable income.

Marginal propensity to import: The fraction of each additional dollar of disposable income spent on imports.

Marginal propensity to save: The fraction of each additional dollar of disposable income that is saved.

Market economy: An economy that relies on markets for basic decisions about what to produce, how to produce it, and for whom to produce. A market is an abstract area in which buyers and sellers negotiate the exchange of goods and bads.

Medicare: A compulsory hospitalization insurance program plus a voluntary insurance plan for doctors' fees for people over 65, included under the Social Security program.

Medicaid extends to the poor who are not yet 65 the same medical services already available to the elderly through Medicare.

Microeconomics: The study of individual household and firm behavior. See *Macroeconomics.*

Mixed economy: An economy that uses both market and nonmarket signals to allocate goods and resources.

Models: Formal presentations of theories, often mathematical or graphic.

Monetarism: The viewpoint that monetary instability is the dominant cause of output fluctuations and that growth of the money supply is the dominant cause of inflation. Economists who share the view that money exerts a dominant effect on economic activity and that a capitalistic economy has an effective self-regulating mechanism are called monetarists. They consider the use of stabilization policies to be destabilizing and therefore reject it. See *Policy ineffectiveness theorem.*

Monetary aggregates: The various measures of the nation's money supply. See *Money.*

Monetary economy: An economy that uses money in the exchange of goods and services. "Goods buy money, and money buys goods—but goods do not buy goods in any organized market" (Clower, 1970, p. 14). See *Barter.*

Monetary policy: A plan or course of action implemented by the Federal Reserve to influence macroeconomic goals—unemployment, price stability, economic growth, and the balance of international payments—by influencing interest rates and the money supply. The monetary instrument most often used by the Fed is open-market operations; other instruments are discount rate, reserve requirements, credit restrictions, and moral suasions. See *Federal Reserve System; Discount.*

Monetization: Central bank expansion of the money supply to pay for the national debt.

Money: Anything that serves as a medium of exchange, a standard of value, and a store of value; the unit in which the prices of goods and services are measured. M_1 is currency held by the public, plus checkable deposits; M_2 is a broader definition of money that includes savings deposits.

Money illusion: A belief that nominal values are the same as real values; the use of nominal dollars rather than real dollars to gauge changes in one's income or wealth.

Money income: Income measured in current dollars, or actual money amounts; identical to nominal income. See *Real income.*

NAIRU: (Non-Accelerating Inflationary Rate of Unemployment): The long-term rate of unemployment determined by structural forces in labor and product markets and associated with potential national income; the long-term rate of unemployment at which a steady rate of inflation can be sustained indefinitely; also called the natural rate of unemployment. See *Phillips curve.*

National debt: Accumulated net deficits of the federal government; the sum of past federal budget deficits minus the sum of past surpluses. To cover the difference between its expenditures and its tax revenues, the government sells bonds, notes, and other forms of IOU's.

National income: The sum of the four components of factor incomes (wages, rent, interest, and profits); roughly, GNP less depreciation and indirect business taxes.

National income accounting: The set of rules and procedures used to measure the total flow of output produced by a nation, together with the income generated by this production. The full name of these accounts is the national income and product accounts—national accounts or national income accounts, for short.

National Industrial Recovery Act (NIRA): Legislation enacted in 1933 containing a variety of emergency programs designed to help the economy recover from the Great Depression. It made price collusion by firms legal. Major portions of the act were ruled unconstitutional by the Supreme Court. See *Demand-side economics; New Deal.*

Natural rate of unemployment: See *NAIRU.*

Negative income tax: A tax program in which households with incomes below a certain break-even level would receive, rather than make, a government income-tax payment. That subsidy would be reduced as the family's income from other sources increased. See *Taxes.*

Neo-Ricardian: See *Ricardian-equivalence theorem.*

Net exports: The value of total exports minus the value of total imports. See *Investment, net foreign.*

Net investment: See *Investment.*

Net national product (NNP): Sum of wages, rent, interest, profits, and indirect taxes minus subsidies. It is also gross national product minus capital consumption allowances (or depreciation). See *Capital consumption allowance.*

Net worth: The difference between assets and liabilities. Net worth is net wealth, the residual equity or claim of the owners.

New Classical economics: The theory that, although unanticipated price level changes may create macroeconomic instability in the short run, the economy is stable at the full-employment level of national output in the long run if prices and wages are flexible. See *Classical theory of employment; Expectations; Keynesian economics; Monetarism.*

New Deal: The economic programs of the first two administrations of President Franklin Roosevelt (1933–1941). See *National Industrial Recovery Act.*

Newly industrialized countries (NICs): A few of the formerly underdeveloped countries that have become major industrial exporters since World War II; the Second World. See *Worlds of development.*

Nominal: Value that is stated or measured in terms of some monetary unit and that has not been adjusted for changes in the general price level.

Nominal GNP: The value of gross national product—final output produced in a given period—measured in the prices of that period (current prices). See *Gross national product.*

Nominal income: The amount of income received in a given period, measured in current dollars; identical to money income. See *Real income.*

Nominal interest rate: Market rate of interest. See *Real interest rate.*

Normative economics: Statements, propositions, and predictions about what ought to be or about what a person, organization, or nation ought to do; value judgments. See *Positive economics.*

Obsolescence: The process of becoming less and less useful or economically feasible for some intended purpose.

Official settlements balance: A concept in the balance of international payments that combines all the entries in the capital account with all the entries in the current account and shows the net effect of all transactions except those in official government reserves. See *Balance of international payments.*

Okun's Law: Arthur Okun's generalization that each percentage-point rise in the unemployment rate above the natural unemployment rate will increase the actual GNP gap by 2.5 percent of the potential GNP of the economy. See *NAIRU.*

OPEC: See *Organization of Petroleum Exporting Countries.*

Open-market operations: The Federal Reserve System's purchases and sales of U.S. government securities for the purpose of influencing monetary and credit conditions. See *Federal Reserve System; Monetary policy.*

Opportunity cost: The cost of the most desired goods or services that are rejected; the best alternative to the option chosen.

Organization of Petroleum Exporting Countries (OPEC): The cartel formed in 1970 by thirteen oil-producing countries to control the price and quantity of crude oil sold. They account for a large proportion of the world's oil exports. The cartel's control has varied greatly.

Other things (being) equal: See *Ceteris paribus.*

Per-capita GNP: GNP divided by total population.

Permanent-income hypothesis: A hypothesis of Milton Friedman's that the level of a household's planned consumption expenditure is based on what it believes to be its long-run or "permanent" level of income rather than, as in Keynes' original theory, its current income. See *Consumption.*

Personal consumption expenditures: See *Consumption.*

Personal income: Current income received by persons from all sources, including transfers from government and business but excluding transfers among persons. Personal income less taxes is personal disposable income, which is income available to households for consumption and saving.

Phillips curve: Originally a historical (inverse) relationship between the percentage of the labor force that is unemployed and the rate of change of money wages; now usually drawn as an inverse relationship between the unemployment rate and the rate of inflation in the short run and a vertical line in the long run.

Expectations-augmented Phillips curve takes into account the demand and expectational components of inflation. The long-run Phillips curve is part of the policy ineffectiveness theorem's apparatus; it uses NAIRU, also called the natural rate of unemployment. See *Expectations; NAIRU.*

Policy ineffectiveness theorem: A proposition advocated by proponents of New Classical economics (or Rational Expectations) that only surprise or unanticipated policies have an effect on such real economic variables as output and employment. Ricardian equivalence theorem is a variant of this belief. See *Expectations; Monetarism.*

Portfolio decision: Mirrors the adage "Don't put all your eggs in one basket"; making implicitly or explicitly ranked choices based on your best judgment.

Positive economics: Statements, propositions, and predictions based on facts that are generally testable. See *Normative economics.*

Positive time preference: A desire to do things now rather than wait.

Post hoc, ergo propter hoc **fallacy:** Incorrect reasoning that the historical timing of events is always related to causation: When one event precedes another event, the first event is the cause of the second.

Potential gross national product (GNP): See *Gross national product.*

Poverty line: The amount of income necessary to maintain a minimally acceptable standard of living; a level of income below which a family is classified as poor.

Precautionary demand for money: Money held because of uncertainty about the timing and size of future expenditures and revenues. See *Demand for money.*

Present value: The value now of a payment or series of payments to be received in the future; the discounted value at the present time of a sum of money to be received in the future. It is often referred to as the discounted present value of future payments. The present-value equation determines the present value of an asset by dividing (discounting) the expected income flow by some mathematical relation involving the rate of interest. See *Capitalization of assets; Discount.*

Price index: The ratio of a weighted average of the prices of goods and services in current dollars to the value of the same set of goods and services in constant dollars. If the goods and services are purchased by consumers, it is a consumer price index; if purchased by producers, it is a producer price index; and if the goods and services are those making up gross national product, it is a (implicit) GNP deflator. See *Index number.*

Private sector: That portion of an economy in which production is owned and operated by private units, such as households and firms.

Productivity growth: More output, and consequently real income, per hour of work; the main source of rising living standards.

Protectionism: A system of tariffs, subsidies, quotas, other restrictions on imports, and sometimes also aid to export industries by direct or hidden subsidies, aimed at defending a country's industries from foreign competition.

Public assistance programs: Programs, financed by general tax revenues, that pay benefits to those who are poor and unable to earn income (because of permanent handicaps or because they are dependent children). See *Transfer payments.*

Public choice: An area of study that combines economics and political science to gain a better understanding of how the public sector actually operates. Economists who specialize in the rational self-interest of decision makers and voters are called public-choice economists.

Public debt: See *National debt.*

Public goods and services: Goods and services supplied either wholly or in large part through the government sector, because of nonrivalry (once provided for one person can be provided for others at no additional cost) and nonexcludability (cannot be provided for one person without being available to others) or because of difficulties in providing them through the market (for example, national defense). See *Government purchases.*

Public sector: That portion of an economy in which production is owned and operated by the government or bodies appointed by it, such as nationalized industries. See *Private sector.*

Purchasing power of the dollar: The reciprocal of the index number for the consumer price index, or the goods and services that a dollar will buy in a given year compared to what it would buy in the base year.

Purchasing power parity (PPP) exchange rate: See *Exchange rate.*

Quantity theory of money and prices: The theory that the velocity of circulation of money times money equals nominal gross national product. A crude version of the theory states that if velocity is constant and real net national product remains fixed at its full-employment level, the price level will be proportional to the money supply. See *Monetarism; Velocity of money.*

Rate of return: The interest rate earned on the investment in a particular asset.

Rational behavior: Acting in a manner consistent with a decision maker's objectives. See *Expectations.*

Reaganomics: The so-called supply-side economic policies of the Reagan administration (1980–1988), based on the Laffer curve. It was intended to reduce inflation and balance the budget. See *Laffer curve; Supply-side economics.*

Real: Denotes quantities and prices expressed in constant dollars. Nominal (or money) quantities and prices are expressed in current dollars. The national income accounts are expressed in real and nominal terms. See *Money illusion.*

Real income: Real purchasing power.

Real interest rate: The nominal (market) interest rate minus the expected rate of inflation.

Recession: A decline in total output (real GNP) for two or more consecutive quarters. The recessionary gap is the amount by which equilibrium GNP falls short of the full-employment GNP level. See *Depression.*

Regressive tax: See *Taxes.*

Repudiation: Decision to not pay the amount due on a loan; a catchall word that includes defaults, debt moratoriums, monetizations, reschedulings, and taxes on interest.

Ricardian equivalence theorem: Hypothesis that increased federal budget deficits induce an equivalent increase in private saving, thus leaving the gross pool of saving (government plus private) unchanged. If valid, most of the alleged adverse consequences of budget deficits are nonexistent. An application of the rational-expectations theory. See *Expectations; Keynesian economics; New Classical economics; Policy ineffectiveness theorem.*

Saving: Net personal saving (NPS), gross business saving (GBS), and net government saving or surplus (NGS). The federal-budget deficit is negative NGS. For national income accounts, both gross and net saving are defined as gross and net investment. Gross national saving is the sum of households' disposable personal income not spent on current consumption, firms' net business saving plus capital consumption allowances, the government's budget surplus or deficit, and the statistical discrepancy. Net national saving is gross national saving less capital consumption allowances. See *Business saving; Deficit; Investment.*

Savings: See *Net worth.*

Say's Law: The macroeconomic generalization for a barter economy, which states that the production of goods and services (supply) results in the generation of an amount of income precisely sufficient to buy that output; often quoted as "Supply creates its own demand." See *Keynes' Law.*

Secular: Referring to economic impacts caused by the passage of time. See *Cyclical.*

Social Darwinism: The belief that the survival and prosperity of individuals, families, nations, and races are determined, like those of animal species, by their biological and psychological fitness in the struggle not only against one another but also against the environment.

Social Security programs: A compulsory system of retirement and survivors' benefits, established by the Social Security Act (1935) and financed by payroll taxes from employers and employees, which are viewed as earned rights (rather than charity). The programs have been expanded since 1935 to include certain disability, hospital, and medical care benefits. Unemployment insurance, which covers employers and makes income available to workers who are unable to find jobs, is financed by state payroll taxes. See *Medicare.*

Special drawing rights (SDRs): Financial liabilities of the International Monetary Fund established in 1968 and held in a special fund generated by contributions of member countries; also known as paper gold. Members can use SDRs to meet their international obligations. See *International Monetary Fund.*

Speculative demand for money: Money held for speculative purposes, or later financial opportunities. See *Demand for money.*

Stabilization policy: Any policy designed to reduce the economy's cyclical fluctuations and thereby to stabilize national income at, or near, a desired level.

Stagflation: The coexistence of high rates of unemployment with high, and sometimes rising, rates of inflation.

Sterilization: Operations undertaken by the central bank to offset the effects on the money supply of balance-of-payments surpluses or deficits.

Structural unemployment: See *Unemployment.*

Supplemental Security Income (SSI): A federally financed and administered program that provides a uniform, nationwide minimum income for the aged, blind, and disabled who do not qualify for benefits under Old Age, Survivors, and Disability Health Insurance.

Supply-side economics: The use of tax rates, (de)regulation, and other mechanisms to increase the ability and willingness of firms to produce goods and services. See *Demand-side economics; Laffer curve; Reaganomics.*

Tariff: A tax (duty) imposed on imported goods.

Tax Act of 1981: Also known as the Kemp-Roth tax cut. See *Economic Recovery Tax Act.*

Tax Act of 1982: See *Tax Equity and Fiscal Responsibility Act.*

Tax Act of 1984: See *Deficit Reduction Act.*

Tax Equity and Fiscal Responsibility Act (1982): Curtailed some of the Kemp-Roth tax cut for businesses.

Taxes: Revenues generated by government. Income taxes are federal, state, or local taxes imposed directly on personal income and corporate profits. Inheritance taxes are imposed directly on wealth at death. Indirect business taxes—such as general sales taxes, excise taxes (on each unit sold of a particular product, such as cigarettes or liquor), and customs duties—are imposed not directly on business profits but on products or services and hence are treated by firms as costs of production.

Regressive tax permits the rich to pay a smaller proportion of their income in taxes than do the poor.

Progressive tax increases as a percentage of income as the taxpayer's total income increases.

Proportional tax or "flat" tax is the same percentage of income paid in tax, regardless of the taxpayer's income. See *Ability-to-pay principle, Social Security programs.*

Tax farming: Originally the collection of taxes on state-owned (often royal) lands by an agent, the infamous tax farmer, on a fee-for-service basis. The agent often bid for the right to collect (farm) the taxes. The state's revenue came from the sale of these privileges, the agent's from the "overage" collected. The United States obtained its first loan (1777) from the Farmers General, a consortium of French tax farmers.

Tax incidence: Distribution of the real burden of a tax.

Tax rate: The "marginal" tax rate, or the tax rate imposed on the last dollar of income.

Tax Reform Act of 1986: Federal legislation that broadened the personal income tax base but also lowered tax rates and the number of tax brackets.

Terms of trade: The ratio of the average price of a country's exports to the average price of its imports, both averages usually being measured by index numbers; the quantity of imported goods that can be obtained per unit of goods exported.

Third World: See *Less-developed countries.*

Tradeoff: An exchange of one thing for another; especially, the quantity of one good or service that must be given up to gain a certain quantity of another good or service. See *Tradeoff; equality vs. efficiency.*

Tradeoff, equality vs. efficiency: The fundamental economic tradeoff; the presumption that decreases in economic efficiency accompany an increase in income (wealth) equality; the assumption that income equality causes inefficiency. See *Economic efficiency; Income equality.*

Trade-weighted basis: Domestic currency value determined as an average of foreign exchange rates weighted by the foreign nations' share of international trade.

Transactions demand for money: Money held for the purpose of making everyday market purchases. See *Demand for money.*

Transfer payments: Government payments to individuals for which no current goods or services are exchanged—for example, Social Security, welfare, and unemployment benefits. Net foreign transfer payments are the personal and government transfer payments made to residents of foreign nations less the personal and government transfer payments received from residents of foreign nations.

Underemployment: A situation in which people seeking full-time paid employment work only part-time or are employed at jobs below their capability.

Underground economy: Income and production, both criminal and otherwise, that are not reported in official statistics, often because people want to evade regulations, union rules, or taxes.

Undistributed corporate profits: See *Business saving.*

Unemployment: According to the Bureau of Labor Statistics, a situation in which a person 16 years of age or older is actively looking for work and would take a job if one were offered.

> *Keynes-defined unemployment* falls into three categories: frictional (or structural), voluntary, and involuntary. Frictional unemployment is temporary joblessness that arises because time is required to change from one job to another. It is caused by mismatched skills (or location), by voluntary job changes, by people looking for their first job, and by temporary layoff. Voluntary unemployment is due to the refusal or inability of laborers to accept a job, because of legislation, social practices, strikes, slow response to change, or mere human obstinacy. Involuntary unemployment, the inability of qualified persons who are seeking work to find jobs at the going wage rate, is one goal of stabilization policy, because Keynes did not believe it would disappear automatically, as did classical theorists. See *Say's Law.*

Unemployment rate: Unemployment expressed as a percentage of the labor force.

Unfavorable balance of trade: See *Balance of trade; Deficit.*

Value-added tax (VAT): A tax on the difference between the value of the goods sold by a firm and the value of the goods purchased by the firm to produce the goods. See *Taxes.*

Velocity of money: The rate per year at which the money supply is used to make transactions for final goods and services; the average number of times per year that a dollar is used to buy the final goods and services produced by the economy. See *Quantity theory of money and prices.*

Vertical equity: See *Ability-to-pay principle.*

Visibles: Merchandise. See *Balance of trade; Invisibles.*

Voluntary unemployment: See *Unemployment.*

Wage-price controls: Limits placed by the government on the amount by which wages and prices can increase. Wage-price guideposts allow labor unions and business firms to voluntarily cooperate with wage-price policy; the purpose of establishing guideposts is to stop a wage-price inflationary spiral before it starts.

Wildcat banking: Banking practices of the early 1800s that made printing of bank notes profitable because the "redemption centers" were located far from where their circulation took place—where only wildcats roamed.

World Bank: An organization established in 1944 that sends out development missions to identify cultural, legal, social, and psychological barriers to growth. Loans are furnished to undertake education programs, legal reform, resource development, negotiation of trade treaties, or actual investment that may smooth the way to more rapid growth. See *Bretton Woods system.*

Worlds of development: The First World (industrially advanced countries), Second World (newly industrialized countries), and Third World (less-developed countries). See *Industrially advanced countries; Less-developed countries; Newly industrialized countries.*

Yield: The rate of return on a bond; the annual interest payment divided by the bond's price.

References

Aaron, Henry J. 1989. "Politics and the Professors Revisited" (1988 Richard T. Ely Lecture to the American Economic Association). *American Economic Review* 79 (May 1989): 1–15.

Aaron, Henry J. 1990. "Costs of the Aging Population: Real and Imagined Burdens." In *Social Security and the Budget,* ed. H. J. Aaron, 51–62. New York: University Press of America.

Aaron, Henry J., Barry P. Bosworth, and Gary Burtless. 1989. *Can America Afford to Grow Old?: Paying for Social Security.* Washington, D.C.: Brookings Institution.

Anderson, Gary. 1988. "Public Finance in Autocratic Process: An Empirical Note." *Public Choice* 57 (April 1988): 25–37.

Aschauer, David Alan. 1988. "Rx for Productivity: Build Infrastructure." *Chicago Fed Letter,* Federal Reserve Bank of Chicago (September 1988): 1–3.

Aschauer, David Alan. 1989. "Is Public Expenditure Productive?" *Journal of Monetary Economics* 23 (March 1989): 177–200.

Atkinson, Richard C. 1990. "Supply and Demand for Scientists and Engineers: A National Crisis in the Making." *Science* 248 (April 1990): 425–32.

Avery, Robert, Gregory Elliehausen, Glen Canner, and Thomas Gustafson. 1984. "Survey of Consumer Finances, 1983." *Federal Reserve Bulletin* (September 1984): 679–92.

Balkan, Erol, and Kenneth V. Greene. 1990. "On Democracy and Debt." *Public Choice* 67: 201–211.

Barnes, Roberta, John Jeffries, and Joseph Minarik. 1989. "Policies to Help Disadvantaged Children: Financing Options for the 1990s." Urban Institute Discussion Paper.

Barro, Robert J. 1974. "Are Government Bonds Net Wealth?" *Journal of Political Economy* 82 (November/December 1974): 1095–1117.

Barro, Robert J. 1979. "On the Determination of the Public Debt." *Journal of Political Economy* 87 (October 1979): 940–71.

Barro, Robert J. 1987. "Government Spending, Interest Rates, Prices, and Budget Deficits in the United Kingdom, 1701–1918." *Journal of Monetary Economics* 10 (September 1987): 221–47.

Barro, Robert J. 1989. "The Ricardian Approach to Budget Deficits." *Journal of Economic Perspectives* 3 (Spring 1989): 37–54.

Barro, Robert J. 1990. *Macroeconomics*. 3rd ed. New York: John Wiley & Sons.

Barro, Robert J., and Xavier Sala i Martin. 1990. "World Real Interest Rates." In *NBER Macroeconomics Annual 1990*, forthcoming. Cambridge, MA: M.I.T. Press in association with National Bureau of Economic Research.

Baumol, William J., and Alan S. Blinder. 1988. *Economics: Principles and Policy*. 4th ed. San Diego: Harcourt Brace Jovanovich.

Becker, Gary S. 1975. *Human Capital*. 2nd ed. New York: Columbia University Press.

Bernheim, B. Douglas. 1989. "A Neoclassical Perspective on Budget Deficits." *Journal of Economic Perspectives* 3 (Spring 1989), 55–72.

Blanchard, Olivier J., and Lawrence H. Summers. 1986. "Hysteresis and the European Unemployment Problem." In *NBER Macroeconomics Annual 1986*, 15–78. Cambridge, MA: M.I.T. Press in association with National Bureau of Economic Research.

Blinder, Alan S. 1986. *Hard Heads, Soft Hearts*. Boston: Addison-Wesley.

Blinder, Alan S. 1989. "Is the Deficit Too High? Yes. Should It Be Higher? Maybe." *Business Week* (February 20, 1989): 17.

Bloom, David, and Neil Bennett. 1989. "Future Shock." *New Republic* (June 19, 1989): 18–21.

Boskin, Michael. 1986. *Too Many Promises*. Homewood, IL: Dow Jones-Irwin.

Bowles, David, Holly Ulbrich, and Myles Wallace. 1989. "Default Risk, Interest Differentials and Fiscal Policy: A New Look at Crowding Out." *Eastern Economic Journal* 15 (July/September 1989): 203–12.

Briggs, Vernon M. 1987. "The Growth and Composition of the U.S. Labor Force." *Science* 238 (1987): 176–80.

Broder, David. 1990. "Getting the Government Its Due." *Washington Post Weekly* (February 26/March 4, 1990): 4.

Buckley, William. 1990. "U.S. Hits Hurdle in Latin Obstacle Course." *The Salt Lake Tribune* (January 8, 1990).

Buiter, Willem H., and James Tobin. 1979. "Debt Neutrality: A Brief Review of Doctrine and Evidence." In *Social Security Versus Private Saving*, George M. von Furstenberg, ed. 39–63. Cambridge, MA: Ballinger.

Buiter, Willem H., Kenneth Kletzer, and T.N. Srinivasan. 1989. "Some Thoughts on the Brady Plan: Putting a Fourth Leg on the Donkey?" *World Development* 17 (October 1989): 1661–4.

Bulow, Jeremy, and Kenneth Rogoff. 1989. "Sovereign Debt: Is to Forgive to Forget?" *American Economic Review* 79: 43–50.

Bulow, Jeremy, and Kenneth Rogoff. 1990. "Cleaning Up Third World Debt Without Getting Taken to the Cleaners." *Journal of Economic Perspectives* 4 (Winter 1990): 31–42.

Burkhauser, Richard J. 1990. "Morality on the Cheap: The Driving Force Behind the Americans with Disability Act." Nashville, TN: Vanderbilt University (February 1990).

Caldwell, Lynton K. 1988. *The Administrative Theories of Hamilton & Jefferson.* 2nd ed. New York: Holmes & Meier.

Calvo, Guillermo A. 1988. "Servicing the Public Debt: The Role of Expectations." *American Economic Review* 78 (September 1988): 647–61.

Carroll, Chris, and Lawrence H. Summers. 1987. "Why Have Private Savings Rates in the United States and Canada Diverged?" *Journal of Monetary Economics* 20 (September 1987): 249–79.

Center on Budget and Policy Priorities. 1989. "Poverty Rate and Household Income Stagnate as Rich-Poor Gap Hits Post-War High." Washington, D.C.: Center on Budget and Policy Priorities, October 1989.

Center on Budget and Policy Priorities. 1990. "Falling Through the Gap," Washington, D.C.: Center on Budget and Policy Priorities, July 1990.

Children's Defense Fund. 1990. *The Nation's Investment in Children.* Washington, D.C.: Children's Defense Fund.

Chirinko, Robert S. 1987. "The Ineffectiveness of Effective Tax Rates on Business Investment." *Journal of Public Economics* 32 (April 1987): 369–87.

Chirinko, Robert S., and Robert Eisner. 1983. "Tax Policy and Investment in Major U.S. Macroeconomic Econometric Models." *Journal of Public Economics* 20 (March 1983): 139–66.

Clower, Robert W. 1970. "Introduction." In *Monetary Theory: Selected Readings,* ed. R.W. Clower, 7–21. Baltimore, MD: Penguin Books.

Coleman, Peter J. 1974. *Debtors and Creditors in America.* Madison, WI: State Historical Society of Wisconsin.

Conan, Arthur R. 1952. *The Sterling Area.* London: Macmillan.

Cooke, Jacob E., ed. 1964. *The Reports of Alexander Hamilton.* New York: Harper & Row (Torchbook edition).

Courant, Paul N., and Edward M. Gramlich. 1986. *Federal Budget Deficits: America's Great Consumption Binge.* Englewood Cliffs, NJ: Prentice-Hall, Inc.

Cukierman, Alex, and Allan H. Meltzer. 1989. "A Political Theory of Government Debt and Deficits in a Neo-Ricardian Framework." *American Economic Review* 79 (September 1989): 713–32.

Cutler, David M., James M. Poterba, Louise M. Sheiner, and Lawrence H. Summers. 1990. "An Aging Society: Opportunity or Challenge," *Brookings Papers on Economic Activity* (1990): 1–73.

Danziger, Sheldon. 1989. "Antipoverty Policies and Child Poverty." University of Wisconsin, Madison, Discussion Paper.

Darity, William. 1989. "Is to Forgive the Debt Divine?" In *Debt Disaster? Banks, Governments, and Multilaterals Confront the Crisis,* ed. John F. Weeks, 233–42. New York: New York University Press.

Darity, William, and Bobbie Horn. 1988. *The Loan Pushers: The Role of Commercial Banks in the International Debt Crisis.* Cambridge, MA: Ballinger.

Devarajan, Shanta, and Jaime de Melo. 1987. "Evaluating Participation in African Monetary Unions: A Statistical Analysis of the CFA Zones." *World Development* 15 (April 1987): 483–96.

Devlin, Robert. 1980. *Los Bancos Transnacionales y el Financiamiento Externo de America Latina: La Experiencia del Peru, 1965–1976.* Santiago, Chile: CEPAL.

Devlin, Robert. 1989. "Disyuntivas Frente a la Deuda Externa." *Revista de la CEPAL* 37 (1989): 29–50.

Dooley, Martin. 1989. "Demography of Child Poverty in Canada: 1973–1986." Presented to the Population Association of America, McMasters University, March 28, 1989.

Dornbusch, Ridiger. 1987. "Collapsing Exchange Rate Regimes." *Journal of Development Economics* 27 (October 1987): 71–83.

Drazen, Allan. 1978. "Government Debt, Human Capital, and Bequests in a Life Cycle Model." *Journal of Political Economy* 86 (June 1978): 505–6.

Durant, Will and Ariel. 1968. *The Lessons of History.* New York: Simon & Schuster.

Eaton, Jonathan. 1990. "Debt Relief and the International Enforcement of Loan Contracts." *Journal of Economic Perspectives* 4 (Winter 1990): 43–56.

Economic Commission for Latin America and the Caribbean (ECLAC). "Magnitud de la Probreza en Ocho Paises de America Latina en 1986." ECLAC, 1989.

Economic Commission for Latin America and the Caribbean (ECLAC). 1990. *Preliminary Overview of the Latin American Economy.* Santiago, Chile: ECLAC.

Eisner, Robert. 1978. *Factors in Business Investment.* Cambridge, MA: Ballinger (for the National Bureau of Economic Research).

Eisner, Robert. 1983. "Social Security, Saving and Investment." *Journal of Macroeconomics* 5 (Winter 1983): 1–19.

Eisner, Robert. 1986. *How Real Is the Federal Deficit?* New York: The Free Press, A Division of Macmillan.

Eisner, Robert. 1987. "Burden of the Debt." In *The New Palgrave: A Dictionary of Economics,* vol. I. ed. John Eatwell, et al., 294–96. New York: Groves Dictionaries, A Division of Macmillan.

Eisner, Robert. 1988. "Extended Measures of National Income and Product." *Journal of Economic Literature* 26 (December 1988): 1611–84.

Eisner, Robert. 1989a. "Divergences of Measurement and Theory and Some Implications for Economic Policy" (1988 Presidential Address to the American Economic Association). *American Economic Review* 79 (March 1989a): 1–13.

Eisner, Robert. 1989b. "Budget Deficits: Rhetoric and Reality." *Journal of Economic Perspectives* 3 (Spring 1989b): 72–93.

Eisner, Robert. 1989c. *The Total Incomes System of Accounts.* Chicago: University of Chicago Press.

Eisner, Robert. 1990a. "National Saving and Budget Deficits."

Eisner, Robert. 1990b. "Economic Policy for Today and Tomorrow: Debunking Some Conventional Wisdom." *Challenge* (May/June 1990b): 4–11.

Eisner, Robert. 1991. "The Real Rate of National Saving." *Review of Income and Wealth* 36 (1991).

Eisner, Robert, and M.I. Nadiri. 1968. "On Investment Behavior and Neoclassical Theory." *Review of Economics and Statistics* 50 (August 1968): 369–82.

Eisner, Robert, and Paul J. Pieper. 1984. "A New View of the Federal Debt and Budget Deficits." *American Economic Review* 74 (March 1984): 11–29.

Eisner, Robert, and Paul J. Pieper. 1988. "Deficits, Monetary Policy and Real Economic Activity." In *The Economics of Public Debt*, eds. Kenneth J. Arrow and Michael J. Boskin, 3–40. London: Macmillan Press in association with the International Economic Association.

Eisner, Robert, and Paul. J. Pieper. 1990. "'The World's Greatest Debtor Nation'?" *North American Review of Economics and Finance* (Fall 1990): 9–32.

Evans, Paul. 1987a. "Interest Rates and Expected Future Budget Deficits in the United States." *Journal of Political Economy* 95 (February 1987a): 34–58.

Evans, Paul. 1987b. "Do Budget Deficits Raise Nominal Interest Rates? Evidence from Six Industrial Countries." *Journal of Monetary Economics* 20 (September 1987b): 281–300.

Evans, Paul. 1988. "Do Budget Deficits Affect the Current Account?" Ohio State University, August 1988.

Fallows, James. 1989. *More Like Us: Making America Great Again.* Boston: Houghton Mifflin.

Federal Reserve Bank of Philadelphia. 1964. *50 Years of the Federal Reserve Act.* Philadelphia.

Feldstein, Martin S. 1974. "Social Security, Induced Retirement, and Aggregate Capital Accumulation." *Journal of Political Economy* 82 (September/October 1974): 905–26.

Feldstein, Martin S. 1982. "Social Security and Private Saving: Reply." *Journal of Political Economy* 90 (June 1982): 630–42.

Feldstein, Martin S., and Phillipe Bacchetta. 1989. "National Saving and International Investment." Cambridge, MA: National Bureau of Economic Research Working Paper #3164 (November 1989).

Fischer, Stanley. 1982. "Seigniorage and the Case for a National Money." *Journal of Political Economy* 90 (April 1982): 295–313.

Ford Foundation. 1989. *The Common Good.* Project on Social Welfare and the American Future.

Foxley, Alejandro. 1983. *Latin American Experiments in Neoconservative Economics.* Berkeley, CA: University of California Press.

Friedman, Benjamin M. 1988. *Day of Reckoning: The Consequences of American Economic Policy Under Reagan and After.* New York: Random House.

Friedman, Milton. 1957. *A Theory of the Consumption Function.* Princeton, NJ: Princeton University Press for NBER.

Friedman, Milton. 1968. "The Role of Monetary Policy" (1967 Presidential Address to the American Economic Association). *American Economic Review* 58 (March 1968): 1–17.

Galbraith, John Kenneth. 1975. *Money—Whence It Came, Where It Went.* Boston: Houghton-Mifflin.

Gambetta, Diego. 1988. "Can We Trust Trust?" In *Trust: Making and Breaking Cooperative Relations,* ed. Diego Gambetta. New York: Basil Blackwell.

Garten Jeffrey. 1989. "Trading Blocs and the Evolving World Economy." *Current History* 88 (January 1989): 15–56.

Gates, Paul W. 1957. "Frontier Estate Builder and Farm Labors." In *The Frontier in Perspective,* ed. Walker D. Wyman and Clifton B. Kroeber. Madison: University of Wisconsin Press.

Glick, Mark. 1989. "A History of Corporate Bankruptcy." Department of Economics, University of Utah, Working Paper.

Gottschalk, Peter, and Sheldon Danziger. 1989. "Increasing Inequality in the U.S.: What We Know and What We Don't." *Journal of Post-Keynesian Economics* (Winter 1989): 175–95.

Gould, Stephen Jay. 1987. *Time's Arrow, Time's Cycle.* Cambridge, MA: Harvard University Press.

Gramlich, Edward M. 1984. "How Bad Are the Large Deficits?" In *Federal Budget Policy in the 1980s,* eds. Gregory B. Mills and John L. Palmer, 43–68. Washington, D.C.: Urban Institute Press.

Gramlich, Edward M. 1989. "Budget Deficits and National Saving: Are Politicians Exogenous?" *Journal of Economic Perspectives* 3 (Spring 1989a): 23–36.

Gramlich, Edward M. (1990): 75–80. "U.S. Federal Budget Deficits and Gramm-Rudman-Hollings." *American Economic Review* 80 (May 1990): 75–80.

Guillamont, Patrick, Sylviane Guillamont, and Patrick Plane. 1988. "Participating in African Monetary Unions: An Alternative Evaluation." *World Development* 16 (May 1988): 569–76.

Haberler, Gottfried. 1941. *Prosperity and Depression*. 3rd ed. Geneva: League of Nations.

Hamilton, Alexander. 1790. *Report of the Secretary of the Treasury to the House of Representatives, Relative to a Provision for the Support of Public Credit of the United State, in conformity to a Resolution of the Twenty-First Day of September, 1789. Presented to the House on Thursday the 14th Day of January, 1790. Published by Order of the House of Representatives*. New York: Printed by Francis Childs and John Swaine.

Heilbroner, Robert L., and Peter L. Bernstein. 1990. *The Debt and the Deficit: False Alarms/Real Possibilities*. New York: Norton.

Hendershott, Patric H., and Joe Peek. 1989. "Aggregate U.S. Private Saving: Conceptual Measures and Empirical Tests." In *The Measurement of Saving, Investment, and Wealth*, eds. Robert E. Lipsey and Helen Stone Tice, 185–223, Chicago, University of Chicago Press.

Hendrickson, Susan, and Isabel V. Sawhill. 1989. "Assisting the Working Poor." Urban Institute Working Paper.

Hicks, Sir John. 1969. *A Theory of Economic History*. Oxford: Clarendon Press.

Hicks, Sir John. 1974. *The Crisis in Keynesian Economics*. New York: Basic Books.

Howard, David H. 1989. "Implications of the U.S. Current Account Deficit." *Journal of Economic Perspectives* 3 (Fall 1989): 153–65.

Hudson Institute. 1988. *Workforce 2000, Work and Workers for the 21st Century*, Indianapolis, IN: Hudson Institute, July 1988.

Humphrey, Thomas M. 1986. *From Trade-Offs to Policy Ineffectiveness: A History of the Phillips Curve*. Richmond, VA: Federal Reserve Bank of Richmond.

Interamerican Development Bank (IDB). 1985, 1988. *Economic and Social Progress in Latin America*. Washington, D.C.: IDB.

International Bank for Reconstruction and Development (IBRD or World Bank). 1987, 1988, 1989. *World Development Report*. New York: Oxford University Press.

International Monetary Fund (IMF). 1987, 1989. *International Financial Statistics*. Washington, D.C.: IMF.

International Monetary Fund (IMF). 1989. *International Financial Statistics Yearbook*. Washington, D.C.: IMF.

Jameson, Kenneth P. 1989. "Austerity Programs Under Conditions of Political Instability and Economic Depression: The Case of Bolivia." In *Paying the Costs of Austerity in Latin America*, eds. Howard Handelman and Werner Baer, 81–103. Boulder, CO: Westview.

Jencks, Christopher. 1989. "What Is the Underclass and Is It Growing?" *FOCUS*, Institute for Research on Poverty 12 (Spring and Summer 1989): 14–26.

Jencks, Christopher, John Palmer, and Timothy M. Smeeding. 1988. "The Uses and Limits of Income Comparisons." In *The Vulnerable*, eds. John Palmer, Timothy M. Smeeding, and Barbara Boyce Torrey, 9–28. Washington, D.C.: Urban Institute Press.

Johnson, Roger T. 1977. *Historical Beginnings . . . The Federal Reserve*. Boston: Federal Reserve Bank of Boston.

Kendrick, John W. 1972. *Economic Accounts and Their Uses*. New York: McGraw-Hill.

Kenen, Peter B. 1990. "Organizing Debt Relief: The Need for New Institutions." *Journal of Economic Perspectives* 4 (Winter 1990): 7–18.

Keynes, John Maynard. 1919. *The Economic Consequences of the Peace*. London: Macmillan, 1971.

Keynes, John Maynard. 1932. "Economic Possibilities of Our Grandchildren." *Essays in Persuasion*. New York: Harcourt Brace, 358–73.

Keynes, John Maynard. 1936. *The General Theory of Employment, Interest and Money*. New York: Harcourt Brace.

Keynes, John Maynard. 1973. *The General Theory and After*. In *The Collected Writing of John Maynard Keynes*, vol. IV, ed. Donald Moggridge. London: Macmillan.

Kimmel, Lewis H. 1959. *Federal Budget and Fiscal Policy, 1789–1958*. Washington, D.C.: Brookings Institution.

Kingson, Eric, Barbara A. Hirshorn, and John M. Cornman. 1986. *Ties that Bind*. Cabin John, MD: Seven Locks Press.

Koopmans, Tjalling C. 1947. "Measurement Without Theory." *Review of Economics and Statistics* 29 (August 1947): 161–72.

Kotlikoff, Lawrence J. 1986. "Deficit Delusion." *Public Interest* 84 (Summer 1986): 53–65.

Kotlikoff, Lawrence J. 1988. "The Deficit Is Not a Well-Defined Measure of Fiscal Policy." *Science* 241 (August 12, 1988): 791–95.

Kotlikoff, Lawrence J., Torsten Persson, and Lars E.O. Svensson. 1988. "Social Contracts as Assets: A Possible Solution to the Time-Consistency Problem." *American Economic Review* 78 (September 1988): 662–77.

Krueger, Anne, Arnold Harberger, Sebastian Edwards, and Ronald McKinnon. 1990. "Developing Countries' Debt Problems and Efforts at Policy Reform." *Contemporary Policy Issues* 8 (January 1990): 1–38.

Lange, Oscar. 1938. "The Rate of Interest and the Optimal Propensity to Consume." *Economica* 5 (February 1938): 12–32. Reprinted *Readings in Business Cycle Theory*, ed. Gottfried Haberler, 169–92. Philadelphia: Blakiston in association with the American Economic Association, 1944.

Levy, Frank. 1986. *Dollars and Dreams*. New York: Basic Books.

Liddell, Andrew. 1979. "Financial Co-operation in Africa—French Style." *The Banker* 129 (September 1979): 105–11.

Longman, Philip J. 1990. "Costs of the Aging Population: Financing the Future." In *Social Security and the Budget,* ed H. J. Aaron, 51–62. New York: University Press of America.

Macaulay, Thomas Babington. 1899. "The Origin of the National Debt," *History of England,* vol. 8. New York: Houghton Mifflin, 62–74. Reprinted in *Challenge* 21 (September/October 1978): 3–6.

Meyers, Margaret G. 1970. *A Financial History of the United States.* New York: Columbia University Press.

Modigliani, Franco. 1961. "Long-Run Implications of Alternative Fiscal Policies and the Burden of the National Debt." *Economic Journal* 71 (December 1961): 730–55.

Modigliani, Franco. 1977. "The Monetarist Controversy or, Should We Forsake Stabilization Policies?" (1976 Presidential Address to the American Economic Association). *American Economic Review* 69 (March 1977): 1–19.

Modigliani, Franco, and Richard Brumberg. 1954. "Utility Analysis and the Consumption Function: An Interpretation of Cross-Section Data." In *Post-Keynesian Economics,* ed. Kenneth J. Kurihara, 388–436. New Brunswick, NJ: Rutgers University Press.

Moon, Marilyn, and Timothy M. Smeeding. 1990. "Can the Elderly Afford Long-term Care?" In *The Care of Tomorrow's Elderly: Encouraging Initiatives and Reshaping Public Programs,* eds. Sean Sullivan and Maria Lewin, 137–60. Washington, D.C.: University Press.

Munnell, Alicia. 1990. "Why Has Productivity Growth Declined? Productivity and Public Investment." *New England Economic Review,* Federal Reserve Bank of Boston (January/February 1990): 3–22.

Murnane, Richard. 1988. "Education and the Productivity of the Labor Force: Looking Ahead." In *American Living Standards,* eds. Robert Litan, et al., 215–46. Washington, D.C.: Brookings Institution.

Musgrave, Richard A. 1988. "Public Debt and Intergenerational Equity." In *The Economics of Public Debt,* eds. Kenneth J. Arrow and Michael J. Boskin, 3–40. London: Macmillan Press, in association with the International Economic Association.

Musumeci, James J., and Joseph F. Sinkey, Jr. 1990. "The International Debt Crisis, Investor Contagion, and Bank Security Returns in 1987." *Journal of Money, Credit and Banking* 22 (May 1990): 22, 209–20.

Myers, Robert, and Bruce Schobel. 1989. "A Money's Worth Analysis of Social Security Retirement Benefits." *Transactions* (1989): 537–61.

Naylor, R.T. 1987. *Hot Money and the Politics of Debt.* New York: Simon and Schuster.

Newcomb, Simon. 1865. *A Critical Examination of Our Financial Policy During the Southern Rebellion.* New York: D. Appleton, 1865. Reprinted by New York: Greenwood Press, 1969.

Nourse, Edwin G. 1953. *Economics in the Public Service.* New York: Harcourt Brace.

Oberg, Christopher N. 1988. "Children and the Uninsured." *Social Policy Report,* Society for Research in Child Development (Spring 1988).

O'Driscoll, Gerald P. 1977. "The Ricardian Nonequivalence Theorem." *Journal of Political Economy* 85 (February 1977): 207–10.

Okun, Arthur. 1975. *Equality and Efficiency: The Big Tradeoff.* Washington, D.C.: Brookings Institution.

Ozler, Sule. 1989. "On the Relation Between Reschedulings and Bank Value." *American Economic Review* 79 (December 1989): 1117–31.

Pastor, Manuel. 1990. "Capital Flight from Latin America." *World Development* 18 (1990): 1–18.

Patinkin, Don. 1948. "Price Flexibility and Full Employment." *American Economic Review* 38 (September 1948): 543–64. Reprinted with revisions in *Readings in Monetary Theory,* eds. Friedrich A. Lutz and Lloyd W. Mints, 252–83. New York: Blakiston in association with the American Economic Association, 1951.

Pechman, Joseph. 1990. "Federal Tax Policy" (1989 Presidential Address to the American Economic Association). *American Economic Review* 80 (March 1990): 1–20.

Phelps, Edmund S. 1961. "The Golden Rule of Accumulation: A Fable for Growthmen." *American Economic Review* 51 (September 1961): 638–43.

Pigou, Arthur C. 1928. *A Study in Public Finance.* London: Macmillan.

Pigou, Arthur C. 1943. "The Classical Stationary State." *Economic Journal* 53 (December 1943): 343–51.

Pigou, Arthur C. 1947. "Economic Progress in a Stable Environment." *Economica* 14 (August 1947): 180–88.

Plosser, Charles I. 1982. "Government Financing Decisions and Asset Returns." *Journal of Monetary Economics* 9 (May 1982): 325–52.

Plosser, Charles I. 1987. "Further Evidence on the Relation between Fiscal Policy and the Term Structure." *Journal of Monetary Economics* 20 (September 1987) 343–67.

Plumb, J.H. 1970. *The Death of the Past.* Boston: Houghton Mifflin.

Pole, J.R. 1978. *The Pursuit of Equality in American History.* Berkeley, CA: University of California Press.

Rae, Douglas. 1981. *Equalities.* Cambridge, MA: Harvard University Press.

Reischauer, Robert. 1990. "The Costs of the Deficit." Presented to the Vanderbilt Institute for Public Policy Studies, Nashville, TN, February 19, 1990.

Ricardo, David. 1951. *"Funding System."* In *Pamphlets and Papers, 1815–1823.* Vol. IV, *The Works and Correspondence of David Ricardo,* ed. Piero Sraffa. Cambridge: Cambridge University Press.

Rogoff, Kenneth. 1990. "Symposium on New Institutions for Developing Country Debt." *Journal of Economic Perspectives* 4 (Winter 1990): 3–6.

Roubini, Nouriel, and Jeffrey Sachs. 1988. "Political and Economic Determinants of Budget Deficits in Industrial Democracies." Working Paper #2682, National Bureau of Economic Research. Cambridge, MA, August 1988.

Sachs, Jeffrey. 1987. "The Bolivian Hyperinflation and Stabilization." *American Economic Review* 77 (May 1987): 279–83.

Sachs, Jeffrey. 1990a. "A Strategy for Efficient Debt Reduction." *Journal of Economic Perspectives* 4 (Winter 1990a): 19–30.

Sachs, Jeffrey. 1990b. "Interview." *Challenge* 33 (January/February 1990b): 22–30.

Schultz, Theodore W. 1961. "Investment in Human Capital" (1960 Presidential Address to the American Economic Association). *American Economic Review* 51 (March 1961): 1–17.

Schultze, Charles L. 1989. "Of Wolves, Termites and Pussycats." *The Brookings Review* (Summer 1989): 26–33.

Schultze, Charles L. 1990. "Setting Long-Run Deficit Reduction Targets: The Economics and Politics of Budget Design." In *Social Security and the Budget,* ed. H. J. Aaron, 51–62. New York: University Press of America.

Sen, Amartya. 1987. *On Ethics and Economics.* Oxford: Blackwell.

Slemrod, Joel. 1986. "Saving and the Fear of Nuclear War." *Journal of Conflict Resolution* 30 (September 1986): 403–19.

Smeeding, Timothy M. 1990a. "Poverty in the United States and Other Nations: Toward a Fund for American Children and Their Families." *FORUM for Applied Research and Public Policy* (1990a). Forthcoming.

Smeeding, Timothy M. 1990b. "Mountains or Molehills: Just What's So Bad About Aging Societies Anyway?" In *Consequences of Aging Societies for Individuals,* ed. J. Huber. Newbury Park, CA: Sage Publishers.

Smeeding, Timothy M., and Barbara Boyce Torrey. 1988. "Poor Children in Rich Countries." *Science* 242 (1988): 874–77.

Smeeding, Timothy M., Barbara Boyce Torrey, and Martin Rein. 1988. "Patterns of Income and Poverty: The Economic Status of the Young and the Elderly in Eight Countries." In *The Vulnerable,* eds. John Palmer, Timothy M. Smeeding, and Barbara Boyce Torrey, 89–119. Washington, D.C.: Urban Institute Press.

Smiles, Samuel. 1889. *Happy Homes and the Hearts That Make Them.* Chicago: U.S. Publishing House.

Smith, James P., and Finis R. Welch. 1989. "Black Economic Progress After Myrdal." *Journal of Economic Literature* 27 (June 1989): 579–64.

Smolensky, Eugene, Sheldon Danziger, and Peter Gottschalk. 1988. "The Declining Significance of Age in the U.S.: Trends in Well-Being of

Children and the Elderly Since 1939." In *The Vulnerable,* eds. John Palmer, Timothy M. Smeeding, and Barbara Boyce Torrey, 29–54. Washington, D.C.: Urban Institute Press.

Solow, Robert M. 1956. "A Contribution to the Theory of Economic Growth." *Quarterly Journal of Economics* 70 (February 1956): 65–94.

Sommers, Albert. 1990. *The Sommers Letter.* New York, March 1, 1990.

Stekler, Lois. 1988. "Adequacy of International Transactions and Position Data for Policy Coordination." International Finance Discussion Papers, #337, Board of Governors of the Federal Reserve System, Washington, D.C., November 1988.

Strange, Susan. 1971. *Sterling and British Policy: A Political Study of an International Currency in Decline.* London: Oxford University Press.

Taylor, George Rogers, ed. 1959. *Hamilton and the National Debt.* Boston: D.C. Heath.

Tobin, James. 1972. "Inflation and Unemployment." *American Economic Review* 62 (March 1972): 1–18.

Tocqueville, Alexis de. 1969. *Democracy in America.* Translated by George Lawrence. Edited by J.P. Mayer. New York: Doubleday, 12.

Tullock, Gordon. 1987. "The General Irrelevance of the General Theory?" In *Deficits,* eds. James M. Buchanan, Charles K. Rowley, and Robert D. Tollison, 173–79. Oxford: Basil Blackwell.

Ulan, Michael, and William G. Dewald. 1989. "The U.S. Net International Investment Position." In *Dollars, Deficits, and Trade,* eds. James A. Dorn and William A. Niskanen, 363–94. Boston: Kluwer Academic Publishers.

U.N. Department of Economic and Social Affairs, Statistical Office. 1964. *National Accounting Practices in Sixty Countries.* Supplement to the *Yearbook of National Accounts Statistics.* Provisional Issue, Studies in Methods, ser. F, no. 11, New York.

U.N. Office of Economic Cooperation and Development (OECD). 1985. *Social Expenditure 1960–1990: Problems of Growth and Control.* Paris: OECD.

U.N. Office of Economic Cooperation and Development (OECD). 1987. *National Accounts, 1970–1985.* Paris: OECD.

U.N. Office of Economic Cooperation and Development (OECD). 1988. *Aging Populations: The Social Policy Implications.* Paris: OECD.

U.N. Office of Economic Cooperation and Development (OECD). 1989. *Quarterly National Accounts.* Paris: OECD.

U.S. Bureau of the Census. 1988. *Measuring the Effects of Benefits and Taxes on Income and Poverty: 1986.* Current Population Reports, Series P-60, No. 164-RD-1.

U.S. Congress, Committee on Ways and Means. 1989. *Background Materials and Data on Programs Within the Jurisdiction of the Committee on Ways and*

Means. Washington, D.C.: U.S. Government Printing Office, March 15, 1989.

U.S. Congressional Budget Office. *Reducing the Deficit: Spending and Revenue Options*. Washington, D.C.: U.S. Government Printing Office, Annual.

U.S. Congressional Budget Office. 1987. *Trends in Public Investment*. Washington, D.C.: U.S. Government Printing Office.

U.S. Congressional Budget Office. 1988. *The Changing Distribution of Federal Taxes*. July 1988.

U.S. Congressional Budget Office. 1990. *The Federal Deficit: Does It Measure the Government's Effect on National Saving?* Washington, D.C.: U.S. Government Printing Office.

U.S. Congressional Budget Office. 1990. *The Economic and Budget Outlook: Fiscal Years 1991–1995*. Congress of the United States, 1990 Annual Report.

U.S. Office of Management and Budget. 1988. *Special Analyses, Budget of the United States Government, Fiscal Year 1989*. Washington, D.C.: U.S. Government Printing Office.

U.S. Office of Management and Budget. 1990. *Budget of the United States Government, Fiscal Year 1991*. Washington, D.C.: U.S. Government Printing Office, February 1990.

U.S. President. 1990. *Economic Report of the President*. Washington, D.C.: U.S. Government Printing Office, February 1990.

U.S. Treasury Department. 1984. *The Effect of Deficits on Prices of Financial Assets: Theory and Evidence*. Washington, D.C.: U.S. Government Printing Office.

Ward, Barbara. 1962. *The Rich Nations and the Poor Nations*. New York: Norton.

Webber, Carolyn, and Aaron Wildavsky. 1986. *A History of Taxation and Expenditure in the Western World*. New York: Simon and Schuster.

Wolff, Edward N. 1988. "Estimates of Household Wealth Inequality in the U.S., 1962–1983." *Review of Income and Wealth* 34 (September 1988):

Index

Page numbers in bold face refer to glossary definitions.